D1570089

Microfinance 3.0

Doris Köhn
Editor

Microfinance 3.0

Reconciling Sustainability with Social
Outreach and Responsible Delivery

 Springer Open

Editor
Doris Köhn
Senior Vice President Africa and Middle East
KfW
Frankfurt am Main
Germany

ISBN 978-3-642-41703-0   ISBN 978-3-642-41704-7 (eBook)
DOI 10.1007/978-3-642-41704-7
Springer Heidelberg New York Dordrecht London

Library of Congress Control Number: 2013953713

Printed on acid-free paper

Springer is part of Springer Science+Business Media (www.springer.com)

Preface

Fifteen years ago, microfinance was looked upon as one of the most promising concept to lift poor people out of poverty. Microfinance was perceived to be "good per se". Many institutions proved successful both in development and in financial terms. Today, after an impressive pushing of the "financial frontier", financial inclusion seems to have a mixed record: While it is true that many people in developing countries still lack access to finance, we have also witnessed the opposite "too much/easy access" led to overindebted clients, unable to serve their several microcredits offered by (too) many institutions. In some markets, this implied a move into pure consumer lending, partly replacing the traditional lending to micro-entrepreneurs. "Good" responsible microfinance institutions were not able to continue to operate in these "contaminated markets". In this context, the question (re-)emerged: isn't it, after all, unrealistic to believe that pursuing a development mission can go hand in hand with financial success, particularly in the context of commercial microfinance?

I do not share this view. In fact, I believe the two goals are intertwined in the sense that without financial viability, clients cannot be served in a sustainable way, and that institutions which do not understand their clients with their financial needs will hardly be financially successful. However, this does not happen automatically: on the contrary, it takes a lot of efforts to achieve both objectives: a high degree of professionalism and a strong commitment to a responsible service delivery. It also takes responsible regulators and more efforts to promote financial literacy of clients.

This book is part of a publication series initiated by KfW on selected topics in the field of financial systems development, one of the core competencies of KfW. This edition addresses the ethics of financial systems development which have been under scrutiny in "developed" markets as well as in developing countries. As "banking" seems to have become a questionable activity, we will take a special look at the institutions that provide microfinance services. "Microfinance 3.0" intends to provide a new "framework" for the future of microfinance which builds upon past success stories as well as upon lessons learnt from bad practices and errors. It contains nine contributions, written by different microfinance experts, distinguished practitioners as well as observers and analysts of microfinance for more than a decade. Some of these contributions were presented at the KfW Financial Sector Symposium in late 2012 in Berlin, where the future landscape of microfinance was discussed.

These contributions touch upon some of the "ingredients of "microfinance 3.0": the values needed to provide financial services responsibly, the appropriate business models needed to serve a large number of unbanked people, the right role of funders to promote professional and responsible service delivery, and the question as to how to measure the impact of microfinance.

As this publication is also available online (via Open Access), my special wish is that it contributes to a fruitful learning process around the globe and familiarizes financial institutions in KfW's partner countries with our ideas of microfinance 3.0. May this book provide new insights for the reader and promote knowledge sharing among all stakeholders.

August 2013

Doris Köhn
Director General, Africa and the Middle East
KfW Entwicklungsbank

Table of Contents

Chapter 1

Microfinance in India: Lessons from the Andhra Crisis...........................1

Vijay Mahajan and T. Navin

Chapter 2

**Armageddon or Adolescence? Making Sense of Microfinance's
Recent Travails** 13

David Roodman

Chapter 3

Core Values of Microfinance Under Scrutiny: Back to Basics?.............41

Reinhard H. Schmidt

Chapter 4

Microcredit Interest Rates and Their Determinants: 2004–2011 69

Richard Rosenberg, Scott Gaul, William Ford, and Olga Tomilova

Chapter 5

**Financial Services That Clients Need: The 3.0 Business Models,
Reconciling Outreach with Sustainability** 105

Robert Peck Christen

Chapter 6

**"Microfinance 3.0" – Perspectives for Sustainable Financial
Service Delivery** 123

Matthias Adler and Sophie Waldschmidt

Chapter 7

**Microfinance Beyond the Standard? Evaluating Adequacy and
Performance of Agricultural Microcredit**..139

Ron Weber

Chapter 8

**The Role of DFls in the Emerging 3.0 Responsible Funding
Landscape – Responsible Corporate Governance and Beyond**............155

Klaus Maurer

Chapter 9

The Microfinance Approach: Does It Deliver on Its Promise? 181

Eva Terberger

Index..197

Abbreviations

ABM	AccèsBanque Madagascar
ABT	AccessBank Tanzania
AfDB	African Development Bank
AFR	Africa
AG	Company limited by shares
AP	Andhra Pradesh
APR	Annual Percentage Rate
ATM	Automated Teller Machine
BLP	Bank Linkage Programme
BRI	Bank Rakyat Indonesia
CDC	Commonwealth Development Corporation
CEO	Chief Executive Officer
CGAP	Consultative Group to Assist the Poor
CIDA	Canadian International Development Agency
CLO	Collateralized Loan Obligation
CMEF	Council of Microfinance Equity Funds
COCA	Code of Conduct Assessment
COFIDE	Corporación Financiera de Desarrollo
CSR	Corporate Social Responsibility
DFI	Development Finance Institution
DfID	Department for International Development
EAP	East Asia and Pacific
EBRD	European Bank for Reconstruction and Development
ECA	Eastern Europe and Central Asia
ECB	European Central Bank
EFSE	European Fund for Southeast Europe
EIB	European Investment Bank
ESG	Environment Social Governance
EUR	Euro
EZ	Entwicklungszusammenarbeit (German Development Cooperation)
FMO	Netherlands Development Finance Company
GBB	Grameen Bank Bangladesh
GDP	Gross Domestic Product
GIZ	Deutsche Gesellschaft für internationale Zusammenarbeit GmbH
GLP	Gross Loan Portfolio

GNP	Gross National Product
GNI	Gross National Income
GoI	Government of India
GPFI	Global Partnership for Financial Inclusion
IFC	International Finance Corporation
IIMPS	Invest India Micro Pension Services
INR	Indian Rupee
IPO	Initial Public Offering
IRDP	Integrated Rural Development Programme
JRY	Jawahar Rozgar Yojana
KfW	Kreditanstalt für Wiederaufbau
KYC	Know Your Customer
LAC	Latin America and the Carribean
MEF	Microfinance Enhancement Facility
MENA	Middle East and North Africa
MF	Microfinance
MFI	Microfinance Institution
MFIN	Microfinance Institutions Network
MILK	MicroInsurance Learning and Knowledge Project
MIS	Management Information System
MIV	Microfinance Investment Vehicle
MIX	Microfinance Information Exchange
MSME	Micro, Small and Medium Enterprises
NABARD	National Bank for Agriculture and Rural Development
NBFC	Non-Banking Financial Company
NBFI	Non-Bank Financial Institution
NGO	Non-Governmental Organization
NPS	National Pension Scheme
NREP	National Rural Employment Programme
NREGA	National Rural Employment Guarantee Act
NRLM	National Rural Livelihoods Mission
OECD	Organization for Economic Cooperation and Development
PAR	Portfolio at Risk
PSL	Priority Sector Lending
RBI	Reserve Bank of India
RCB	Rural Cooperative Bank
RCT	Randomized Controlled Trial(s)
REGMIFA	Regional Microfinance Fund for Africa
RMK	Rashtriya Mahila Kosh
ROA	Return on Assets
ROE	Return on Equity

RRB	Regional Rural Bank
RSBY	Rashtriya Swasthya Bima Yojana
SBF	Small Business Finance
SBLP	SHG-Bank Linkage Programme
SERP	Society for Elimination of Rural Poverty
SEWA	Self Employed Women's Association
SFDA	Small Farmers Development Agency
SGSY	Swaranjayanti Gram Swarozgar Yojana
SHG	Self-Help Group (Programme)
SIDBI	Small Industries Development Bank of India
SKS	Swayam Krishi Sangam
SME	Small and Medium Enterprises
SRO	Self-Regulating Organisation
SSA	Sub-Sahara Africa
TCX	The Currency Exchange Fund
TDP	Telugu Desam Party
UN	United Nations
UNCDF	United Nations Capital Development Fund
UNDP	United Nations Development Programme
USAID	United States Agency for International Development
USD	US-Dollar
YSR	YS Rajashekhar Reddy

CHAPTER 1

Microfinance in India: Lessons from the Andhra Crisis[*]

Vijay Mahajan[**] *and T. Navin*[***]

1 The Two-Model Microfinance Industry in India

The Indian economy was able to witness high levels of economic growth follow-ing the economic reforms that were introduced in the 1990s. The GDP grew at the rate of 8.45 % per annum between the years 2004 till 2011[1]. Despite this, India continued to see high degree of poverty and low human development. While growth did create zones of prosperity, and reduce poverty and hunger, the residue was still very large – 37.2 % of the Indian population continued to be poor[2], while 77 % of the population remained vulnerable to income shocks[3]. This proportion was even higher for the socially disadvantaged groups such as the Scheduled Castes, the Scheduled Tribes and Minorities. India continued to occupy a low rank – 134 – in the UNDP Human Development Index which takes into account health, education, income, inequality, poverty, gender, sustainability and demographic indicators[4]. With an estimated 385 million employed population, unemployment in India was estimated to be about 9.4 %. [5]

The post independent Indian state adopted various means for addressing poverty and livelihood challenges. This began with land reforms, followed by increasing

---

[*] This is an updated version of an earlier article by the authors, titled Microfinance in India – 2012 – Growth, Crisis and Future, which was published by the French Association d'Economie Financière in the Revue de Economie Financiere, No 102, Sep 2012.

[**] Founder and CEO of the BASIX Social Enterprise Group; President of the Microfi-nance Institutions Network of India; Chair of the Ex-Com of CGAP.

[***] Faculty member of The Livelihood School, Hyderabad, a BASIX Group entity. His fields of interest include the political economy of livelihoods and social performance of mi-crofinance institutions.

[1] Planning Commission: Indian Economy: Some Indicators (as on 1st June, 2011).

[2] Tendulkar committee puts the figure at 37.2 % based on the NSSO study 2004–05.

[3] India's Common People: Who are they, How many are they and How do they live, EPW March 15, 2008, Arjun Sen Gupta, KP Kannan, G Raveendran.

[4] Human Development report 2011: Sustainability and Equity A better Future for all.

[5] Report on Employment & Unemployment Survey (2009–10), GOI, Ministry of Labour & Unemployment, Labour Bureau, Chandigarh.

the area under irrigation, culminating in a dramatic rise in agricultural production through the introduction of high yielding varieties of wheat and rice, dubbed the "Green Revolution" of the late 1960s. But this only exacerbated inequalities between the large and the small farmers, the landed and the landless, and irrigated and rainfed regions. Thus, the then Prime Minister, Indira Gandhi launched a "direct attack on poverty" in the mid 1970s, with large government funded programs of wage employment in public works and self-employment through credit-based asset acquisition. These two strategies have remained the main planks of poverty alleviation, with names changing from NREP to Food for Work to JRY to NREGA for wage-employment programs and from SFDA to IRDP to SGSY to NRLM for self-employment programs.

The need to enhance agricultural production, and promote self-employment for the landless, led to the role of credit becoming significant. Banks were nationalized in 1969 and used throughout the 1970s and 1980s as instruments of development. But once again, it became clear that despite the priority sector lending obligation and the mandated credit for schemes for self-employment of the poor like the IRDP, banks did much less than what was needed. Then, in 1990s, with economic reforms redrawing the banks' priorities in favour of sustainability, they turned their backs to the poor. It was left to NGOs to work out new modalities for providing the poor with access to credit[6]. This is what led to the emergence of the two predominant microfinance models in the last two decades. In both, banks play the lenders' role, but the front-end is tackled either by a "self-help group" (SHG) or by a microfinance institution (MFI).

Access to credit has for ever been a major constraint for the poor in India. Traditionally the poor depended on large farmers, merchants and middlemen, pawn brokers and moneylenders for meeting their credit needs. Unable to pay high interest rates, the poor often ended up forfeiting their land and eventually becoming bonded labourers to money lenders. Many attempts were made to break dependence on money lenders through provision of institutional credit, starting from the British colonial period. The need to produce enough food to feed the growing population was a priority for the newly independent India. In the initial two decades 1947–67, cooperatives became less and less important as an answer to provision of credit for agriculture. In 1969, the then Prime Minister Indira Gandhi nationalized the top ten banks and mandated them to open a large number of rural branches. Then in 1975, after money-lending was abolished during the Emergency, the government set up a network of Regional Rural Banks to reach out to the rural poor, specifically small and marginal farmers, rural artisans and agricultural labour. With a focus on physical expansion of banking services the branches grew rapidly during 1969 to 1990.

---

[6] The others included building large scale infrastructure projects for irrigation and power, creating large scale extension network and promotion of modern agricultural practices, community development works, integrated development projects, area level development projects based on specific geographies etc.

Table 1. Expansion of Banking Services

Year	Rural branches	Total branches	Population per branch (in 1000s)	Priority sector credit as % of total credit
1969	1833	8262	64	14.0
1980	15105	32419	21	33.0
1990	31114	55410	14	43.8
1995	33004	62367	15	33.7
2000	32734	65412	15	35.4
2010	32624	85393	13.8	35.1

Source: Progress of Commercial Banking at a Glance – RBI Statistical Returns

Though the last column in the table above looks impressive, the fact is that the so-called priority sector includes many non-poor sectors, such as large farmers, commercial agriculture, small-scale industry, self-employed professionals and exports. The banking system had limited ability to reach the small borrowers as was evidenced by the fact that in 2004, only about 5 percent of bank credit went to small borrowers.

1.1 Self Help Group – Bank Linkage Model – Achievements and Shortcomings

In order to enhance access to credit to the poor, since the mid 1980s, NGOs started experimenting with credit groups. MYRADA, an NGO in Karnataka since 1986 and PRADAN in Rajasthan since 1987, began setting up Self Help Groups (SHGs) for encouraging savings and credit and training on the principles of self help[7]. The German technical agency, then called GTZ, took many Indian officials from the Government of India (GoI), the Reserve bank of India (RBI) and the National Bank for Agriculture and Rural Development (NABARD) to Indonesia to show them the possibilities of lending to the poor through groups. In 1992, the RBI approved a pilot project of linking SHGs to banks, which eventually led to the SHG-Bank linkage program (SBLP) in 1996. The SBLP received major policy and promotional support, both from the central and various state governments, in particular, Andhra Pradesh. It was scaled up nationwide through support from NABARD and World Bank loans[8]. By March 2011, around 7.46 million SHGs

---

[7]   Consultative Group to Assist the Poor (CGAP), Andhra Pradesh 2010: Global Implications of the Crisis in Indian Microfinance, 2010.

[8]   Johnson, D. and Meka, S., Access to Finance in Andhra Pradesh, Institute for Financial Management and Research—Centre for Microfinance, 2010.

around India have been linked with banks in what is the world's single largest microfinance program. About 4.78 million SHGs have loans outstanding worth INR 312 billion[9] (about Euro 4 billion). In the following year, 2011–12, banks disbursed INR 84 billion in AP and INR 165 billion all over India, including AP.

The direct benefit of the SBLP, in terms of income enhancement of poor households, and the indirect benefit in terms of women's empowerment, has been enormous. Though a great leap forward in terms of enhancing credit access by the poor, the SHG model suffers from a major lacuna – it is subsidy driven, with at least three types of subsidies –

First, is the cost of organizing the SHGs. In the early days, this was done by NGOs, a role increasingly taken over by government agencies as the scale went up. But both required subsidies. In AP, the funding largely came from World Bank loans of USD 600 million to the AP government run Society for Elimination of Rural Poverty (SERP).

The second subsidy comes in the form of lower interest loan funds. While in the early years, banks lent to SHGs at 12% per annum, successive state governments tried to subsidise the rate at which SHGs got funds. In AP it came down successively from 12% in 1996 to 9% before the 1999 state elections, to 3% after the 2004 elections in which the SHGs were promised "*paavla vaddi*" (quarter percent per month interest or 3% pa). In 2011, the subsidy was increased to cover the full interest, so the cost of funds to SHGs has been reduced to 0%[10].

The third subsidy is in the form of bad debts that banks have to write off. The recovery rates of SHGs in early years were 95% plus and have steadily fallen as the poor sensed the program becoming one of political patronage. In the wake of the MFI Ordinance in AP, which led to mass default of MFI loans, initially SHG loan repayments increased but have in a year fallen to 60–70%. The increasing subsidy has also led to increasing cornering of credit by the better-off members, corruption and reduction in repayment rates in expectation of loan waivers.

1.2   Emergence of MFIs After Banking Sector Reforms Were Launched

The introduction of financial sector reforms since 1992 saw a reduction in the share of small borrowers (below Rs. 25,000) to total bank credit decline from 18.3% in 1994 to 5.3% in March 2002 and 1.3% in March 2010. Even the number of small borrower accounts reduced from 55.8 million to 37.3 million in March 2002 to merely 1.9 million in March 2010[11]. This is partly because most

---

[9] National Bank for Agriculture and Rural Development (NABARD), Status of Microfinance in India, 2010–11, Mumbai.

[10] http://www.serp.ap.gov.in/AWFP/FrontServlet?requestType=BudgetLineReportRH&actionVal=Budgetline1&Year=20122013&FunctionalHead=-1&District=-1&Mandal=-1&CostCentre=-1.

[11] Mahajan, Vijay and Ramola, Bharti Gupta, Microfinance in India – Banyan Tree and Bonsai – A review paper for the World Bank, 2003.

small loans are now being given through SHGs or MFIs rather than directly by banks. After rising for three decades from 1951 onwards, the share of institutional credit to total credit declined during the period 1991 till 2001. It reduced from 64% to 57% for rural areas. Over 70% among the poorer households (less than Rs. 60,000 assets) were dependent on non-institutional sources for meeting their credit needs[12].

The need for physical collateral, high transaction costs involved in processing small amounts and concerns related to loan recovery discouraged banks from lending to small borrowers. This demanded an alternative system to meet their needs. The Grameen Bank, Bangladesh (GBB) demonstrated a successful model of microcredit steadily since 1976. Initially donor subsidised, the GBB model reached a volume where it could help meet the financial needs of the poor in a sustainable manner. By the mid 1990s, the GGB model was being seen with great interest by other countries.

The then Finance Minister of India, Dr Manmohan Singh announced in 1995 that India should have a bank for the poor like the GBB. Indian financial institutions, led by NABARD, however, rejected the GBB model in favour of the home-grown SHG model. Many Indian NGOs, however, experimented with both the models and found that using the GBB model, they could themselves become sustainable. Once SIDBI and later private sector banks like the ICICI Bank started funding NGOs in a big way for microcredit, the GBB model was widely adopted by most Indian MFIs, with a few exceptions like BASIX.

1.3 International Development Policy Thrust on Sustainability

The success of the Grameen Bank, Bangladesh led to demands for its replication all over the world and this was first done systematically at the Microcredit Summit in Washington DC in February, 1997. Thousands of organisations from developing countries joined the movement, and worked towards increasing outreach. Microcredit was also beginning to find favour among the donors such as the USAID, DfID of UK, Canadian CIDA, the German, the Dutch and the Scandinavian donors and European donors all began to give substantial amount of funding to promote microfinance in developing countries. In India, apex lenders such as Small Industries Development Bank of India (SIDBI) and the Rashtriya Mahila Kosh (RMK) turn gave wholesale loans to MFIs, most of which began as developmental NGOs but quickly adopted the mantra of sustainability.

The private sector arm of the World Bank, the International Finance Corporation (IFC) and other development banks like the German KfW, the Dutch FMO and the British CDC all began to develop an interest in microfinance and began to invest in more commercially oriented MFIs, such as banks and non-bank finance

---

[12] All India Debt and Investment Survey, 59th Round, National Sample Survey Organization, December 2005.

companies. They also invested in a whole range of new funds, specializing in lending to and investing in the equity of microfinance institutions. These bodies, the earliest of which were set up in 2000, were called "microfinance investment vehicles" (MIVs) and there were as many as 150 MIVs listed on the Mix Market data base in 2012. Many of them raised funds from socially motivated investors who were willing to take a lower return if they saw their money helping the poor. By 2005, investors in microfinance had a motley mix of motivations, all way from those seeking no returns to those seeking high returns.

The year 2005 was declared by the United Nations as the 'International Year of Microcredit' and the Nobel Peace Prize for 2006 was awarded to Prof Mohammed Yunus and the Grameen Bank of Bangladesh. Compartamos, a Mexican MFI which had begun as an NGO and transformed first to a non-bank credit company and then to a microfinance bank, made on Initial Public Offer and the IPO was 13 times oversubscribed and considered a huge success by any financial market standards. This led to an upsurge of investment in MFIs and new classes of investors came in – those willing to take on structured debt obligations and private equity investors. They brought with them lots of expertise and funds, but also lots of expectations of high returns. They also spawned the ambitions of several MFI promoters who realised they could make a lot of money by offering high growth rates and high profitability in their MFIs.

2   Achievements and Shortcomings of MFIs in India

The growth of MFIs was supported by state owned Small Industries Development Bank of India (SIDBI) and loans from commercial banks under the priority lending quotas since 2000. Initially they leant to NGO-MFIs but within a few years, as the amounts outstanding increased, they sought some equity as a risk cushion. This is when the larger NGO-MFIs began transforming into for-profit NBFCs. In the next step, by 2006, these NBFCs started attracting equity investments from specialized microfinance investment vehicles and private equity funds[13]. For example, SHARE got equity from Legatum, Spandana from JM Financial and SKS from Sequoia, by 2007, within a few years of having been NGOs. By 2010 the MFI growth in India had reached its peak growing at 80% per annum and the outreach had reached around 27 million.

2.1   Achievements of MFIs

MFIs could achieve what the banking sector could not achieve over the years. Within a short period of 15 years borrowers from MFIs increased from merely

---

[13] Sparreboom, Pete, Indian Microfinance crisis, 2010, Working Group on inclusive finance in China, April 2011.

3,000 in 1995 to 31.7 million in 2010. In the corresponding period, the banking sector with its huge infrastructure only showed a decline in terms of lending to small borrowers[14]. MFIs brought down dependence on money lenders. MFIs offer a variety of loans for agriculture, animal husbandry and non-farm activities as well as for housing needs. MFIs introduced micro-insurance for life and health cover of borrowers, and some innovative ones also added weather insurance for crops and livestock insurance.

In the run up to the SKS IPO in August 2010, a few MFIs participated in a reckless rush to build portfolio and the resultant multiple and higher ticket lending led to over-indebtedness in a small proportion of the borrowers. Many poor families were overwhelmed by the repayment obligations. As they began to skip installments, MFI staff, accustomed to near 100% on-time repayment, increased pressure on recoveries. Reports of coercive recoveries and in some cases, suicides by borrowers, began to appear in the media. This led to a political backlash and the AP state government enacted a law in October 2010 to curb MFIs.

2.2   Shortcomings of MFIs

Indian MFIs, particularly the four in AP – SKS, Spandana, SHARE and Asmitha – witnessed high levels of growth from 2006 onwards and could not manage that process well. A vast majority, with the exception of SEWA and BASIX, were following the Grameen Bank, Bangladesh model, offering a single product – a year-long loan repayable in 50 equated weekly instalments. They recruited a large number of people, but did not train them or monitor them adequately. The only parameters to which the MFI managements and Boards seemed to pay attention to were growth in and health of the loan portfolio, and reduction in operating costs. The field staff quickly learnt to respond to that which was being monitored and incentivised and ignored all the rest, including, going to remote villages, searching for the really poor clients, handholding and training of client groups before giving them the powers to approve each other's loans, and ensuring client education, or even adequate disclosure about interest rates and other terms.

3   The Politics Behind the Microfinance Crisis in Andhra Pradesh

The microfinance crisis in AP can be traced to the simultaneous expansion of SHG Bank Linkage Model promoted by the State and the MFI model by private players. By 2010, it was estimated that there were about 6.25 million MFI borrow-

---

[14]   Figures derived from MIX Market Data.

ers in Andhra Pradesh and 19.11 million SHG Bank Linkage members[15]. Clearly, in percentage terms bank loans to MFIs had been growing faster than bank loans to SHGs. According to N. Srinivasan, in 2010 growth in MFI loans outstanding also overtook growth in SHG loans outstanding in absolute terms[16]. The growing pace of expansion of MFI meant that it could outpace SHG as a popular model for microfinance.

This was not acceptable to the political class as they would lose hold over an important vote bank. The civil servants were in agreement with the political leaders as they would lose hold of a major program and the related budget if MFIs occupied the dominant space. The hostility of the staff of the government sponsored Andhra Pradesh Society for Elimination of Rural Poverty (SERP) towards MFIs is largely based on this anxiety.

While the SHG movement was initially a grass root driven movement in Andhra Pradesh, it was sought to be co-opted by political parties. Since 1999, when the then incumbent Chief Minster Chandrababu Naidu of the Telugu Desam party (TDP), used women's SHGs as his vote bank and returned to power, microfinance has become increasingly important to the electoral politics in Andhra Pradesh. Beginning with the TDP, women's SHGs were seen as a political constituency, a potential vote bank[17]. Mr Naidu persuaded banks to lower interest rates on loans to women SHGs to 9% from 12% before the 1999 elections. The Congress, under the leadership of late YS Rajashekhar Reddy (YSR) sought to win the game of electoral politics during 2004 elections by offering to provide women loans at 3% pa interest[18], a promise which he kept on coming to power, with the *Pavala Vaddi* scheme[19].

In 2009 elections, the interest rates again became an issue of populist politics. TDP sought to win back the women vote base by agreeing to offer interest free loans upto a ceiling of Rs. 25,000 and 3% loans for loans above Rs. 25,000[20]. However, in the face of the popularity of the YSR, Naidu could not make much impact. The recovery rates for bank lending to SHGs declined during the period.

---

[15]   Srinivasan, N., Microfinance India: State of the Sector 2010, Presentation to ACCESS Microfinance India Summit 2010.

[16]   Srinivasan, N., Microfinance India: State of the Sector 2010, Presentation to ACCESS Microfinance India Summit 2010.

[17]   http://telugudesam.org/cbn/velugu.html.

[18]   Andhra Pradesh Congress Committee Manifesto 2004.

[19]   G.O.Ms. No. 271, G.O.Rt.No.5, PR&RD (RD III) Department, Dated 17.09.2004. Pavala refers to quarter of a rupee i.e., quarter rupee interest per month which equals 3% interest per year.

[20]   TDP Election Manifesto, 2009.

While recovery was over 95 % in 2007–08, by 2010–11 this had declined considerably to a reported 60–70 %.[21]

Unfortunately, YSR died in a helicopter crash within six months of getting re-elected in 2009. His son Jagan Mohan Reddy was widely expected to become the Chief Minster, but the Congress High Command decided to appoint old loyalist Rosaiah. This led Jagan to rebel. He kept looking for issues to raise and the one about microfinance borrowers feeling so harassed that some committed suicides caught his attention. He found the perfect issue to embarrass Rosaiah and the High Command in Delhi – a picture of Rahul Gandhi sitting with Vikram Akula in a SKS women borrowers' group meeting, which was carried in the media in 2006. There was also a photo of Smt Sonia Gandhi, the Congress party president, presenting Akula with an award for Social Entrepreneur of the Year at the World Economic Forum's India Economic Summit.[22] Jagan's newspaper *Sakshi* and his TV channel by the same name hammered the point – "Why would Rosaiah's government act against MFIs, when the Gandhis are their friends?". The other media picked up the issue. This led to acute embarrassment for the Congress and they even issued a denial but the charge stuck[23].

In October 2010, when media criticism against the MFIs was at its peak, the statements by leaders of political parties had its affect and the Congress government in AP had to enact a harsh law curbing MFIs. The Government of Andhra Pradesh brought in the Andhra Pradesh Microfinance Institutions (Regulation of Money Lending) Ordinance, 2010[24] which was later passed as the Andhra Pradesh Microfinance Institutions (Regulation of Money Lending) Bill 2011. This law had several features which effectively made it impossible for MFIs to function in the state. For example, MFI staff could not go to the residence or workplace of the borrower for recoveries, but instead had to go and sit at a central public place, hoping for borrowers to come and repay. No additional loans were permitted without prior approval by the government.

Though the law was ostensibly aimed to protect MFI borrowers from coercion and over-indebtedness, it virtually stopped MFIs from functioning in AP, Two crucial provisions were – visits by MFI staff to the residence or work place of the borrowers for recovery could be construed to be a coercive practice, so instead they had to sit in a "central place" hoping for borrowers to come there. Second, no further loans were allowed with government permission for each individual loan. This by itself slowed down recoveries drastically. But Opposition leaders, particularly former Chief Minister Chandrababu Naidu, used this as an opportunity to

---

[21]   Based on the Status of Microfinance Survey, NABARD Reports 2008, 2009, 2010 and 2011.

[22]   http://blogs.ft.com/beyond-brics/2010/11/01/indias-microfinance-crisis-the-rahul-gandhi-factor/#axzz1sqxBojDc.

[23]   http://www.ysryouthcongress.in/2011/06/blog-post_23.html.

[24]   G.O.M.S. 356, Panchayat Raj & Rural Development (RD-1), 19th October 2010.

win popularity by saying the law had not done enough and told people not to re-pay MFI loans[25]. Similar statement was also made by Narayana of Communist Party of India[26].

This led to a mass default. Over 9.2 million loans worth Rs 72000 million (about USD 1.5 billion at that time) became overdue and 90 % remain unpaid till Apr 2012. Banks panicked and stopped lending to MFIs all over India and the out-standings of the MFIs shrank by half.

People took the convenient interpretation and stopped repaying MFI loans. In the aftermath of the AP MFI Act, 2011, the credit flow from banks to SHGs in AP also came down. This led the AP government to set up a special institution. Titled Sthree Nidhi[27], this is an apex cooperative credit society that has been formed to provide interest free loans to women[28]. Using a high-tech platform, it disbursed Rs 660 crore in loans to members of women's SHGs. But this has had hardly any im-pact on the overall credit availability as bank credit became tighter and money lenders continued to be the main source of funding at 5–10 % per month (60–120 % per annum) interest rate. Thus, in a last act of political desperation, to make itself look like the champion of the poor, the AP Government announced "*vaddi leni runam*" i.e., interest free loan[29].

4   Emerging Scenario – Responsible Finance

The AP crisis led to several regulatory reforms and operational improvements. The larger MFOIs, which are NBFCs, formed as self-regulatory organisation – the Microfinance Institutions network (MFIN) and all of them joined the RBI ap-proved credit bureaus, contributing over 70 million loan records and following a code of conduct, which prevented over and multiple lending. MFIN also system-atically started interacting with political and administrative leaders to obviate cri-ses before those arose.

4.1   RBI Upgraded the Regulatory Framework for MFIs

Following the AP Microfinance crises, the RBI appointed the Malegam Commit-tee to study the MFI regulatory environment in India. The Malegam Committee after a consultative process with all stakeholders, including the Government of

---

[25]   http://www.indianexpress.com/news/dont-repay-microfinance-loans-tdp/706093/.

[26]   http://www.siasat.com/english/news/cpi-leader-tells-mfi-borrowers-not-repay-loan.

[27]   https://www.sthreenidhi.ap.gov.in.

[28]   G.O.Ms.No. 285, PANCHAYAT RAJ & RURAL DEVELOPMENT (RD-II) DEPART-MENT, Dated:26.08.2011.

[29]   G.O.Ms.No. 403, PANCHAYAT RAJ & RURAL DEVELOPMENT (RD.II) DEPART-MENT, Dated:26.12.2011.

India, select State Governments, major NBFCs working as MFIs, industry associations of MFIs working in the country, other smaller MFIs, and major banks etc., recommended (i) defining microfinance loans as up to Rs 50,000 per household, of which no more than 25 % could be for consumption purposes and placed an income limit of the clients (Rs. 50,000 pa); (ii) imposed a margin cap and an interest rate cap on individual loans; (iii) transparency in interest charges; (iv) lending by not more than two MFIs to individual borrowers; (v) creation of one or more credit information bureaus; (vi) establishment of a proper system of grievance redressal procedure by MFIs; (vii) creation of one or more "social capital funds"; and (viii) continuation of categorisation of bank loans to MFIs, complying with the regulation laid down for NBFC-MFIs, under the priority sector. The Committee also made a number of recommendations regarding MFI supervision, corporate governance etc.[30] The RBI accepted the broad framework of regulations. Loans to MFIs will remain under the classification of priority sector lending provided they fulfil the Malegaon conditions. Besides a limit has been placed on the maximum income of the clients (Rs. 60,000 for rural and Rs. 1,20,000 for urban), size of indebtedness (not to exceed Rs. 50,000), extent of loan that can be used for consumption (maximum 25 %), etc. The RBI also imposed both a cap on interest rate (max 26 %), as well on the net interest margin (12 %). The acceptance of the framework of Malegam Committee by the RBI provided much needed orderliness to the sector.

4.2   Microfinance Institutions (Development and Regulation) Bill 2012

The GoI introduced the Microfinance Institutions (Development and Regulation) Bill 2012 in the Parliament to further strengthen the regulatory framework in the microfinance industry. Drafted with extensive inputs from MFIs, SIDBI and NABARD, features of the Bill include: (i) defining microfinance broadly – beyond just lending, to include savings, insurance, money transfers, etc.; (ii) inclusion of NBFC MFIs in its purview, in addition to NGO-MFIs; (iii) recognition of the RBI as the sole regulatory of NBFC MFIs and exclusion of MFIs from the purview of Money Lender Act; and (iv) Strengthened client protection norms – establishment of advisory councils at the central, state and district levels and restrictions on pricing and profitability; and an Ombudsman system. Greater insistence of transparency in pricing and fees.

---

[30]   Ramesh S Arunachalam, http://microfinance-in-india.blogspot.in/2011/05/rbi-acceptance-of-malegam-committee.html.

5 Conclusion

The current phase of microfinance sector could be viewed as the beginning of a period of qualitative transformation. While the first phase (1996–2010) could be characterized as a period of rapid expansion of the MFI sector with a quantum jump in micro-lending to small borrowers, the current phase (2011– onwards) could be seen as a period of qualitative consolidation of the microfinance industry with the strengthening and increased clarity on regulatory framework and consumer protection norms – in other words, the phase of "responsible finance".

While the first phase placed a larger emphasis on micro-credit, the second phase will expand the range of financial services offered by MFIs to also include thrift, insurance, pension services and money transfer. In the second phase, consumer protection norms are stronger. With Credit Information Bureaus having access to over 70 million MFI loans, instances of multiple lending and over-indebtedness will reduce sharply. With the institution of Ombudsmen, the instances of misbehaviour with customers and coercive recovery practices are bound to get minimised. The high growth, high profit regime prevailing from 2006–10 has been curbed by the RBI capping interest margins on the one hand, and the banks squeezing the extent of credit they give to MFIs. Even the investor mania is long since over after the SKS shares plunged from a high of INR 1400 to a low of Rs 60. But more sober investors are coming back and investing in more solidly run MFIs.

The AP crisis was not caused either by the reckless actions of a few MFI promoters not by over-zealous bureaucrats out to protect SHG women from coercion. It was the failure of the complete eco-system – from the rich investor in Europe to the poor borrowers in AP villages. All played their part in the unfolding of this tragedy. The investors saw microfinance as a way of doing good while doing well, expecting high returns when this was unrealistic. The MFI promoters, CEOs and managements, desperate for capital to grow, fell in line to fulfil these expectations. Banks fuelled this growth with a lot of leveraged loan funds, as they found this to be an easy way to meet their priority sector lending obligation, with a high margin. MFI field staff were incentivised to lend more and recover tightly. Borrowers could not resist the temptation of easy loans till they realised that repaying one loan by taking another gets them into more and more indebtedness. The regulator, RBI, followed a policy of benign neglect.

But there is still a lot to be learnt by all these stakeholders. MFIs have to learn that they cannot deal with the poor – the vote bank of the politicians – on just their own terms. Banks have to learn that they will never be able to reach the poor as efficiently as dedicated MFIs and so they must support this channel instead of setting up their own mimic channels. Multilaterals like the World Bank have to learn that they cannot help the poor by providing funding which is used by politicians to subsidise interest rates to unsustainable levels. Its investment arm, the IFC and other investors must learn to curb their expectations of returns or seek those elsewhere. Most importantly, politicians have to learn the simple principle that they cannot drive down the price (interest rate) of a commodity and yet expect its supply to go up.

CHAPTER 2

Armageddon or Adolescence?
Making Sense of Microfinance's Recent Travails

*David Roodman**

Abstract

The pendulum of public perception is swinging against microfinance. That leaves the thoughtful observer, wary of extreme claims in any direction, with a puzzle. Is microfinance a bane or a boon or in between? This paper reviews the triumphs and troubles of the microfinance industry. It then sets forth a frame for assessing the impact of microfinance, one that helps put the recent challenges in perspective. And it offers some thoughts, in light of these difficulties, about key tasks going forward. It concludes that microcredit stimulates small-scale business activity, but that the best available evidence fails to show it reducing poverty. Its ability to empower people, especially women, is also ambiguous. Still, there is no question that all people need financial services. The main achievement of the microfinance movement has been the founding of businesses and businesslike non-profits that are delivering these services to millions of people on a sustainable basis.

The core problem facing the industry is that just as a stable banking system is more than a bunch of banks, a microfinance industry is more likely to be safe and resilient if it contains not just microfinance institutions, but credit bureaus, consumer protection laws, effective regulators, and more; and many of these other institutions are weak or absent in poor nations. It is hard (though not impossible) for donors and social investors to improve them. Yet the stronger they are, the higher is the safe speed limit for growth of microfinance institutions. The weaker they are, the more that microfinance institutions will need to internalize limits on their behavior and growth. Key steps may include giving those with an institutional commitment to the "social bottom line," such as representatives of non-governmental organizations, public agencies or social investors, a formal role in microfinance institution governance; creating systems for defining and enforcing responsible lending behavior; and building collective arrangements such as an international credit bureau to monitor and modulate aggregate investment flows into microfinance markets.

---

* Senior Fellow, Center for Global Development.

1   Introduction

Speaking in India just after the government of Andhra Pradesh had ambushed the microcredit industry amid reports of suicide, Sam Daley-Harris observed that the movement he had done so much to build was undergoing a "near-death experience." Indeed, recent years have delivered harsh shocks to the global microfinance industry and to the broader movement that incubated and supports it. Microcredit bubbles have inflated and popped. "Successful" initial public offerings (IPOs) have sparked heartfelt debates about the proper balance between price and profit. Star academics have found the impact of microcredit on poverty to be merely neutral. New works in print and film have accused microcredit of impacts far worse than neutral, portraying the microfinance investment industry as morally corrupt.

Clearly the pendulum of public perception is swinging against microfinance. That leaves the thoughtful observer, wary of extreme claims in any direction, with a puzzle. Is microfinance a bane or a boon or in between?

There were good reasons why in 2006 the Nobel Committee awarded a peace prize to Muhammad Yunus and the Grameen Bank, with its millions of female owner-clients. Not for nothing did the United Nations declare 2005 the Year of Microcredit. For by then, the microfinance industry had stood up robust financial institutions delivering useful financial services to millions of deserving women and men who otherwise lacked access to such services. It had demonstrated that outsiders could help these institutions become financially self-sufficient. And as the industries have matured they have generally cut prices and diversified their offerings, in particular moving into savings. This success in building whole industries is rare in the annals of foreign aid and philanthropy. Meanwhile, a distinct industry has developed to channel at least a billion dollars per year of private investment into microfinance.[1] This investment helped finance an expansion from some 11 million microcredit borrowers worldwide in 2000 to 94 million in 2010.[2]

This paper reviews the triumphs and troubles of the microfinance industry. It then sets forth a frame for assessing the impact of microfinance, one that helps put the recent challenges in perspective. And it offer some thoughts, in light of these difficulties, about key tasks going forward.

Overall, microcredit does stimulate small-scale business activity, but going by the best available evidence, it does not reliably reduce poverty. Its ability to empower people, especially women, is also ambiguous since while it can give women more economic power, in some cases it has burdened them with the fear of default and loss of face in public group setting. Nevertheless, just as mainstream finance is essential despite its shortcomings, so are micro-financial services inherently

---

[1]   Figure is net new commitments from individual and institutional investors based on author's analysis of CGAP Cross-Border Funding Surveys (Roodman 2012, p. 241).

[2]   Author's calculations, based on data downloaded August 22, 2012. Figures exclude some large institutions that are heavily subsidized or up-market on the credit side: Banco Caja Social Colombia, Banco Popular do Brasil, Kenya Post Office Savings Bank, Khushhali Bank of Pakistan, Postal Savings Bank of China, and Vietnam Bank for Social Policies.

valuable even when they do not help every client they touch. The greatest achievement of the microfinance movement has been the founding of businesses and businesslike non-profits that are delivering these inherently useful services to millions of people on a sustainable basis.

In this view, the greatest concern arising out of the recent travails is that in some places the industry has strayed from this core strength primarily by growing too fast. The result in some countries has been a collective eagerness to lend that has made microcredit less safe, and led to bubbles and political backlashes that damaged or destroyed microfinance institutions.

The core problem facing the industry is that just as a stable banking system is more than a bunch of banks, a microfinance industry is more likely to be safe and resilient if it contains not just microfinance institutions, but credit bureaus, consumer protection laws, effective regulators, and more. Many of these other institutions are weak or absent in poor nations (not to mention many rich nations). And it is not easy for donors and social investors to improve them. The stronger they are, the higher is the safe speed limit for growth of microfinance institutions. The weaker they are, the more that microfinance institutions will need to internalize limits on their behavior and growth.

2   The Triumphs

Since 2000, microfinance has expanded remarkably. Going by data from the Microfinance Information Exchange (MIX), total outstanding microloans rose from $2.2 billion in 2000 to $80 billion in 2011, a 37-fold increase overall, and equivalent to 39 % growth per year. (See Fig. 1.) Regions with higher GDP/capita—Latin

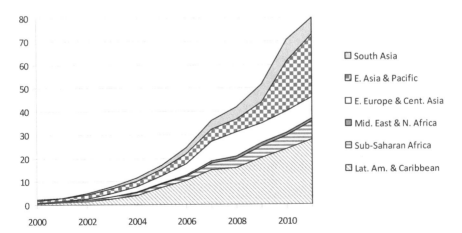

Fig. 1. Billions in Outstanding Microloans by Region, 2000–11

Source: MIX

America, Eastern Europe, and East Asia—accounted for most of this expansion because on average people there can absorb larger loans.

The trends in the total number of loans, rather than the total value, differ in a few ways, primarily because South Asia, where loans are small but numerous, moves to the fore. Worldwide, the tally climbed from 10.8 million in 2000 to 95 million in 2010, but then dropped to 81 million in 2011 because of the near shutdown of the industry in the Indian state of Andhra Pradesh.[3] (See Fig. 2. Section 3 describes that event.) Less evident from the graph is the shrinkage in the Middle East and North Africa from 2.2 million to 1.5 million borrowers, which was driven by the implosion of the Moroccan industry, from 680,000 to 230,000 loans.

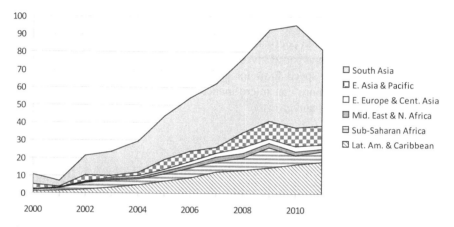

Fig. 2. Millions of outstanding microloans, 2000–11
Source: MIX

The arrival of microcredit as a major business can be measured in other ways. Half of outstanding microloans at the end of 2011 were made by microfinance institutions (MFIs) reporting operating expenses below 14% of the loan stock. (See Fig. 3, which plots the distribution of outstanding microloans by lender's expense ratio.[4]) Fourteen percent exceeds levels typically found in conventional retail credit, but is lean given the administrative challenges of lending in small quanta to people operating in the informal economy.

---

[3]   These and subsequent graphs exclude some large institutions that are heavily subsidized or up-market on the credit side: Banco Caja Social Colombia, Banco Popular do Brasil, Kenya Post Office Savings Bank, Khushhali Bank of Pakistan, Postal Savings Bank of China, and Vietnam Bank for Social Policies.

[4]   This and subsequent graphs omit the Grameen Bank for lack of data and BRAC for lack of reliable data. For clarity, these graphs also omit a small number of institutions outside the plotted ranges.

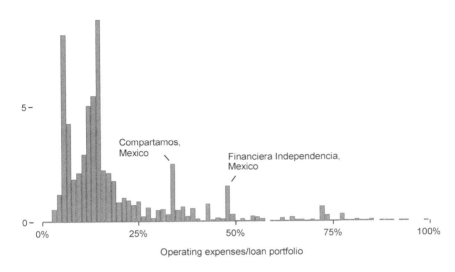

Fig. 3. Number of outstanding loans by operating expense ratio of MFI, 2011
Source: MIX

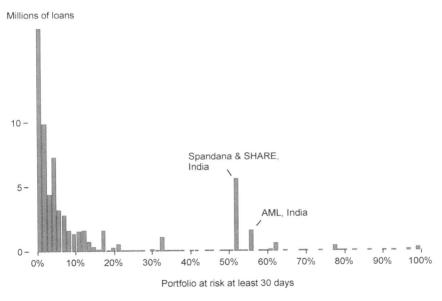

Fig. 4. Number of outstanding loans by Portfolio at Risk more than 30 days, 2011
Source: MIX

Outside of India, portfolio quality is generally high too. The share of outstanding credits on which payments are at least 30 days late (portfolio at risk, 30 days, or PAR 30) is generally low: half of all outstanding microloans at end-2011 were from MFIs with a PAR30 below 4 % and three-quarters were from lenders below 10 %. (See Fig. 4.) The major exception is Andhra Pradesh, where Spandana, Share, and AML carried large stocks of delinquent loans on their books. (As a publicly traded company, SKS is subject to stricter accounting rules, and had already written off most of its Andhra Pradesh delinquencies).

The prevalence of efficiency helps explain why most microloans come from MFIs with positive profit margins (net operating income as a share of financial revenue; see Fig. 5). For most, weighting by number of loans, the profit margin lay between 0 % and 25 % in 2011.

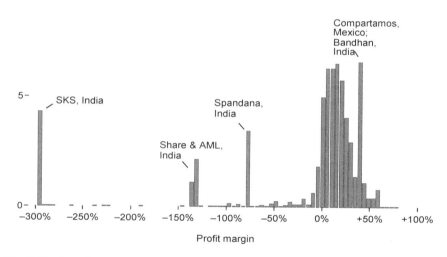

Fig. 5. Number of outstanding loans by profit Margin of MFI, 2011
Source: MIX

The story is similar if one examines return on assets (ROA; Fig. 6) or return on equity (ROE; Fig. 7). Many major MFIs make 4 % ROA or more, which is impressive by banking industry standards. The outliers on the negative end include the Andhra Pradesh MFIs, especially SKS because of large write-offs. High-ROE MFIs include Compartamos in Mexico at 34 %, and India's Bandhan at 38 %.

These figures overestimate the self-sufficiency of MFIs that obtain debt financing on favorable terms from socially motivated investors. Forced to operate on the same playing field as other firms of similar size and risk, their expenses would be

Millions of loans

10 –

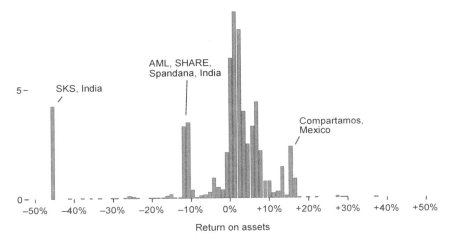

Fig. 6. Number of outstanding loans by return on assets (ROA) of MFI, 2011
Source: MIX

Millions of loans

10 –

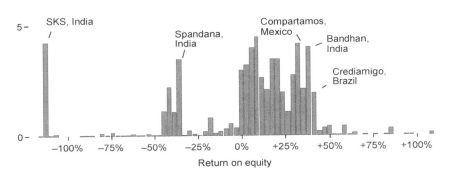

Fig. 7. Number of outstanding loans by return on equity (ROE) of MFI, 2011
Source: MIX

higher and profits lower. That said, while the extent of the overestimate is hard to know, it is unlikely to fundamentally change the picture of the microfinance industry as operating under its own power. Financing costs are only about a quarter of operating costs for individual lenders, and about a sixth for the group lenders that serve most microcredit clients. If withdrawal of grants and concessional investment elements doubled financing costs that would increase total costs by one-fourth to one-sixth.[5] Some of this cost increase could be offset by increases in efficiency or interest rates. Thus it seems likely that the majority of microfinance clients are served by institutions that are self-sufficient or within striking distance of being so.

The microfinance investment industry has grown too. The first dedicated microfinance investment vehicle (MIV) was Profund: founded in 1995, it focused on Latin America and turned a profit over its ten-year life. By 2000, 15 MIVs operated; by 2010, 101 did (Symbiotics 2012a, see Fig. 8). However, three MIVs closed in 2010 and another nine followed in 2010, so that the total number of active MIVs fell on net in 2011, to 99.) While MIVs have invested predominantly in debt (more than 80 % of their funding Symbiotics 2012a), microfinance securities have become more variegated: there are direct loans, tradable bonds, equity, collateralized debt obligations, and more. Creativity in finance of course has its pitfalls; but the arrival of such tools marks a kind of maturation for the industry.

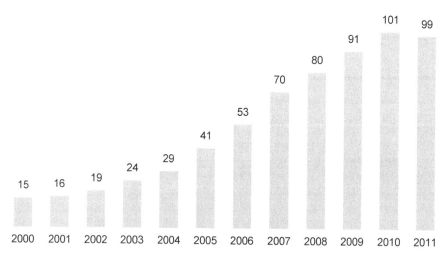

Fig. 8. Number of microfinance investment vehicles, 2000–11

Source: Symbiotics

---

[5]   Cost figures from Roodman (2012, Table 5–2), which is based on MIX (2010). For a more refined analysis of the contribution of subsidies to profits, see Cull, Demirgüç-Kunt, and Morduch (2009).

Microfinance has been most successful, in the business sense of expanding operations, in the domain of credit—but not only there. As for deposit-taking, the data are too spotty to plot trends reliably, but figures for a recent year suggest that many mature microfinance institutions are taking savings on a large scale. (See Table 1, a top-20 list of savings-takers in 2009, the last year with relatively complete data.) Bank Rakyat Indonesia looms over all, with more than 21 million accounts. The Bangladeshi big three (Grameen Bank, BRAC, and ASA) also cluster near the top. After them come institutions from elsewhere in South Asia, Latin

Table 1. Number of Voluntary Savings Accounts, Twenty Largest Account Providers, 2009 (most recent year with relatively complete data)

Name	Country	Accounts (thousands)
BRI	Indonesia	21,229
Grameen Bank	Bangladesh	79,701
BRAC	Bangladesh	5,447
Equity Bank	Kenya	4,038
Caja Popular Mexicana	Mexico	3,514
Khan Bank	Mongolia	2,500
ASA	Bangladesh	1,324
Capitec Bank	South Africa	12,972
UNACOOPEC	Cote d'Ivoire	925
Crediscotia	Peru	8,081
BURO	Bangladesh	747
FECECAM	Benin	708
RCPB	Burkina Faso	673
ACSI	Ethiopia	612
CMS	Senegal	607
ACLEDA	Cambodia	586
PRODEM	Bolivia	568
WDB	Sri Lanka	555
BancoEstado	Chile	504
Sabaragamuwa	Sri Lanka	448

Notes: 1Includes an unknown number of involuntary accounts, required as part of borrowing. 2Number of depositors rather than accounts. Excludes the Banco Caja Social Colombia and the Kenya Post Office Savings Bank as institutions that do not emphasize financial self-sufficiency.

Source: MIX

America, and Sub-Saharan Africa. These include PRODEM in Bolivia, which along with its urban cousin BancoSol (the two descend from the same non-profit), holds nearly 1.2 million savings accounts (MIX 2012)—that in a nation of 10 million people and perhaps 2 million households.

The microfinance movement has achieved notable successes over the last decade with another financial service, money transfers. The leading example is M-PESA, the extraordinarily successful phone-based system in Kenya. Run by a mobile telephone operator, M-PESA is not part of the microfinance industry as usually conceived. But it is part of the historical *movement*, for it began as a way to service microloan payments electronically (Hughes and Lonie 2007). And it embodies the dominant philosophy in the industry, that the best way to serve the poor is to operate in a businesslike, cost-covering way, in order to scale up. In its first five years of life, M-PESA has grown to 15 million adults. To date, it has transferred some $15 billion.[6] No microfinance institution has ever grown so fast.

In sum, while certain failings of microcredit have become clear in recent years, and must be reckoned with, in assessing the industry's past and shaping its future, it is important to recognize its successes too.

3   The Troubles

Despite all these achievements, the six years since the symbolic accolade of the Nobel Prize have been tough on the microfinance industry. ROE on investible MFIs fell from +20 % at the end of 2007 to −5 % at end-2009 (Symbiotics 2012b). The first MIV closures occurred in 2010 and accelerated in 2011. The country with the most loans, India, saw a major microcredit setback; and the number-two country, Bangladesh, is witnessing a government take-over of its leading MFI. The tone of press coverage has flipped from positive to negative. Investment growth is slowing to the low single digits (MicroRate 2012).

Four principal challenges have emerged: rigorous academic studies on the impact of microcredit; public stock flotations that stoked controversy by arguably enriching a few investors and founders at the expense of the poor; coercive loan collection practices; and microcredit bubbles in some markets. Environmental factors also turned against the industry, including the global financial crisis and political antibodies in Nicaragua, India, and Bangladesh. But since the latter are complex and idiosyncratic and largely beyond the control of the industry, they will not be discussed in this short review.

---

[6]   Squad Digital (2012).

3.1 Randomized Impact Studies

In 2009, the first two randomized studies of the impact of microcredit appeared. As discussed below, the studies' conclusions should not be devastating for microfinance. But the new research, by questioning the popular perception of microcredit as a powerful weapon against poverty, did cause negative press. "Perhaps microfinance isn't such a big deal after all," ran a headline in the *Financial Times*, for example (Harford 2009).[7] And bad press is a threat in itself.

One of the studies looked at group credit in Hyderabad, the capital of Andhra Pradesh; the other, individual loans in Manila. Neither new analysis found an impact on average poverty, at least within 12–18 months of availability (Banerjee et al. 2009; Karlan and Zinman 2011). "Poverty" is proxied in the studies by such indicators as number of children in school and monthly per-capita household spending. The Hyderabad experiment, however, did reveal a stimulus to microenterprise starts, investment, and profits. Perhaps the profit increase did not measurably increase household spending because families devoting more time to business activities earned less wages outside the home. Or perhaps such translation did occur but outside the study's short timeframe. (A three-year follow-up is due out soon.)

Table 2. Summary of results from randomized microcredit impact studies

Authors	Where	When	Female % of sample	Level of randomization	Credit type (group or individual)	Follow-up (months)	Investment/ enterprise	Wellbeing
Banerjee, Duflo, Glennerster, and Kinnan	Hyderabad, India	2006–08	100	District	G	12–18	+	0
Karlan & Zinman	Manila, Philippines	2006–08	85	Individual	I	11–22	–	0
Crépon, Devoto, Duflo, & Parienté	Morocco	2006–09	100	Village	G (mostly)	24	+	0
Attanasio, Augsburg, De Haas, Fitzsimons, & Harmgart	Mongolia	2008–10	100	Village	G, I	8–17	Group: + Individulal: 0	Group: +food spending
Augsburg, De Haas, Harmgart, & Meghir	Bosnia & Herzegovina	2008–10	39	Individual	I	~14	+	Lower food spending

Source: Banerjee et al. (2009); Karlan and Zinman (2011); Crépon et al. (2011); Attanasio et al. (2011); Augsburg et al. (2012).

---

[7] Harford went on to tweet: "Note to all microfinance enthusiasts: I DO NOT WRITE MY OWN HEADLINES," j.mp/WIHnR7.

Further studies in a variety of contexts—Africa, Europe, and Asia; for-profit and non-profit; rural and urban; individual- and group-based lending—have generally corroborated the findings of stimulus to microenterprise and lack of short-term impact on poverty. (See Table 2.) The diversity of the study settings makes it harder to argue that the 2009 results were anomalous. The burden of proof is now on those who would argue that microcredit in some form or in some contexts does reliably reduce poverty.

3.2   Initial Public Offerings and Charges of "Usury"

Initial public offerings (IPOs) of stock in MFIs have triggered larger earthquakes of controversy. In 2007, Mexico's Compartamos sold some 30% of itself to the public. The transaction valued the company at more than $1.5 billion (Rosenberg 2007), a financial prize owing almost entirely to the MFI's ability to charge poor women interest rates of 92–195%/year (Roodman 2011) and thereby earn an ROA of 18% and ROE of 39%.[8] While conceding that most of the capital gains went to the non-profit institutions that were Compartamos's main early investors—Accíon International and the World Bank's International Finance Corporation—critics have questioned the morality of earning such high profits off the poor. Compartamos co-founder Carlos Danel has defended the high profits as demonstrating the business viability of banking the poor.[9] But critics asked: if this is not usury, what is?[10]

The IPO of India's SKS in 2010 scored a full point higher on the Richter scale. Individual investors and venture capitalists, not non-profit institutions, reaped the capital gains. At the peak stock price, the stakes of founder Vikram Akula and billionaire venture capitalist Vinod Khosla were estimated at $90 million each (Chen et al. 2010). Although microcredit costs far less in India than Mexico—SKS charged 25–32% per annum (MF*Transparency* 2011)—SKS and other for-profit microlenders still came in for severe criticism for combining aggressive disbursement with aggressive collection practices.

3.3   Reports of Abusive Credit Methods

In the months before the SKS IPO television channels in the company's home state of Andhra Pradesh began broadcasting stories of women forced, by the burden of microdebt, into prostitution or suicide. As in many countries, media companies in India tend to sensationalize to get attention, and sometimes in order to advance the political agendas of their owners. And in India, microcredit is political, because elected officials have long competed with each other to offer lower

---

[8]   The high number, unlike the low one, compounds the interest cost and factors in the potential indirect cost of a 10% savings requirement. Both numbers include value added tax.

[9]   Interview with author, June 24, 2008.

[10]   See Yunus criticism in Keith Epstein and Geri Smith, "Compartamos: From Nonprofit to Profit," *BusinessWeek*, December 13, 2007.

interest rates through government-run lending programs. One of those—the Self-Help Group (SHG) program—competes directly with microfinance.

Despite the suspect source, the stories of abuse proved hard to completely dismiss. An organization that helps administer Andhra Pradesh's SHG program compiled a list of 54 allegedly microcredit-linked suicides (SERP 2010). Bereaved family members told their stories to reporters, who captured them on video.[11] Allegations also emerged of loan officers visiting the homes of defaulters and publicly haranguing them to shame them into repaying. Suicides were evidently so rare among microcredit clients (a reported 54 out of millions) that the small loans may have *prevented* as many deaths as they caused, by giving a handful of cornered people a way to go on; but their stories will never be told on TV. Nonetheless, the stories of multiple borrowing, abusive collection practices, and frenetic growth of microcreditors taken over by investors looking for a quick exit were all signs that something had indeed gone seriously wrong in Indian microcredit. That belief appears shared by a majority of the microfinance industry, even SKS founder Vikram Akula (Hanna 2012).

What then do the suicides signify for microfinance? The combination of easy offers of credit and tough demands for repayment, enforced through public embarrassment of group meetings, probably put many Indians in a tough spot—perhaps only the minority of all borrowers, but far more than 54. The likely difficulties of this larger but less well-defined group cannot be dismissed as regrettable rarities.

3.4   Bubble Troubles

The boom and bust in Andhra Pradesh did not follow the storyline of a classic bubble—one that implodes under its own weight—because the crash was brought about by sudden government action. Nevertheless, growth that in retrospect appears dangerously rapid, on the order of 100 % per year, is an important element of the story. And Andhra Pradesh is not unique in this respect. Experts at CGAP documented and analyzed similar reversals in 2008–09 in Bosnia and Herzegovina, Morocco, Nicaragua, and the Punjab region of Pakistan (Chen, Rasmussen, and Reille 2010). Each case is distinctive in certain respects. Politics was a major factor in Nicargua, for example, as President Daniel Ortega endorsed the *no pago* movement. Ripples from the global financial crisis also may have hurt repayment rates. Yet the authors judged these three common threads to be primary:

1. Concentrated market competition and multiple borrowing.

2. Overstretched MFI systems and controls.

3. Erosion of MFI lending discipline.

---

[11]   See for example "India's Microcredit Meltdown," Assignment, BBC, January 29, 2011, bbc.in/l6H2tI; and Tom Heinemann, "The Micro Debt," 2010, j.mp/UCwUE9.

The three can be further distilled as: an imbalance between the rate of expansion of the quantity of lending and the capacity of the systems needed to assure the quality of lending. With the partial exception of Morocco, socially motivated foreign investors, public and private, fueled the rapid growth (Roodman 2012, p. 278). They therefore bear some responsibility for these failures.

4   Does Microfinance Work?

Recent events raise fundamental questions about the efficacy of microfinance. But the best answers to the questions cannot be reached merely by reacting piecemeal to the pinpricks and body blows. We must think systematically. What constitutes success in microfinance? That is, when we ask whether microfinance works, what does "work" mean? Given a definition, or definitions, of "works," what evidence is available on whether success is being achieved? Is the evidence of high quality? How safely can one generalize from it? What do the answers to these questions imply for an overall assessment of microfinance, and for strategy going forward?

Roodman (2012) discerns three distinct conceptions of success in microfinance. Each corresponds, at least in English, to a different definition of "development"; and each tends to lead one to different kinds of evidence for testing.

4.1   Escape from Poverty

The first conception of success is "development as escape from poverty." This corresponds to the widespread perception that microfinance, microcredit in particular, helps people out of poverty. That perception owes to stories of women taking loans to raise goats or sew saris, gain independence from husbands, and better their lives and their children's lives. The perception was importantly bolstered by academic research seeming to show that microcredit reduces poverty.

However, recent studies have significantly shifted our understanding of the impacts of microcredit. The new generation of work is randomized, just like the best drug trials. For lack of randomization, the older studies could not as credibly rule out such statistical problems as reverse causation. That is: if people who use microcredit are better off, perhaps that is not because the microcredit helped them but because being more affluent made them more able to borrow. And replication of some leading studies of the old generation shows that methodological sophistication meant to attack problems such as reverse causality mostly obscured them (Roodman and Morduch 2011).

As Table 2 showed, five randomized trials of microcredit have been released. They are reasonably consistent in showing that microcredit *does* stimulate microenterprise, as measured by business starts, investment, and profits. But as mentioned before, they are equally consistent in finding no impact on poverty. In this respect, the literature has confirmed Peter Rossi's (1987) Stainless Steel Law of Evaluation, which distilled his decades of experience evaluating programs: "The better designed the impact assessment of a social program, the more likely is the resulting estimate of net impact to be zero." Worse studies tend to show bigger impacts and better studies smaller impacts.

Randomized studies of microsavings have produced more positive results. Among vendors in a Kenyan market town and a group of tobacco farmers in Malawi, the availability of a formal deposit account has increased investment *and* household income over 12 months (Dupas and Robinson 2009; Brune et al. 2010).

It is worth bearing in mind that each of these studies examines just a small dot on the microfinance landscape—a particular product offered at a particular time in a particular place to a particular population, tracked for one to two years. The studies cannot prove that microcredit has never reduced poverty anywhere, nor that microsavings is always better in this respect.

That said, decisions that must be made today should be made based on conservative generalizations from the best evidence available today. And the best evidence available today says that microcredit cannot be relied up on to cause development-as-escape-from-poverty.

4.2 Freedom

The second conception of success borrows from the work of Amartya Sen, author of *Development as Freedom* (1999). For Sen, the essence of development is not just economic growth. It is expanding agency in one's life, control over one's circumstances. Such freedom flows from many sources: income, assets, education, health, civil rights, political rights. Central to Sen's theory is the observation that freedoms tend to support one another. Education leads to more income, which leads to more education. At the macro level, he has famously argued that in India freedom of the press prevented famine (freedom from want) in the 1960s, whereas in China lack of political freedom facilitated the 30 million deaths of the Great Leap Forward. Freedoms are thus both ends and means.

Financial services for the poor are inherently empowering. They are for helping poor people manage their money, which is central to economic survival. No work makes this clearer than *Portfolios of the Poor* (Collins et al. 2009). Through stories and data from detailed financial diaries, the book illustrates how those who "live on $2 a day" *don't* live on $2 a day, but on $3 one day, 50 cents the next, $3 the day after, and so on. The volatility and unpredictability of income, along with the greater vulnerability to health emergencies, means that poor people need financial services *more* than the rich, in order to set aside money in good times and draw it out in bad. Informally, out of necessity, they develop credit, savings, insurance, and transfer services to meet this core need. Forms of microfinance are additional options, with disadvantages (rigidity) and advantages (reliability, impersonality).

But *inherently* does not mean *automatically*. Credit can entrap. As a result, when and how much various kinds of microfinance empower or disempower is an empirical question. This question about impacts is hard to answer, for the reasons given earlier.

One kind of research relevant here is *qualitative* work, done by anthropologists who immerse themselves for a month or a year in communities where microfinance is offered, closely following the lives of some of those affected. The strength of such work is the rich insight it can give into the lives of human beings, which is particularly helpful when studying a subtle and complex concept such as "empowerment." The disadvantages are that the samples are small, usually in the dozens; and it is rarely experimental, thus lacking the capacity of randomized trials to reliably identify causality.

The qualitative findings on empowerment and microcredit are mixed, with the most negative results emerging for group loans. Helen Todd (1996) tells of a woman in Bangladesh labelled Begum who, along with her husband, invested her Grameen loans in cows and fertilizer, and climbed up a rung on the income ladder. And surely there have been women for whom it was a breakthrough to do serious financial business in public. But there are also worrying stories. Karim (2008) describes a "house-breaking" in Bangladesh in which a peer group carted off the belongings of a defaulting woman in order to repay her loan. Individual loans, which are free of the yoke of joint liability, appear more empowering (Kabeer 2001).

Savings appears rather differently from credit in the development-as-freedom light. It is harder to get in trouble by saving too much than by borrowing too much—unless the savings institution becomes insolvent. As an empirical matter, deposit-takers within the mainstream microfinance movement have so far lived up to the trust placed in them. If anything, the responsibility of holding deposits has led MFIs to lend more conservatively. Fear of unleashing a bank run may also deter politicians from interfering in operations (Chen 2011). Were a major deposit-taking MFI to go under, and were savers not kept whole, the empirical picture would change radically.

4.3 Industry Building

It is interesting to note that for savings to empower, they must be *safe*—and that requires high-quality institutions, specifically, some combination of sound banks and effective supervisors. This brings us to the last conception of success in microfinance, "development as industry building." Though overshadowed in the public imagination by the other two conceptions, it was fully articulated early in the movement (von Pischke 1991; Otero and Rhyne 1994; Krahnen and Schmidt 1994). Within economics, it resonates with the thinking of Austrian economist Joseph Schumpeter. Writing 100 years ago, Schumpeter (1934 [1911]) reacted against the supply-and-demand graphs made famous by Alfred Marshall, which explained how prices helped the economy find equilibrium. Schumpeter wanted to understand why the economy he lived in operated in *dis*equilibrium as a steady stream of new firms and technologies perpetually disrupted the status quo. For

Schumpeter the essence of development lay in this "creative destruction." Indeed, the constant churning of industrialization is what has reduced poverty in Europe over the last two centuries and in China over the last three decades.

Microfinance has not turned many clients into heroes of creative destruction. Typically, they sell more tomatoes or raise more goats. However, the microfinance movement has built impressive institutions and industries in many countries. BRI in Indonesia; the Grameen Bank, BRAC, and ASA in Bangladesh; Pro Mujer in Peru; Bancosol in Bolivia; D-MIRO in Ecuador; Equity Bank in Kenya. These and others do something once thought impossible: they employ thousands, they serve millions, they compete, and as result they innovate, offering more flexible and diverse services at lower prices. If the randomized studies were showing microcredit to be the financial equivalent of cigarettes, we would not celebrate this flourishing; but the case is otherwise.

And while the contributions to development may not be significant macroeconomically, they are respectable against the checkered history of foreign aid and philanthropy, in which failure is common. The public and private donors who supported the creation of the BRI program, the Grameen Bank, Bancosol, and others, made real contributions to development.

But not all growth of microfinance has been worthy of the label "development." Sometimes creative destruction has been more destructive than creative. Examples include the apparent microcredit overshoots in Bosnia and Herzegovina, Morocco, Nicaragua, and parts of India and Pakistan, all of which burst within the last four years (Chen, Rasmussen, and Reille 2010).

5   Interpreting the Past and Present

5.1   A Realistic Vision of Success

This systematic review of the impact of microfinance according to different definitions of success is rather like a guidance counselor perusing a student's report card. It is not a conclusion, but an *input* to a comprehensive assessment that can help make sense of current difficulties and plot a path forward.

In light of this evidence, what strategies should those wanting to support financial services to the poor adopt? Just as one might engage a tutor for a student struggling to read, one logical response is to zero in on the weaknesses of microfinance, such as the inherent but dangerous tendency to press for near-perfect repayment rates. The Smart Campaign is one effort of this type. It has obtained hundreds of endorsements for a definition of responsible lending and is now piloting an audit system for compliance. Someday investors could condition their funding on such audits.

However, the more mature the student, the more important it becomes to recognize that her nature is to some degree fixed, and to cultivate her manifest strengths. Microfinance is a mature enough industry that the latter metaphor is apt.

We are most likely to do good if we help the industry play to its strengths, to guide it along its natural grain. And the evidence suggests that its strength is not in systematically lifting people out of poverty, but *building dynamic institutions to mass-produce inherently useful services for the poor*.

To discern this aptitude is not to imply that microfinance has always succeeded at what it does best. But it has done so often, and can do so more.

This conclusion sides with the "institutionalist" school associated with prominent German thinkers (J.D. von Pischke (1991); Jan Pieter Krahnen and Reinhardt Schmidt (1994); the work of C.P. Zeitinger and the ProCredit group), with the Ohio School (Dale Adams, Claudio Gonzalez-Vega, and again J.D. von Pischke), and with Acción International (e.g., Otero and Rhyne 1994). It implies that donors and social investors involved in microfinance should prioritize building financially self-sufficient institutions and stable industries. Subject to the constraint of financial self-sufficiency, they should support the delivery of financial services characterized by safety, diversity, flexibility, transparency, and prices appropriate to vulnerable people. Updating the philosophy, they should look to digital technologies in the hope that these will loosen the strictures of that binding constraint of self-sufficiency, allowing institutions to provide more diverse, safe, and flexible services at lower cost than once possible.

5.2   An Anchored Perspective on Recent Difficulties

This perspective anchors an analysis of most of the recent difficulties in microfinance.

It accepts the failure of the latest studies to demonstrate that microcredit reduces (or increases) poverty; it responds by observing that financial services, including credit, are inherently useful and that economic development has always involved the construction of institutions to deliver such services, however imperfect, on a large scale.

And it is dismayed, but not crushed, by the recent credit overshoots and reports of irresponsible lending practices. Much more than the impact studies, these signify serious flaws—direct challenges to the claimed core strength of microfinance in building institutions. However, to give up on microfinance at this point would be like giving up on mortgages because of the mortgage crises. Not only would it frustrate the continuing demand for microfinance, it would ignore and destroy the institutions that have been delivering it year in and year out, proving that safe, durable, large scale microfinance is possible.

As usual in credit crises, rapid growth appears to have been a core problem. This raises the question of what constitutes appropriate growth in microfinance. When is expansion healthy like the growth of a child and when is it unhealthy like cancer? A comparison between economy and ecology offers a way to think about this question (Roodman 2012). Asking when the arrival or growth of a microfinance institution enriches the economic fabric is like asking when the arrival of a new species adds resilience and productivity to an ecosystem. Answers to the ecological question arguably include: when the new species interconnects with other species in diverse ways, such as through predation, competition, and symbiosis; and when, as a result, the species' drive for growth is roughly counterbalanced by limits. Likewise, microfinance growth is most likely to enrich the economic fabric when MFIs link to many other economic actors—clients, regulators, domestic and foreign investors—and in many ways, including various forms of investment and financial service. Notably, relative to the common operating model that focuses on borrowing abroad and lending locally, a move into deposit-taking diversifies in two ways at once, connecting to a new source of capital and enriching service offerings.

The ecological analogy also suggests the value of broadening our concerns from the function of institutions to the functioning of industries. A *financial system* is more likely to be stable when it contains diverse and interacting players. In addition to the financial institutions, there generally must be an enabling regulatory environment, credit bureaus, consumer protections, supervisors that monitor capital adequacy and lending propriety, investors, rule of law (requiring accessible courts and police), perhaps deposit insurance, and more. In the ideal, and in practice, the exact configuration of a financial system will vary by context. Regardless, a lesson of history is that a sustainable system must consist of more than retail service institutions.

Ergo a sustainable microfinancial system, one that extends formal financial access to poorer people, must consist of more than MFIs. Historically, financial systems have typically begun with retail institutions; then, through bitter experience, governments and industry actors have added components such as credit bureaus and deposit insurance. Microfinance appears to be no exception to this pattern of often learning the hard way. But in some cases, donors and social investors can help governments learn from the past mistakes of others—instituting deposit insurance before a local bank run makes the need tragically obvious—or at least help governments learn faster once a crisis occurs.

5.3   The Lessons of Recent Troubles

A natural first step in trying to learn from a financial crisis is identifying what caused it. As we have seen in the financial crises in wealthy nations, the search for the cause is inherently muddled, and for two reasons.

First, the focus on causes ignored the question of agency. Suppose it was determined that sunspots contributed to the mortgage meltdowns in Ireland and Spain. Blaming sunspots would not help. Better to blame the parts of the system that humans control for not being robust to sunspots. That is a fanciful example, so replace sunspots with human greed, which is also a fact of nature. Arguably, it does not do us much good to blame the mortgage bubbles (or the Andhra Pradesh overshoot) on the greed of investors. More practical is to blame the bubbles on rules that did not fully take into account the consequences of inevitably greedy behavior. Now, the distinction between greed and rules to contain it is simplistic. After all, the rules are also made by self-interested people such as politicians. Still, politicians, regulators, donors, and social investors do often act in the public interest, so it is on them that our best hopes rest for agency in the public interest. Thus, as a practical matter, the search for causes converges to a focus on what these legislators and regulators should do differently next time, taking human greed as given.

The second factor muddling the search for a cause is that causes interact. The global financial crisis hit many countries, with diverse regulatory systems, so it is not credible to blame it purely on idiosyncratic national factors as Alan Greenspan and the Greek government's affinity for side deals with Goldman Sachs. Seemingly, the universal cause was the huge swell of capital, much of it from certain developing countries. On the other hand, thanks to regulations that made Canadian banking relatively boring and safe—in particular, inhibiting loan securitizations—Canada escaped major damage, even though it was tied to the same global capital markets (Atlantic Council and Thomson Reuters 2012). So, arguably, poor policies in the United States and Greece were the root cause after all. How to square this circle? At the risk of oversimplifying, the crises can be seen as arising from the *combination* of easy money and bad policies. If either had been eliminated, the crises would have been prevented. Thus we could blame—and adopt policies to redress—either factor alone and be partly right. But ideally, those seeking to act in the public interest would recognize both factors, survey possible policy changes that could affect either, then choose from among them in light of what is known about costs, effectiveness, and political and administrative constraints. The upshot is that it is important to distinguish the search for who or what to blame from the search for practical steps to prevent a repeat.

In the sweep of history, countries that are wealthy today have had the most time to learn hard lessons (and sometimes forget them). In these nations, the lending system includes such actors as retail lenders; investors therein; credit information bureaus; and regulatory bodies that limit and monitor aspects of credit products such as term, term disclosure, even pricing. For institutions that take deposits, additional regulators come knocking—to insure those deposits or ensure that under ordinary circumstances capital is on hand to absorb losses and meet withdrawal demands.

A truth often overlooked in excitement about microfinance as a retail service model is that it is no exception to this need for companion institutions. If anything, the need is greater when targeting the poor. The Economist Intelligence Unit annually surveys experts in order to assess the business environment for microfinance in dozens of countries. Implied in this work is a broad agenda for building microfinancial ecosystems. In contrast with the more famous Doing Business index, the Global Microscope survey puts roughly equal weight on the need for legal space to do operate—the need to avoid prohibitively burdensome regulation—and the need for well-functioning institutions of restraint (EIU 2012). The compilers of the Microscope cull data from relevant legal texts, scholarly articles, interviews with country experts, and other sources. On this basis, they make qualitative

Table 3. Results of 2012 Microscope Survey

Country	Regulatory framework for					Supporting institutions for				
	Microcredit portfolios	Forming microcredit institutions	Non-regulated institutions	Deposit-taking	Regulator admin. capacity	Accounting transparency	Pricing transparency	Dispute resolution	Credit bureaus	Transacting through agents
Peru	4	3	2	3	4	3	4	3	4	3
Bolivia	3	2	3	3	3	3	4	3	4	2
Pakistan	3	3	2	3	4	3	3	2	2	3
Philippines	4	3	3	3	3	2	3	2	1	4
Kenya	4	3	3	3	2	3	2	1	1	1
El Salvador	2	2	3	3	2	3	2	2	3	1
Colombia	2	2	3	2	2	2	2	3	3	2
Cambodia	4	3	2	3	2	3	3	0	2	1
Mexico	3	2	2	2	2	3	2	2	2	1
Panama	3	2	2	2	2	3	2	2	3	1
Ecuador	2	2	2	2	3	2	2	2	4	1
Paraguay	3	3	3	2	2	2	1	2	2	2
Chile	3	1	2	2	1	3	2	3	2	2
Uganda	4	3	2	3	3	2	2	1	1	1
Ghana	3	2	2	2	1	2	2	3	1	3
Brazil	2	2	2	2	2	2	2	2	2	2
Rwanda	3	3	2	2	2	1	1	2	2	1
Armenia	2	2	0	0	3	3	4	2	3	1
Tanzania	3	1	4	2	2	3	1	1	0	2
Honduras	2	2	3	2	2	2	2	1	2	1
Dominican Republic	2	2	3	2	1	2	2	1	3	1
India	2	2	2	1	2	3	3	0	3	2
Bosnia & Herzegovina	1	2	2	0	2	3	4	2	3	0
Indonesia	3	1	2	2	2	3	1	1	1	2
Uruguay	2	1	1	2	2	2	2	3	2	1
Mongolia	3	2	1	3	3	1	2	1	0	2
Mozambique	2	2	3	2	2	2	2	1	1	1
Nicaragua	2	2	2	1	2	3	3	1	2	1
Nigeria	3	2	2	2	1	1	2	2	1	2
Kyrgyz Republic	3	2	4	1	2	2	1	1	2	0
Guatemala	3	1	2	2	1	3	1	1	2	1
Costa Rica	2	2	2	2	1	1	2	2	2	0
Azerbaijan	3	3	0	2	1	3	1	0	2	1
Tajikistan	3	3	0	2	2	3	2	0	0	0
Madagascar	3	3	0	3	2	2	0	0	1	1
China	2	2	1	3	2	2	1	0	1	0
Senegal	2	2	0	3	2	2	1	1	0	0
Georgia	3	3	0	0	2	3	1	1	1	0
Morocco	2	3	0	0	2	3	0	0	3	1
Lebanon	2	2	2	0	1	2	2	2	0	1
Bangladesh	2	2	2	1	1	2	3	0	0	1
Cameroon	3	2	1	2	1	2	1	0	0	1
Jamaica	1	1	1	1	1	3	1	2	1	1
Nepal	2	3	1	1	0	1	2	0	1	2
Yemen	2	3	2	1	1	2	0	0	1	1
Haiti	2	1	3	1	0	1	2	1	0	1
Argentina	2	1	1	0	1	2	1	2	2	0
Dem. Rep. of Congo	2	2	1	2	1	1	1	1	0	1
Sri Lanka	1	2	2	1	0	1	1	1	1	2
Egypt	1	1	2	1	2	1	0	1	2	1
Turkey	2	1	1	0	1	3	1	1	1	0
Thailand	1	1	1	2	0	1	2	1	1	1
Venezuela	1	1	0	1	1	3	2	1	0	1
Trinidad & Tobago	1	0	1	1	0	2	1	1	3	0
Vietnam	2	1	1	2	1	1	1	0	0	0
Average	2,4	2,0	1,7	1,7	1,7	2,2	1,8	1,3	1,6	1,2

judgments, for example assigning a 0 if "regulated institutions may not take deposits," a 1 if "Regulated institutions can take deposits, but are limited in the types they may accept and most regulations are burdensome," a 2 if "regulated institutions may take a reasonably broad range of deposits and regulation is only moderately burdensome," and so on up to 4.

The results for 55 countries in 2012 show the potential for excellence—the mature markets of Peru and Bolivia top the list—and room for improvement in many countries. The 55 average above 2 on the 4-point scale only in connection with regulation and supervision of microcredit portfolios and institutional support for accounting transparency. (See Table 3.) Eleven countries lost ground in the 2012 survey but 28 gained, lifting the global average overall. The biggest improvements were in setting up functioning credit bureaus and in permitting agents to retail financial transactions, notably in "mobile money."Despite the progress, the global capacity to regulate retail microfinance institutions lags the capacity to build and invest in such institutions. Indeed the microfinance investment vehicles and securitization deals are world-class. The result is microfinance ecosystems in many countries with robust, energetic MFIs, and few other constituents nearly so vital: lots of growth drive and little countervailing force. This imbalance is worrisome given finance's especial propensity for instability. It makes microfinance industries fragile and potentially destructive to others and themselves.

The imbalance arises in part from the historical tendency of microfinance promoters to focus on supporting institutions and, starting in the mid-1990s, ways to invest in them.[12] The tendency was understandable, even necessary, for several reasons. In the 1960s and 1970s donors lent billions to developing-country governments for credit programs and mostly met with failure as local political economy distorted who received the subsidized credit. The microfinance movement arose in part as a reaction against this top-down, government-centered approach. It favored an adaptive, bottom-up strategy of experimenting and replicating success. It operated in the grey zone between the formal and informal economies, taking the relative lack of regulatory infrastructure as given. It accepted that countries that still have far to go in economic development also have far to go in institutional development. It discovered that it was easier for outsiders to stand up nongovernmental lending institutions than to install functioning credit bureaus, regulators, and supervisors. And it made extraordinary progress, reaching tens or hundreds of millions of people.

Still the imbalance is there, and must be reckoned with. True to the earlier warnings about the difficulty of isolating causes, it is not useful to simply *blame* the recent excesses in microcredit on the imbalance. None of us is a god who can reach down and directly adjust the balance. Nevertheless, viewing the industry as out of kilter in this way helps to organize the search for practical improvements. It points up the value of three practical steps:

---

[12] The focus has not been exclusive. CGAP and some donors have also partnered with governments to improve the regulatory environment for microfinance.

1. *Wherever possible, support the development of a richer institutional environment for microfinance.* Channels include traditional "North-South" technical assistance and "South-South" learning activities such as those run by the Alliance for Financial Inclusion.[13] Codified principles of financial inclusion (Claessens, Honohan, and Rojas-Suarez 2009; G20 2010) and distillations of best practices (Christen, Lyman, and Rosenberg 2003) can guide the work.

2. Recognizing that progress on the first item will be slow, attempt to compensate in domains where outsiders have more control, notably in the governance of MFIs and the functioning of the international microfinance investment industry. The more impoverished the microfinance ecosystem, the less that MFIs and their investors can depend on other institutions to check their worst collective tendencies. The Smart Campaign, which seeks to define and monitor responsible lending, can be seen in this light. If responsible lending can be credibly measured, then funders can factor it into their allocations of capital.

   In addition, as Krahnen and Schmidt (1994, p. 108) argue, MFIs that seek the "double bottom line" would do well to institutionalize this pursuit by infusing their governance with pluralism. In particular, they can give representatives of each bottom line a strong voice on the governing board. Advocates for the social bottom line might be drawn from the NGOs out of which for-profit MFIs spring (in cases of transformation) or from relevant public agencies, foreign or domestic, or from social investors. Elisabeth Rhyne (2010) has noted that many transformations of MFIs from non-profit to for-profits status have given the founding NGOs ownership and board voice in their for-profit offspring. Indian law, however, prevented this from happening in Andhra Pradesh, handing control of for-profit MFIs to equity investors looking for a quick, lucrative exit.

3. *Confront the problem of rapid growth more systematically.* Since the regulatory environment for microfinance in most countries resembles the American more than the Canadian mortgage lending environment—fragile to large influxes of capital—donors and social investors need to attack the collective action problem of modulating the quantity and character of capital inflow according to market conditions. Otherwise, investment in microfinance will often prove counterproductive from the point of view of industry building. Just look at Spandana in India, which is hanging on by a thread, or Zakoura in Morocco, which had to be merged into another lender, or BANEX in Nicaragua, which went bankrupt. The issue here is primarily one of magnitudes of inflows; however, it should be recognized that the quality matters too. For example, an equity investment made to

---

[13] Perhaps countries such as Greece and the United States could benefit from some North-North or South-North learning.

give an institution adequate capital to take savings may, by enabling deposit-taking, make the institution lend more conservatively. Equity that allows a credit-only MFI to leverage more debt may have the opposite effect. In my experience, many people in investing institutions recognize that too much money of certain kinds has gone into some markets too fast. But beyond this, the only point of consensus among investors is that it was some other investor's fault.

Roodman (2012) proposes the creation of a kind of international credit bureau whose subjects would be microfinance institutions. It could monitor debt levels of individual MFIs, as well as their rates of growth in borrowing, lending, and equity. In could also monitor market conditions in countries and region where the MFIs operated, since rapid market growth can damage even slow-growing MFIs in that market. Just like an ordinary credit bureau, this one would need to be supplied with accurate, timely information on all MFI investment deals, whether involving foreign or domestic investors. Vital too would be data on portfolio quality. The credit bureau would need the right to share this data with potential investors. Based on this information, it could issue "credit scores" or red, yellow, or green lights to investors considering whether to place funds in various MFIs and countries. In issuing guidance, it could distinguish between deposit-taking and non-deposit-taking ones since the former sometimes need equity investment to increase their capital adequacy to protect depositors, as distinct from leveraging equity for more lending growth. Unlike an ordinary credit bureau, it might also take the initiative in publicizing its market assessments to make them harder to ignore. Public investors, for example, might face pressure from politicians and taxpayers to explain why they were investing in red-light countries.

The proposal is not without problems. The body's hypothetical mandate begs many questions about how to determine when a market is at risk of overheating. The body's recommendations would not be binding. And it could even backfire in the manner of the ratings agencies in the United States: at times it would err on the liberal side, creating a misplaced sense of security about some markets, boosting investment flows, and making matters worse than if it did not exist. That argues for keeping the mechanism relatively informal, so that its judgments are not taken as gospel.

The practical question is not whether system would work perfectly, nor even whether it would improve on the status quo (which, seemingly, would not be hard), but whether it is worth trying. The initial funding, which would be modest next to the billions invested in microfinance each year, could come from foundations and donors working on financial services for the poor. If successful, the MFI credit bureau might eventually self-finance through fees to investors or, like a rating agency, MFIs.

Absent credible mechanisms to moderate capital flows, donors and social investors will almost certainly do best by erring on the side of providing *less* funding. This is because the tendency toward instability in credit markets is nonlinear.

Up to some unknown threshold, the economic value of a credit portfolio—the net present value of actual future payments—remains close to the book value. Beyond this threshold, credit goes increasingly into unsustainable uses, including, crucially, the refinancing of older loans. This refinancing inserts a temporary wedge between apparent and actual credit portfolio quality. It delays the transmission of information about the true state of the portfolio. That facilitates further and ultimately destabilizing growth.

Not only will a ratcheting-down of microfinance investment raise the probability that microcredit will grow sustainably. It will also increase the incentive for MFIs to take savings as an alternative source of funds, or to seek regulatory permission to do so.

6 Conclusion

Microfinance has been growing for 35 years and now reaches upwards of 100 million people, who cannot all be wrong in their judgments about the utility of microfinance. Moreover, most of them are served by institutions that are nearly or completely self-sufficient in financial terms; these MFIs do not depend greatly on outside subsidies, and so their fates do not ride on the latest headlines in the *New York Times* or *Die Welt*. Thus all the recent bad press will probably not extinguish the microfinance industry. And just as recent crises in the mainstream financial system do not spell Armageddon for that system, the recent wounds to the microfinance industry—the bubbles and political backlashes—are unlikely to bring down the global microfinance industry.

Nor should they. Because of the vicissitudes of poverty, poor people need financial services more than the rich. Their financial options will always be inferior—that's part of being poor—and microfinance offers additional options with distinctive strengths and weaknesses. The microfinance industry has demonstrated an ability to build enduring institutions to deliver a variety of inherently useful services on a large scale.

Nevertheless, the recent travails are signs that something is wrong in the industry. What is wrong is, ironically, what was once so right about the industry: it largely bypassed governments in favor of an experimental, bottom-up approach to institution building. The industry got so good at building institutions and injecting funds into them that it often forgot that a durable financial system consists of more than retail institutions and their investors. The narrow focus became a widening problem as microfinance grew. The result in some countries is a microfinancial ecosystem that lacks diversity, being dominated by vigorous retail MFIs subject to inadequate external (and, in some cases, internal) controls.

To mature, the industry and its supporters should recognize the imbalance it has created. Where possible, they should work to strengthen institutions of moderation such as credit bureaus and regulators. Accepting that such institutions will often be weak, they should err on the side of investing less. In microfinance funding, less is sometimes more.

References

Atlantic Council and Thomson Reuters (2012) The Finance Crisis: Lessons Learned from Canada and the Way Forward. Washington, DC: Embassy of Canada. j.mp/Qf9bae.

Attanasio, O., Augsburg, B., De Haas, R., Fitzsimons, E., Harmgart, H. (2011) Group lending or individual lending? Evidence from a randomised field experiment in Mongolia. Working Paper 11/20. Institute for Fiscal Studies.

Augsburg, B., De Haas, R., Harmgart, H., Meghir, C. (2012) Microfinance at the Margin: Experimental Evidence from Bosnia and Herzegovina. European Bank for Reconstruction and Development.

Banerjee, A.V., Duflo, E., Glennerster, R., Kinnan, C. (2009) The Miracle of Microfinance? Evidence from a Randomized Evaluation. Massachusetts Institute of Technology, Department of Economics.

Brune, L., Giné, X., Goldberg, J., Yang, D. (2010) Commitments to Save: A Field Experiment in Rural Malawi.

Chen, G. (2011) Does Savings Help Protect MFIs from Political Interference? CGAP blog, June 27.

Chen, G., Rasmussen, S., Reille, X. (2010) Growth and Vulnerabilities in Microfinance. Focus Note 61. CGAP.

Chen, G., Rasmussen, S., Reille, X., Rozas, D. (2010) Indian Microfinance Goes Public: The SKS Initial Public Offering. Focus Note 65. CGAP.

Christen, R.P., Lyman, T.R., Rosenberg, R. (2003) Microfinance Consensus Guidelines: Guiding Principles on Regulation and Supervision of Microfinance. CGAP.

Claessens, S., Honohan, P., Rojas-Suarez, L. (eds.) (2009) Policy Principles for Expanding Financial Access. Center for Global Development.

Collins, D., Morduch, J., Rutherford, S., Ruthven, O. (2009) Portfolios of the Poor: How the World's Poor Live on $2 a Day. Princeton University Press.

Crépon, B., Devoto, F., Duflo, E., Parienté, W. (2011) Impact of microcredit in rural areas of Morocco: Evidence from a Randomized Evaluation. Massachusetts Institute of Technology, Department of Economics.

Cull, R., Demirgüç-Kunt, A., Morduch, J. (2009) Microfinance Meets the Market. Journal of Economic Perspectives 23(1):167–92.

Druschel, K., Quigley, J., Sanchez, C. (2001) State of the Microcredit Summit Campaign Report 2001. Washington, DC: Microcredit Summit Campaign.

Dupas, P., Robinson, J. (2009) Savings Constraints and Microenterprise Development: Evidence from a Field Experiment in Kenya. Working Paper 14693. National Bureau of Economic Research.

Economist Intelligence Unit (2012) Global Microscope on the Microfinance Business Environment.

G20 (2010) Principles for Innovative Financial Inclusion. j.mp/RaasOS.

Hanna, H. (2012) Microfinance Duel: SKS' Akula Gives Advice and Admits Muhammad Yunus Was Right. Hala's Blog. halahanna.com/2012/02/29/microfinance-duel/.

Harford, T. (2009) Perhaps Microfinance Isn't Such a Big Deal After All. Financial Times, December 5.

Hughes, N., Lonie, S. (2007) M-PESA: Mobile Money for the 'Unbanked.' Innovations 2 (1–2):63–81.

Kabeer, N. (2001) Conflicts over Credit: Re-Evaluating the Empowerment Potential of Loans to Women in Rural Bangladesh. World Development 29 (1):63–84.

Karim, L. (2008) Demystifying Micro-Credit: The Grameen Bank, NGOs, and Neoliberalism in Bangladesh. Cultural Dynamics 20(5):5–29.

Karlan, D., Zinman, J. (2011) Microcredit in Theory and Practice: Using Randomized Credit Scoring for Impact Evaluation. Science 332(6035):1278–84.

Krahnen, J.P., Schmidt, R.H. (1994) Development Finance as Institution Building: A new Approach to Poverty-Oriented Banking. Boulder: Westview Press.

MFTransparency (2011) Pricing Data Report: Transparent Pricing Initiative in India.

MicroRate (2012) The State of Microfinance Investment 2012.

Otero, M., Rhyne, E. (1994) The New World of Microenterprise Finance: Building Healthy Financial Institutions for the Poor. Kumarian Press.

Reed, L.R. (2011) State of the Microcredit Summit Campaign Report 2001. Washington, DC: Microcredit Summit Campaign.

Rhyne, E. (2010) On Microfinance: Who's to Blame for the Crisis in Andhra Pradesh? Huffington Post, November 2.

Roodman, D. (2011) Does Compartamos Charge 195% Interest? David Roodman's Microfinance Open Book Blog, January 31.

Roodman, D. (2012) Due Diligence: An Impertinent Inquiry into Microfinance. Washington, DC: Center for Global Development.

Roodman, D., Morduch, J. (2011) The Impact of Microcredit on the Poor in Bangladesh: Revisiting the Evidence. Working Paper 174. Center for Global Development.

Rosenberg, R. (2007) CGAP Reflections on the Compartamos Initial Public Offering: A Case Study on Microfinance Interest Rates and Profits. Focus Note 42. CGAP.

Rossi, P.H. (1987) The Iron Law of Evaluation and Other Metallic Rules. Research in Social Problems and Public Policy 4:3–20.

Schumpeter, J.A. (1934) The Theory of Economic Development: An Inquiry into Profits, Capital, Credit, Interest, and the Business Cycle. Oxford University Press.

Sen, A. (1999) Development as Freedom. Anchor Books.

Society for Elimination of Rural Poverty (SERP) (2010) List of Victims of MFIs in AP State. Available at j.mp/V1K5Oi.

Squad Digital (2012) Celebrating 5 Years of M-PESA. Infographic. https://squad-digital.com/beta/safaricom/facebook/saftimelineiframe/pdf/infograph.pdf.

Symbiotics (2012a) 2012 Symbiotics MIV Survey: Market Data & Peer Group Analysis. Geneva.

Symbiotics (2012b) Data obtained from www.syminvest.com, October 20.

Todd, H. (1996) Women at the Center: Grameen Bank Borrowers after One Decade. University Press Limited.

Von Pischke, J.D. (1991) Finance at the Frontier: The Role of Credit in the Development of the Private Economy. World Bank.

CHAPTER 3

Core Values of Microfinance Under Scrutiny: Back to Basics?

Reinhard H. Schmidt[*]

1   What I Want to Address

During the past decade, what has for a long time been called microfinance (henceforth MF) has changed in a fundamental way. The reality of MF has changed, the terminology has changed[1], the discourse about microfinance has changed, the reputation of MF with the general public has changed, and last but certainly not least the ethical foundations of MF have also begun to change. What has once started as a purely value-driven development aid activity has turned into a new field of business in which commercial values seem to play a much larger role than traditional ethical and developmental values. The various aspects of change are closely connected, and this interplay certainly merits a careful consideration. It is the purpose of this paper to provide a starting point for the discussion of how to assess these changes and whether such an assessment warrants rethinking the ethical foundations of MF and to provide a conceptual structure for this discussion.

Many participants from within the "microfinance community" and even more observers who look at it from the outside seem to believe that "the dark side of microfinance" has recently become visible, that the traditional model of microfinance has been discredited and "needs to be replaced by a new one", that "heroes have turned into villains" and that even the entire concept of microfinance is ill-conceived.[2] The main reason for their change of view is related to the ethical underpinnings of microfinance. Recent developments suggest that this foundation is no longer as firm as it used to be. If this is really the case, what does it imply, and

---

[*]   Professor, University of Frankfurt.

[1]   From rural finance (in the 1970s and 80s) to microcredit (in the 1980s) to microfinance (in the 1990s and into the new century) to access to finance (since the middle of the 2010s) to, most recently, inclusive finance. In spite of these terminological modernizations, I continue using the term microfinance to denote the entire topic.

[2]   The sources referred to are, respectively, Business Week (2006), FAZ (2011), Sinclair/Stanford (2012) and Bateman (2010).

would it require going "back to basics", at least as far as the role of values or even the entire approach to MF are concerned?

During the past five years, developments in the reality of microfinance and the debate about microfinance go more to the roots than comparable debates of past decades. Before 2006, when Muhammad Yunus and his Grameen Bank were awarded the Noble Peace Price, there were already lively debates about MF. However, they referred more to the question of whether the approach to microfinance that was epitomized by Yunus and his bank is more appropriate to reach given social and developmental goals than what has been called the commercial approach to MF. Today, in contrast, the goals or objectives and the values themselves are under debate.

The paper starts out in section 2 by discussing two different notions of value that play a role in microfinance. Then, in section 3, it addresses the goals or objectives of microfinance according to different views, taking up a debate that confronts the approach that Yunus and the Grameen Bank seemed to represent and the so-called commercial approach. Section 4 is dedicated to the question if and why the ethical orientation of MF may have disappeared. In section 5, I want to restate why I think that a firm ethical or value foundation of MF is still needed in spite of the advances brought about by the commercial approach, and how a microfinance institution (henceforth MFI) can try to make sure that it does not lose its value base even though it may seek access to the capital market. The concluding section 6 provides my answer to the question of the subtitle, that is, whether all of this suggests going "back to basics".

2   The Dual Notion of "Value" and the Role of Values

2.1 Two Concepts of "Value"

The term "value" has at least two meanings. I want to call them Value 1 and Value 2, respectively. Both are relevant for MF, and as I will argue, it is important to understand how they are related and what their relative importance and their substance have been in different phases of the development of MF.

The concept of Value 1 is taken from standard economic theory. Generally speaking, something, which may be an action, a decision, a transaction or a firm or similar organization, creates value if it generates a flow of net economic benefits to a certain person or group of persons. Thus, claiming that "MF creates value" (Value 1) means that MF is, by some standard, economically beneficial to a somehow defined group of people.[3]

---

[3] In a more technical sense, value (and thus Value 1) is defined as a stock measure that express the current value of a flow of benefits such as, for example, the net present value of the cash flows resulting from undertaking an investment. This concept goes back at least to the work of Irving Fisher (1904).

The concept of Value 2 refers to an ethical or social or political assessment. People's attitudes and conduct or certain activities or social institutions are candidates for being assessed as valuable in the sense of having or showing Value 2. For instance, an activity can be said to have Value 2 if it is guided by noble, possibly altruistic intentions or if it can be assumed to have positive consequences for some other people than those who undertake it. One can also apply the term Value 2 to certain motives and even to people whose conduct is shaped by these motives. Thus, the claim that "MF has Value 2" means that microfinance activity is inspired by the intention of people or organizations, such as development aid organizations, of benefitting others or creating Value 1 for others than those who undertake this activity and/or that it is good for some people that MF activities are initiated and implemented. Thus, Value 2 of those who fund or provide MF services is based on the assumption that MF benefits or creates Value 1 for those who will obtain these services.[4]

The main focus of this paper is on Value 2, since it seems that the formerly solid ethical foundations of MF, its Value 2 orientation, has eroded in the recent past. However, all debates about the ethical attractiveness and the ethical foundations of MF – i.e. its Value 2 – have always been closely related to controversies concerning the benefits that it really brings to people and nations, that is, to its Value 1. Thus Value 2 and Value 1 considerations are closely intertwined.

2.2 Why Values Matter in Economics, Business and Finance in General ...

Value-1 is at the core of economics, business and finance in general. It is generally assumed that all economic activity is driven by the aspiration to create benefits for those who undertake or initiate it and that competitive markets and the liberty to enter a contract have the function of transforming the individual agents' quest for their own advantage into benefits for all parties involved.[5] The extent to which this transformation is successful depends on a number of conditions that are laid out in any economics textbook.

In the radical version of conventional neoclassical economics, the role of finance is largely neutral. Value 1 creation only depends on the availability of factors of production, technologies employed by firms and know-how available for the transformation of inputs into outputs and thus into economic benefits. Financial institutions and money facilitate welfare enhancing exchange between eco-

---

[4] An attentive reader of an earlier version of this paper suggested using the terms "economic value" instead of "Value 1" and "ethical value" instead of "Value 2". I have decided not to adopt his suggestion because I consider Value 2 to also be an eminently economic concept that is linked to Value 1.

[5] Under certain conditions, voluntary transactions even benefit an economy as a whole. As is well known, the idea goes back at least to Adam Smith.

nomic agents, but this role is considered not to be critical. Thus, there is no need for Value 2 in business and in finance.

In the perfect neoclassical model world, any consideration of fairness, equality, cultural advancement etc, is left to governments, possibly assisted by private philanthropy or charity. While for them Value 2 considerations are of central importance as a means of expressing collective or personal preferences, in the business world, Value 2 is largely irrelevant. Since markets are assumed to be perfect and deviating from unrestricted profit maximization would be sanctioned by economic extinction in the form of firms' bankruptcy, there is also no room for Value 2. As Friedman has said, it is the ethical mandate of firms to maximize their profit.[6]

However, the real world is not like the model world of neoclassical economics. Agents may not be completely rational and markets are not perfect. One of the reasons why markets are imperfect is the uneven or asymmetrical distribution of information between the parties which might enter into a contract. One party to a potential contract may have better information than the other one and the less informed party may be aware of his or her informational disadvantage and therefore refrain from entering into that contract.[7] The second reason is that real-world contracts are almost never complete. Incomplete contracts leave room for later decisions, which the contract party that is better informed can use to her advantage.[8] Broadly defined, institutions are sets of rules that shape agents' decisions by imposing constraints on the actions that people can undertake and by providing sanctions and rewards.[9] To some extent, institutions serve to mitigate the negative consequences that may arise from the asymmetrical distribution of information and the incompleteness of contracts. Institutions include governments, courts, firms, laws and much more.[10] However, not only markets are imperfect. Also governments, judicial systems and other formal institutions do not function perfectly and therefore cannot create an "ideal" world like the one that is assumed to exist in the model world of elementary economics textbooks.

Here, Value 2 comes into play. Value 2 considerations such as a commitment to fair behavior, honesty, a fair sharing of benefits or the desires to reduce other people's suffering and helping them to exploit their human potential have a dual function. One is akin to that of philanthropy and charity in conventional neoclassical economics: it is an expression of what some people want to see implemented in this world. The difference to the neoclassical model is that the imperfection of markets may leave room for these interests being put into practical action within

---

[6]   See Friedman (1970) as the standard source.

[7]   See, e.g. the textbook by Tirole (2006).

[8]   The fundamental ideas concerning the role of contract incompleteness are very well presented in Hart (1995).

[9]   This is the definition of "institutions" used by Douglass North (1991).

[10] See e.g., Furubotn/Richter (2002) on the "new institutional economics".

the business world. The second function of Value 2 is that it creates additional constraints and incentives for action. In his respect, Value 2 is akin to institutions.

2.3 ... and Especially for Microfinance and Small Business Finance

For MF and its variants[11], value has always been of overwhelming importance. However, the relative importance of Value 1 and Value 2 and the specific content that they take on have changed over time. Therefore, a first step in characterizing their role requires a brief look at the history of microfinance. One can distinguish two periods in the development of microfinance. In the spirit of the name of this conference ("Towards Microfinance 3.0"), I call them MF 1.0 and MF 2.0. Alternatively, one could also call them traditional and modern microfinance, respectively.

What marks the transition from MF 1.0 to MF 2.0 is the advent of the concept of commercialization, which occurred towards the end of the 1990s. Initially, commercialization was understood to simply mean that a MFI should strive to cover its full costs and be financially self-sustaining and independent of donor support. In MF 1.0, cost coverage and financial self-sustainability were not considered as an issue, whereas in MF 2.0 it has become a central topic. It needs to be added that in the early years of MF 2.0, almost all MFIs were NGOs and their capital was mainly provided by foreign donor institutions, whereas in the later years, registered and regulated banks in the legal form of corporations became more important and to an increasing extent funding came from private investors.

In MF 1.0, Value 1 was almost exclusively understood as benefits for the clients of MFIs. Donors and local MFIs were assumed to intend creating Value 1 for their clients by making small loans at favorable terms available to them. The term "beneficiaries" that was typically used for the borrowers or clients at that time clearly indicates that benefitting others was the main concern of relevant aid donors. Even at the level of the local MFIs and possibly also of the foreign consultants who were involved in many cases, MF was assumed to be mainly motivated by an intention to help, a clear manifestation of Value 2.

During the MF 1.0 phase, one crucial assumption was regularly made: MF creates Value 1. Getting small loans from an MFI at favorable terms was seen as a benefit for those who were fortunate enough to received these loans. Whether it really improves their lives was hardly ever asked.[12] While reaching and benefitting the target group members played the key role, hardly any concern was given to what the whole undertaking meant for the local institutions that were used as a

---

[11] Such as small enterprise or small business finance, inclusive finance etc.; see note 1 above.

[12] A second assumption underlying this approach was that being able to show that the earmarked development aid funds had really reached the so-called target groups was sufficient in terms of success for the donor institutions. Accomplishing what they were supposed to achieve constituted a form of creating Value 1 for them. But given the deep pockets of foreign donor institutions, this assumption was of lesser concern.

channel for the foreign funds, and for the people working in these institutions. More or less implicitly, it was assumed that they were also motivated by good intentions and thus by Value-2 considerations.

With the advent of the commercial approach in the mid-1990s, the relative weights and the specific forms and contents of Value 1 and Value 2 started to change. However, two things did not change. It was still assumed that MF would have the dominant purpose of creating Value 1 for clients and that it would indeed have this effect. Thus MF was still driven by the Value-2 consideration of foreign donors, consultants and local MFI staff.

The new element concerned the local MFIs that served as conduits for funds from foreign donors and lenders to poor local borrowers. It was now deemed not only legitimate but also important to assure that playing this role would strengthen the local MFIs as institutions or, in other words, that it would create Value-1 for the local MFIs as organizations.

In the early years of modern microfinance, most MFIs were NGOs in the legal form of a foundation or an association. But relatively soon, it became apparent that the legal forms of an NGO, and thus the lack of a true owner, was more of a burden than a blessing since it was no longer considered to be conducive to the overarching objective of benefitting certain target groups. Therefore, during the time between 1995 and 2005, several local NGOs were converted into corporations as the legal basis for an MFI that would be a more professional institution, and MFIs were converted into licensed and registered target group-oriented specialized microfinance banks.[13] Only a little later, donors and consultants started to create microfinance banks "from scratch" or, as it is also called, as "greenfield investments".

The newly created entities had owners who had invested capital, and what used to be distribution channels for foreign funds turned into genuine financial intermediaries. Several among them started to take deposits. All of this expanded the range of stakeholders who had claims to receiving some benefit, or Value 1, in return for their contributions. Value 2 alone was no longer considered to be enough to drive MFI activity. As was intended by the advocates of MF 2.0 and the commercial approach, the agendas and the operations of many MFIs became more and more shaped by Value 1 concerns for themselves. This was, by and large, a positive development, as without a stronger orientation to Value 1 for all parties, the new MFIs of the MF 2.0 era would hardly have been able to expand and provide services at a much larger scale and with much lower costs than those of the MF 1.0 era.

However, one should not overlook the role that Value 2 continued to play. Modern MF looks at transactions as voluntary deals that must create Value-1 for all sides of the transaction. But positive Value 1 for all parties involved is only a necessary condition for the development of MF. It is not a sufficient condition. Some Value 2 was also required for MF to continue being regarded as ethically

---

[13]   The technical term for this conversion was „upgrading". See Nair/Von Pischke (2007) on the limited success of upgrading as a type of institutional development.

valuable and receiving the donor support that was still needed to get commercially oriented MFIs started, and the public support that backs generous donor funding for MF. Similar considerations apply to the people active in MF in their respective roles. Many of them have better-paid outside options for instance in conventional banks. Therefore one can assume that also for them Value 2 still played a role. Moreover, the underlying idea of the commercial approach is not that the interests of the clients should matter less, but rather that commercial microfinance can provide more benefit for the clients because it operates according to a different business model. Thus, over the longer period, the concern for Value-1 for clients and that for the interests of MFIs as institutions complement each other. This sounds like "perfect harmony", but unfortunately this is not the whole story.

In the later part of the MF 2.0 era, private capital has become an essential element of MF, and this has in some cases led to severe negative consequences. Two such cases are particularly noteworthy: the IPO of the Mexican MFI Compartamos in 2006 and that of the Indian MFI SKS in 2010. I will discuss these cases in detail below. In both cases, a large part of the shares that were issued were taken up by private institutional investors.

As these two cases demonstrate, the intrusion of private investors, who can be assumed to be only interested in their own profit, into the domain of MF changes the relative importance of Value 1 and Value 2 as well as the substance of Value 1. At least in these cases, the interests of private investors, the creation of Value 1 for them, seem to have come to completely dominate the former interest in the Value 1 creation for clients or target groups, and Value-2 has been completely sidelined. This far-reaching change in the value orientation of MF poses a challenge for the ethical appeal microfinance. As it seems, the two cases are not going to remain exceptions. As the Indian Financial Economic Times reported on Oct. 5, 2012, "Private Equity Firms Woo Indian Microfinance Institutions" to an extent that can only be called stunning.[14]

To sum up this section: In MF 1.0 (or traditional MF), Value 2 considerations were the driving force behind efforts of foreign donors and the local MFIs that were their partners to create Value-1 for the target groups.

In MF 2.0 (or early modern microfinance), the Value 2 considerations and the Value-1 aspirations of clients are complemented by what one can call the Value-1 interests of the MFIs that play an essential role in creating and distribution MF services for certain target groups, and the people and institutions backing these new-type MFIs.

In recent years, the trend towards increasing commercialization has, at least in some cases, changed the substance of the value orientation of MF. Clients' Value 1 does not seem to count so much anymore. In its place, investors' Value 1 has become the dominant concern; and one might worry that in a number of MFIs all traces of Value-2 are about to disappear.

---

[14] See Financial Times of India, Oct. 6, 2012.

3   Traditional Objectives and Values of Microfinance and How They Were Discussed and Implemented

3.1   Two Competing Approaches to Microfinance and Small Business Finance

The term 'objectives' indicates what a social activity, such as that of MF, is intended to achieve according to a widely shared view among experts or the general public or competent decision makers. At least as far as ultimate or highest ranking objectives are concerned, it is almost impossible to clearly distinguish objectives from underlying values. On a lower level of abstraction, objectives can be considered as a way of expressing different views about how the overarching objectives can best be reached. With the term "traditional values" I refer to values and objectives held at the time until 2006, the year in which the Noble Peace Price was awarded to Yunus and his bank and the year of the first IPO of a MFI and the beginning of what I call excessive commercialization.

At the highest level, there was a general agreement that MF was meant to benefit clients. However, already at the next level of generality, experts disagreed on almost any aspect of what this meant in practice. More specifically, there was disagreement about

- the definition of the target groups that MF was meant to directly benefit: really poor people vs. micro and small enterprises and their owners and their employees;

- the definition of the overall objective: poverty alleviation vs. improving the economic environment in which poor people live and in which small and very small firms operate;

- the kinds and the scope of services MFIs should provide to the target population: all those services that poor people need vs. merely financial services;

- the importance attached to the requirement that MFIs cover their full costs and become financially self-sustaining after a brief initial period vs. the disregard for such considerations;

- the directness of efforts to ultimately benefit the target population: reaching poor people and providing immediate benefits for them vs. strengthening the institutions that would provide financial services to those who formerly lacked access to financial services, or even to strengthening the financial system of certain countries

Combining these features one arrives at the main "battle line" of the 1990s and the early years of the new millennium. One the one side, we have the position of those who opted for immediate and comprehensive support for poor target groups combined with the objective of alleviating poverty. One can call it "the poverty alleviation camp". As it presented itself until 2002, the Grameen Bank was the leading example of a MFI in this camp, and Yunus was its best known proponent. On the other side, we find the advocates of a more indirect support for the target population and a more focused "finance only" approach. This "commercial camp" emphasizes institution building and financial sector development and a commercial orientation of MFIs. The village bank units of Bank Rakyat Indonesia (BRI) and the MFIs supported by ACCION and IPC were the prime examples for this camp of MFIs.

3.2 Outreach and Its Dimensions

As said before, during the 1990s, the debate between these two camps did not refer to the overarching objective of MF but rather to different view concerning how this objective can best be reached. One way of framing this controversy was by using the vague, but intuitive and highly plausible concept of "outreach". Outreach has two dimensions. Having a "deeper outreach" means that an MFI reaches and serves poorer clients; and having a "wider outreach" means that more relatively poor clients are reached.[15] At an early stage of this debate, it was widely believed that there would be a trade-off between depth and width of outreach, and the two camps held contrasting views concerning which dimension of outreach is more important. The inhabitants of the poverty alleviation camp put priority on depth while those of the commercial camp were more concerned about a wide outreach.

The preference ordering of depth versus width touches on several aspects. One aspect is a simple, straight-forward difference in value judgments. The proponents of poverty alleviation regard poverty alleviation as more important than establishing viable financial institutions or strengthening the financial sector; and for many of them it is even ethically unacceptable to make poor borrowers bear the full costs of the financial services offered to them.[16] The advocates of the commercial approach argue that MFIs which emphasize poverty alleviation and follow a soft approach can hardly cover their costs and become stable financial institutions and therefore cannot provide loans and other financial services to their clients on a permanent basis. In their view, the ability to provide services on a permanent basis is of paramount importance for their clients, even if this requires the MFIs to charge slightly higher interest rates.

Another point of disagreement refers to the scope of operations that MFIs of the two types can achieve. Poverty oriented MFIs are notoriously dependent on foreign subsidies and soft loans provided by international financial institutions on concessionary terms, whose availability is limited. This inevitably restricts the scope of their lending business. In contrast, commercially oriented MFIs find it easier to expand. Once they have reached financial self-sustainability, they can take deposits from local clients and access international funding from develop-

---

[15] See e.g. Gonzalez-Vega (1998).

[16] See e.g. Hulme/Mosley (1996) and Waller et al. (1999).

ment finance institutions and even from commercial sources. With a larger scale of operations, they can make more loans and thereby have a larger positive impact on the lives of the people whom they aspire to benefit. Thus, there is in fact no trade-off between depth and width of outreach once the time span and the scope of operations are considered. The impact of MFIs that follows the commercial approach is larger, and this benefits their really poor and also their relatively poor clients.[17]

A third aspect refers to the question of who the main target groups of MFIs should be. For the poverty alleviation camp, really poor people are the preferred clients of MFIs. The inhabitants of the commercial camp find it more important that their loans go to small and very small businesses. The main reason for this preference for micro and small business finance over the direct financing of really poor people is that this ultimately benefits even the really poor more since small enterprises have a capacity to create employment and income from which also the really poor can benefit.

3.3 The Economic Rationale of the Institution Building Approach to Microfinance

There is more substance behind the commercial approach to MF, that one can alternatively call the institution building approach or the financial sector approach, than the mere assertion that it generates a stronger impact than the poverty alleviation approach. It can also be supported by a strong economic argument, which has been developed by Ingo Tschach in his dissertation entitled "the theory of development finance". I find his argument important enough to present it briefly here. [18]

Financial markets do not function like the textbook model of a commodity market in which supply and demand curves intersect and jointly determine a price at which the market clears. Financial markets are strongly affected by information and incentive problems; and this is particularly so in the case of markets for loans to very small and small businesses in developing countries. As Stiglitz and Weiss have shown in a seminal article, information asymmetry leads to moral hazard and adverse selection, and this in turn leads to credit rationing.[19] Credit rationing means that potential borrowers do not get the kind of loans they demand even though they may have economically valuable projects for which they request external financing. Evidently, credit rationing is a pervasive feature in those markets in which MFIs are active. A generalization of the argument developed by Stiglitz and Weiss provides an economic rationale for microfinance in the spirit of the institution building approach.

In any developing country, we find firms of vastly different sizes. Typically, small firms are endowed with little capital, not only in absolute quantities but also relative to the quantity of labor they use. The smaller firms are, the less capital

---

[17] For a simple numerical illustration, see Schmidt (2010).

[18] For details and additional references see Tschach (2002).

[19] See Stiglitz/Weiss (1982).

they tend to have; and therefore the higher the marginal return to capital is for them. This is an empirical fact that has often been observed. As a simplification one can assume that firms want to obtain loans whose size corresponds to firm size.

If markets were perfect, the smallest firms would be those that offer the most attractive applications for loanable funds. However, for two reasons, this is not the case in reality. One reason is that the transaction costs of granting small and very small loans to firms of correspondingly small size are high, and they can be assumed to be the higher the smaller the loans and the loan seeking firms are. The second reason is that it is difficult for lenders to properly assess the credit worthiness of the very small and small firms that would like to obtain loans. These simple considerations permit deriving a demand curve relating interest rates and loan/firm size.

If one looks at the supply side of the loan market in a typical developing country, one can distinguish two segments or two parts of the existing overall supply. One segment is that of the informal and semi-formal loan supply, most of which comes from money lenders. Money lenders can be assumed to be able to assess the credit worthiness of very small and small firms. However, their transaction costs are very high and their capital is limited. Therefore, they can only offer very small loans to very small businesses at very high interest rates. The other segment is the loan supply of conventional banks. These banks offer loans to large firms that are not particularly difficult to evaluate, e.g. because they have collateral and audited balance sheets, and they demand moderate interest rates which would be sufficient to cover their costs including transaction costs. In contrast to money lenders, conventional banks do not have the know-how that would be required to evaluate very small and small firms and their projects. This is why they do not offer loans to them even if these loans would carry higher interest rates.

Combining the loan demand curve and the two segments of loan supply generates a segmented market. This market has three segments. The first segment is that in which money lenders provide very small and very costly loans to very small firms that can take out these costly loans because of their very high marginal return on capital. The third segment is that of large firms getting large loans from conventional banks at moderate interest rates. The second segment is the one in the middle composed of small firms with high, but not very high, returns on capital, which would like to obtain small, though not very small loans. However, the cost of money lender loans is too high for them, and the banks do not finance them because they lack the necessary techniques to assess their credit worthiness. The loan demand of these firms is not met by the two types of suppliers considered so far.

This is where MFIs can find an appropriate and also financially attractive market niche: Since they have more capital available for lending than the typical money lenders and some relevant know-how to assess small firms, which the banks typically lack, the middle segment of small firms is their natural domain. Ideally, they can meet the demand of firms in the middle of the firm and loan size spectrum.

The importance of this role of MFIs in financing small firms goes far beyond simply filling a gap between the loan supply of money lenders and banks and simply funding a class of small, but not extremely small firms that typically do not receive the loans they would need. If the gap were not filled, it would create a serious obstacle to growth and thus also to additional employment and income for all those who would work in the small firms. To see why this is so, consider the case in which the gap is not filled. In this case, the owners of very small firms would be aware that the gap exists, and they would anticipate that if their firms grew they would run into the trap of their business being too large for money lender loans and too small for loans from conventional banks. As a consequence, they would refrain from even trying to make their firms grow, and they would therefore not create employment and income.

This is, in my view, the most convincing argument why MFIs should follow the commercial approach, aspire to become financially viable establishments and aim at financing not the economic activities of the extremely poor but rather those small businesses that are still too small to get normal bank loans. In doing this successfully, they remove a severe obstacle to economic growth and development and thus have a substantial impact on the general economic development. Though only indirectly, this would also lead to a substantial improvement of the situation of really poor people, who could then find employment and derive income from getting newly created jobs.

3.4 The Meta-ethical Debate

It is not enough to argue that the inhabitants of the poverty alleviation camp and those of the commercial camp differ in terms of whether they find poverty alleviation or financial institution building and financial sector development more important and what they believe serves poor people better. There is another dimension in which the two approaches differ, and this dimension refers explicitly to ethical values.[20]

In the general philosophical debate about what constitutes ethical or moral value of human conduct, there are two fundamentally different positions. One of them is a position which was widely spread among German and European philosophers and their followers in the general public in the 19th and early 20th century and which can be traced back to the writings of the eminent 18th century philosopher Immanuel Kant. According to this position, which was later given the name "*ethics of conviction*" (in German: *Gesinnungsethik*) by Max Weber, we call conduct ethically good if it is based on ethically valuable intentions and principles that would be suited to serve as general rules of conduct and as the basis of the legal system in an ideal state.[21] In accordance with this view, MF can be called

---

[20] I have addressed this issue in Schmidt (2010) and therefore only briefly summarize it here.

[21] On page 85 of his highly influential book "Politik als Beruf" (politics as a vocation) from 1919, Max Weber describes this position and introduces the term "Gesinnungsethik" for it, which is by now widely adopted. His implicit reference is to Kant (1788). Later authors, such as Kohl (1990), question whether this is a fair representation of Kant's certainly more complex view, but finally concur with Weber.

ethically good primarily because, and if, it is based on ethically valuable principles like that of aspiring to help those in need. Evidently, MF aiming at poverty alleviation has this appealing feature and can be regarded as a manifestation of the Kantian ethics of conviction.

The competing position is that developed and propagated about one hundred years ago by the equally eminent sociologist and economist Max Weber in an explicit confrontation to the conventional view of Kant and his followers. He called his approach to practical ethics *the ethics of responsibility* (in German: *Verantwortungsethik*). As he argues, human conduct can and should be called ethically good if, and only if, it is based on careful planning and the expectation of achieving effects that can themselves be called good according to some appropriate standard, whereas ethically valuable intentions and underlying guiding principles are less important. Weber criticized the ethics of conviction for ignoring the question of what the effects of adhering to valuable principles really are as long as these principles are considered ethically sound.[22] In a Weberian perspective, MF appears to be ethically good – or have Value 2 – if it can, upon careful analysis, be expected to create net benefits – or Value 1 – for its clients or their countries.

Applied to the debate about MF[23] one can say that the poverty alleviation approach largely conforms to Kant's ethics of conviction. As Yunus has argued in innumerable speeches, what makes MF such an ethically attractive proposition is exactly that it is based on ethically valuable principles and intentions. For him, compared to principles and intentions, facts and figures carry much less weight. The most important issues that he has regularly ignored in his speeches, and often even brushed aside as largely irrelevant, are the questions of what the true impact of the kind of MF is that he advocates, how this impact can be measured in a reliable way and what his concept implies for the role and strategies of MFIs.

Being mainly economists or social scientists, most experts and practitioners in the commercial camp would rather subscribe to Weber's ethics of responsibility. For most of them it is straight forward that consequences are more important than principles. The meta-ethical controversy would strengthen their position, as long as the stronger impact of commercial MFIs can indeed be assumed to exist[24] and as long as the commercial orientation does not go at the expense of ethical principles.

---

[22] See Weber (1919), *loc. cit.*

[23] For details, see Schmidt (2010).

[24] The condition that the consequences are predictable is essential. Weber's position rests on the assumption that the consequences of the conduct that is to be assessed can be predicted. If this is not the case, his meta-ethical argument is much weaker, and correspondingly the Kantian position is stronger in relative terms. In an earlier paper, I have provided one argument why one might question the predictability of the impact of commercial MF. This argument rests on the impossibility to predict the effects of innovations. See Schmidt (2010). Another argument that works in the same direction is that it is much less clear than had formerly been assumed that MF provides direct benefits for poor households, as Roodman (2011) and others argue.

4   The Perceived Loss of Ethical Appeal and Reputation

4.1   Relevant Changes in the Reality of Microfinance

During the past six years, microfinance seems to have fallen from a peak of reputation into a deep trough. Relevant changes that have caused this downfall have
occurred on two levels at the same time: in reality and in the discourse about MF.

The most visible events that have gravely damaged the reputation of microfinance are the IPOs of two large and well known MFIs. Both cases and the controversies surrounding them are so well known that it may suffice to briefly recall
their main features.

In 2006, the Mexican MFI Compartamos went public. 30 percent of the outstanding shares were issued to American and Mexican investors, and the Compartamos shares were listed on the Mexican stock exchange. In the course of the IPO,
no new shares were issued and no new capital was raised for Compartamos. Most
of the shares that were sold had been held by managers of the MFI and two important development oriented institutions, the World Bank's private sector arm IFC
and ACCION, the world's largest and most highly regarded microfinance support
organization.

The IPO of the Mexican MFI was very successful in financial terms. The issue
price of the shares was very high. Valued at the issue price of the shares Compartamos had a market value of approximately 1.5 billion USD. Some observers and
especially the founding shareholders of Compartamos hailed the IPO as an important step showing that microfinance had finally arrived at the "real financial market" and stood its test there.

Others saw it differently and supported their critical view by pointing out that
the high issue price could only be a reflection of the enormous profitability of
Compartamos as an enterprise during the past six years since the time when the
former NGO was transformed into a corporation, and the expectation that it would
maintain its profitability in the foreseeable future by sticking to its policy of
charging exorbitant interest rates. Yunus and others commented that this IPO
demonstrated the moral decay of some players in MF. A feature that appeared as
particularly worrying is that a large fraction of the shares were sold to American
hedge funds, allowing the sellers, which included IFC and ACCION in a prominent position, to pocket financial profits unheard of in MF before.[25]

In 2010, the largest and fastest growing Indian MFI SKS also undertook an IPO
with similarly spectacular financial success. In this case, it were not exorbitant interest rates but extremely high growth rates which seem to have inspired investors
to pay a very high price for the shares. The issue price was indeed so high that it
could only be explained by the assumption of investors that the unbelievable
growth of SKS will continue for an extended period of time. Also in this case,

---

[25]   For details and an equally critical assessment see Rosenberg (2007).

purely profit oriented investors were involved in the financing of this MFI, and top managers used the opportunity to pocket substantial profits for themselves.

The highly problematic aspect of this IPO is that SKS and a handful of other large Indian MFIs seem to have pursued policies of granting loans and of enforcing repayment from its clients that have nothing in common with responsible micro lending. As is well known, a large number of borrowers who were unable to repay the excessive loans that they had obtained from SKS and its peers committed suicide. As is equally well known, this led to a general microfinance crisis in Andhra Pradesh.[26]

Unfortunately, these were not the only events that caused a loss of reputation for MF on a worldwide scale. Other problematic aspects are that, after 2005, a number of purely commercial banks invaded what they called the microfinance market. But instead of granting loans that were in some way related to income generating activities of their clients, they pushed outright consumer lending and thereby caused serious problems for their clients. In addition, in a number of countries, the supply of very small loans to poor clients expanded at a very rapid pace, leading to over-indebtedness of clients and rising default rates of MFIs.

Last but not least, there was a controversy around the activities of the personality who had represented the former positive side of MF like no one else, Noble Laureate Mohammad Yunus. The role of his bank and of other firms in the Grameen Group of enterprises became the topic of very critical reports and comments in the media casting doubt on the ethical and developmental merits of the ever growing range of the group's business activities and of a stunningly close cooperation with large multinational firms. In part fuelled by these accusations, the government of Bangladesh forced Yunus in 2011 to retire from his position as the CEO of Grameen Bank and claimed the right to determine the future CEO of the bank. Even though many of the accusations turned out to be ill-founded, casting a shadow over the most highly respected representative of MF also affected the reputation of MF in general.[27]

---

[26] For details, see Chen et al. (2010).

[27] At least as a footnote it should be added that also another aspect of microfinance changed in a negative way. It concerns the attractiveness of MF for retail investors. Until the middle of the past decade, MF was considered to be particularly attractive for them because the profitability of MFIs and of MF investment vehicles was largely uncorrelated with general economic and stock market developments. Therefore, MF investments were considered as valuable instruments for portfolio diversification (see Krauss/Walter 2009). During the past years, MF has become much more connected to the general financial system. As a consequence, the financial returns of MF investments started to be highly correlated with general market developments and therefore lost an important part of their appeal for investors. For empirical evidence, see Wagner (2012).

4.2 Relevant Changes in the Discourse About Microfinance

While the Compartamos IPO and its problematic aspects did not have a great deal of impact in the general press, the events surrounding the SKS IPO and the ensuing Indian microfinance crisis and the intrusion of purely commercial lenders who pushed consumer lending under the misleading name of MF made headlines in the press. One very prominent American business magazine published several articles about the "dark side of micro lending"; the highly respected German newspaper Frankfurter Allgemeine bluntly declared that the model of microfinance had failed, and others declared that microfinance would be almost dead, at least as far as its ethical appeal is concerned.

Even more important is the change of attitude in the more specialized microfinance-related literature. For the sake of brevity, I only want to briefly comment on three widely read and discussed recent books on MF.

The first one is "Confessions of a Microfinance Heretic" by Hugh Sinclair (2012) As the title suggests, this book is highly provocative in its tone and content. The author recounts his negative experience with several MFIs and MF support organizations for which he had worked. He demonstrates that these organizations and the leading people behind them are irresponsible, profit and power seeking and not in the least socially and developmentally responsible. Of course, there are institutions and individual people in the MF business that deserve to be criticized in the way Sinclair does it in his book and related publications and public appearances. And it is justified to point out that the former MF hype may have encouraged the entry of shady characters into MF. However, Sinclair refrains from explicitly generalizing what he documents for individual cases. Therefore, one might say that he was unfortunate to run into black sheep several time in his career as a MF consultant. But apart from his caution of not explicitly making very sweeping statements, his book conveys the impression that what he reports represents a general feature of today's MF and that there are many black sheep. In this sense he contributes substantially to the current trend of putting MF down.

The second book is more important and richer in substance. In "Why Doesn't Microfinance Work?" Milford Bateman (2010) attacks what he considers to be central weakness of the relatively new breed of MFIs. The subtitle "The Destructive Rise of Local Neoliberalism" suggests what his answer to the title question is. In equally strong words like those of Sinclair, Bateman attacks aid-supported MFIs and donor support for these "new style MFIs" as cementing underdevelopment and poverty instead of fostering development and making a contribution to poverty alleviation, as has again and again been claimed by thousands of MF enthusiasts. As a conclusion, he recommends to simply discontinue the policy of supporting MF with technical and financial assistance from the advanced countries.

I see two main arguments in this study. The first one is that modern MF is a manifestation of a neoliberal policy that grossly underestimates the role that government interventions can and should play for economic development. Much of modern MF is indeed inspired by anti-government and pro-private sector thinking.[28] However, if he had been more versed in the history of development finance and development aid policy Bateman would most probably also have noticed how problematic the kind of government interventions can be that he so strongly advocates.[29] In other words, I tend to accept his diagnosis on this point and still disagree with his conclusions and recommendations.

His second main argument refers to the kind of economic activity that, according to his view, many "new-style MFIs" aspire to support with small loans. As he argues, the economic activities of the very poor do not generate sufficient income to warrant the application of development aid funds. Development would be strengthened and thus also the economic situation of large segments of the population would benefit more if funding were directed to small and medium-sized firms with some growth potential instead of informal and other micro-enterprise activity. With his second argument Bateman is not alone among microfinance experts and, based on similar ideas, some important players in MF have already adapted their strategy to the insight that more development impact can be generated by financing small firms rather than informal and micro-scale economic activity or even pure consumer lending.[30] Moreover, a large part of the commercially oriented MFIs have not or only half-heartedly subscribed to the poverty alleviation rhetoric of Yunus and his followers. It is therefore difficult to understand why Bateman arrives at the sweeping indictment that "microfinance does not work".

The third and by far the most important recent book is David Roodman's "Due Diligence" of 2011. The subtitle "An Impertinent Inquiry into Microfinance" could create the expectation that this is one more book containing a full blown attack on microfinance. Fortunately, this expectation is not justified. The book offers a very serious and thoughtful, indeed "diligent", account of modern MF and a careful assessment of its merits. The standard against which MF is assessed are frequently made claims on what MF could achieve. And by this standard the outcome of the intellectual exercise is somewhat disappointing. One claim, and probably the one that has gained the greatest popularity, is that MF is an ideal instrument to alleviate or even to eradicate poverty. Roodman looks at the facts and on recent econometric studies that seem to support the poverty alleviation claim and comes to the conclusion that there is no evidence that being clients of a MFI does indeed help people get out of poverty. This finding should, however, be taken with a large grain of salt. What Roodman and the researchers whose work he

---

[28] See many of the contributions in Levitsky (1990). This book summarizes the proceedings of the first World Microfinance Conference in Washington in 1989, that is, during the presidency of Ronald Reagan.

[29] See for instance the collection of articles about the old policy of directed credit contained in Adams et al. (1984) with the informative title "Undermining rural development with cheap credit". What Bateman recommends has stunning similarities to the policy that is so forcefully criticized in the book by Adams et al. and similar publications by the same group of authors in the early 1980s.

[30] See, for example, the latest Annual Report of ProCredit Holding (2012).

analyses look at, are immediate and very short-term effects. If such effects cannot be shown, it does not at all imply that MF does not increase welfare of large parts of the population, and thus also including the poor and the very poor. If one looks at the effects that, for instance, German savings banks and cooperative banks have had since the time they were created in the 19th century, one can hardly question that they have had a very positive effect. But this effect took decades to material-ize, and the mechanism through which these financial institutions that opened up the access to finance for formerly excluded clients are more complex than what the recent econometric studies can capture.

The second claim investigated by Roodman is that MF creates empowerment. Here his assessment is similarly skeptical. No immediate effect of empowerment can be identified in serious econometric studies. However, as in the case of pov-erty reduction, the argument is relatively weak in so far as the pertinent studies can only capture short-term and readily observable effects.

Up to this point, one could say that both the developments in the "reality" of microfinance and the popular and academic debate about MF point in the same direction: MF does not, and cannot, keep its promises and therefore has lost a great deal of its appeal. However, this assessment would disregard that Roodman also considers a third claim. It is the claim of those who advocate financial institu-tion building and financial sector development in the direction to more inclusive finance. On this account, his assessment is unambiguously positive. Unfortu-nately, he does not delve into the question to which extent the positive develop-ments in what he calls "microfinance as industry building" have a positive impact on broad segments of the economically active population in developing and transi-tion countries over a longer term. The general literature on the finance-and-growth nexus provide ample reason to think much more positively about MF including its welfare effects for the general population.[31]

5   The Renewed Debate About Objectives and Values of Microfinance

5.1   Values for "Microfinance 3.0"

The recent developments and the widely perceived loss of ethical appeal of MF, as it has been practiced up to now, requires reconsidering the question why values and especially what I have called Value 2 above is important for finance in general and microfinance in particular. The general answer to this question is that values and ethics play a role because they provide orientation and can shape the behavior

---

[31]   For an overview, see World Bank (2001) or Levine (2005). The „theory of development finance", summarized in section 3c above supports the view that good microfinance has the potential to generate not only growth but also a broad-based economic and social development.

of economic agents where markets and politics fail to give unambiguous orientation, lead to undesirable outcomes and leave room for discretion. Real-world (financial) markets do not function as standard economics textbooks suggest. They
invite exploitation and other forms of unethical behavior and lead to exclusion and
discrimination. Policy interventions (regulation, state banks, etc.) cannot compensate this „market *cum* policy failure", leading to a void which needs to be, and can
be, filled by „Values 2" in the forms of personal integrity, professional ethics, etc.
The debate about the role of ethics in general banking and finance after the financial crisis has made this point sufficiently clear: Profit making without ethical restraint has done damage, and even the largest investment bank of this world, such
as Deutsche Bank, are now trying to revive their corporate culture in a way that
puts more emphasis on responsible client service, transparency and fairness, not
least because this would be good for the banks itself.

This applies even more so to development finance, MF and small business finance (henceforth SBF). Endeavors in these fields have always been inspired by
the idea that unrestricted markets do not function as one would hope and that
therefore some intervention is required that is itself guided by Value 2 considerations.[32] These considerations are based on value judgments and beliefs that

- opportunities should be distributed equitably,

- poor people and those excluded from access to finance need support;

- better access to finance fosters economic growth and broad based development and ultimately also democracy and peace; and that in most cases,

- host-country authorities do not support broad based finance enough.

As I have argued above, in order to be effective, MF and SBF require the existence of solid and stable institutions. In order to be effective for a long time, these
institutions must follow a commercial approach. If they are not profitable they cannot survive and grow and create „Value 1" for anybody. But there is the danger that
the commercial approach can go too far. The economically sound and ethically legitimate aim of making a profit or, in other words, to cover their full cost including the cost of equity, may suggest profit maximizing behavior. However, outright
profit maximization would be contrary to the logic why MF and SBF are created in
the first place, since all profit maximizing financial institutions tend to discriminate,
exploit etc if they have the opportunity to do so, as the cases in Mexico and India
clearly show. Therefore, it is particularly important for commercially oriented MFIs
and small business banks that they are solidly based on values in the sense of
Value 2. Values are an antidote to an excessive commercial orientation.

Given that values are very important for sound, commercially oriented MF and
SBF institutions, one needs to take a closer look at what these values and the ob-

---

[32] The conditions under which market failure justifies interventions in markets can be
found in Besley (1994).

jectives of MFIs are today: The dual objective of outreach/impact/benefit (or Value 1 for clients) and institutional sustainability (or Value 1 for the institutions) remain relevant. But this needs to be made more operational for an upcoming age of "Microfinance 3.0". One can distinguish three types of objectives/values:

1. Rules of conduct: Fairness and transparency to clients and other partners; responsibility in lending; transparency to providers of funds, regulators and donors. In particular, the responsibility of MFIs for preventing that their clients borrow more – from one MFI or from different MFIs – than they would ever be able to repay deserves emphasis, since this commitment to responsible lending has been grossly neglected in the recent past. A firm commitment to the value of responsible lending implies that MFIs should avoid getting involved in consumer lending that does not produce economic benefits and in any transaction take extreme care in making sure that their clients are capable of bearing the debt burden they incur when they take out loans.

2. Traditional objectives of MF such as benefitting clients e.g. by expanding the set of options they have, instead of claiming to directly alleviate or even eliminate poverty (since this is not achievable) and strengthening the respective financial system and combating financial exclusion; and

3. fostering economic growth by improving the access to finance for very small, small and even mid-sized businesses that are capable of creating income and employment and that so far do not have access to credit at reasonable terms.

Value considerations in the form of a sound balance between Value 1 for clients and other stakeholders and Value 2 are not only important for those who govern and manage MFIs. They are also criteria that investors and donors should use in their decisions on how to support MFIs with loans, equity and technical assistance. Last but not least they should play a prominent role in the selection, training and evaluation of those who work in MFIs.

5.2   Assuring Value Orientation of MFIs That Want to Access the Capital Market

Still today, there are millions of economically active people and very small and small businesses in this world that do not have access to the kind of financial services they need and want and that would have a positive effect on their personal situation and their countries' development. Therefore, the institutions that provide these services have a moral and developmental obligation to expand the scale of their operations. This complements the requirement for MFIs as business entities to grow in order to be attractive for staff and for their own creditors and investors. For financial institutions that are regulated and supervised as banks, growth creates the need to increase their equity in parallel to their loan portfolios and the level of deposits they may want to mobilize. However, equity is difficult to get, even for formal financial institutions.

One source of equity is self-financing or retained earnings. But given the pace at which most MFIs have grown in the recent past[33] and at which they will hopefully continue to grow, retained profits are typically not enough, especially if the institutions find it important under ethical and developmental aspects not to make as much profit as they would need if they had to rely exclusively on internal financing to satisfy their growing equity needs. Another source of equity are national and international development finance institutions. Their resources are also limited and not enough to meet the equity needs of the growing MFI sector. Therefore, it is inevitable to raise equity from private sources. Here, we first find the type of private "social investor" who want to be rewarded with a financial and a "social" dividend and might be prepared to accept a lower financial dividend if they can count on having the feeling that they contribute to an ethically valuable undertaking. But also this source of equity is limited, especially since it is difficult to organize the external financing from a large number of "social investors". Ultimately, there is hardly a way of avoiding the step of turning to private and institutional investors for whom financial interest dominates social or political interests.

At least for large and growing MFIs, an option worth considering is to address the general market for equity capital by issuing shares in the format of an initial public offering (IPO) and then having their shares listed and traded on an organized stock market. Having the shares issued to the general public (as opposed to a private placement) is important because it provides liquidity for investors and thus makes MFI shares more attractive as an investment.[34]

However, this is not as easy as it may appear. This is not so much the case because an IPO is always a difficult process, especially for firms that have an unconventional business model and operate in a line of business with which the capital market is not familiar. A more important reason is that equity in a public exchange listed company brings with it certain rights for the new shareholders and the legal obligation for the issuing firm to protect their interests and, at least to a certain extent, follow a strategy that conforms to their interests. An IPO changes the character of any institution in a fundamental way. In the case of an institution with a social and developmental mission, it can imply that this mission is lost.

Assuring the lasting social and developmental orientation, which has typically been a driving force behind the original creation of a MFI or a similar organiza-

---

[33] Disregarding cases of excessive and unhealthy growth as it has recently occurred in a number of countries and regions, notably in the Indian state of Andhra Pradesh.

[34] Moreover, having shares traded on an organized market may be important for development institutions like the IFC which have in many cases served as early investors in commercially oriented MFIs and which are required by their internal regulation to exit their investment after a given time span.

tion[35], is a challenge. If after completing an IPO a sufficiently large fraction of the equity is held by the general public or even by institutional investors with purely financial interests, there is a considerable chance – or rather a considerable danger – that the power derived from holding shares will be used to transform the nature of the MFI in a way which would conform more to the financial interest of outside shareholders. For instance, powerful outside shareholders could exert pressure to the effect that a MFI becomes more profit oriented than it had been before, e.g. by raising interest rates, as in the Compartamos case, or by expanding operations faster than would be compatible with the rules of responsible lending, as in the SKS case. Or outside investors might transform a micro and small business oriented MFI into a consumer lending institution, as it recently happened in a number of countries.

Those who have once created a MFI with a social and developmental orientation and who might still lead it face a dilemma if their MFI is set to grow so much that it needs equity capital from outside private investors[36] in order to expand. If they turn to the capital market and thus ultimately to investors whom they cannot hand-pick they endanger the ethical orientation of their MFI. If they therefore avoid attracting outside equity, they forgo the opportunity to expand the operations and limit the positive impact for their potential clients they might otherwise have. However, the decision to go public and to look for outside equity capital and thereby grant decision rights to investors who might not share their developmental orientation is not an all-or-nothing decision. There are several ways of limiting the possibly negative effects of going public.

What comes to mind first is to limit the fraction of the shares sold to outside investors. Another option is to make sure that the shares held by others than the anonymous outside investors are, to use finance terminology, "in stable hand" of investors who can be expected to stick to the original social and developmental mission. A part of this strategy would be to place large blocks of shares with reliable "anchor investors". The third option is to find a legal form for the shares that are issued which entails weaker ownership rights for the outside shareholders than ordinary shares. Non-voting preferred shares are one among several options that can be chosen it the applicable legal regime provides this possibility.

Of course, it has to be anticipated that those who might acquire newly issued shares would understand the implications of any attempt of the incumbent owners or managers of an MFI to restrict the influence they can have on the orientation and strategy of the institution in which they might invest. For instance, they would

---

[35] Such a "similar organization" could be one that owns or controls local MFIs without itself being an MFI. Since by now there are several important networks of MFIs with central institution which might go public, the case of "similar organizations" is of substantial practical importance in the present context.

[36] This is even more so if a MFI tried to satisfy its equity needs by inviting private equity firms or hedge funds to become outside investors. Their business model relies to a large extent on their ability to re-orient a firm in which they invest.

understand that an outright conversion of a small business-oriented bank with limited profitability into a more profitable firm focused on consumer lending would be very difficult if not simply infeasible or that it would be impossible to acquire a sufficiently large majority to take over the entire firm and integrate it into an existing large commercial banking group.

Seeing these restrictions, potential outside investors might refrain from buying shares or they would pay less for the shares than in if there was the option of converting the MFI into a more profitable but ethically or developmentally less valuable financial institution. This is a price to be paid by the present owners – and de facto also by its potential clients since it limits the possible expansion of the MFI's operations. But it might be worth paying this price especially in view of the unpleasant consequences that the de facto take-over by purely profit oriented investors and the ensuing strategic reorientation seem to have had in those two cases mentioned above, in which hedge funds and private equity firms have, respectively, become the dominant shareholders. The price may be so high that an IPO becomes outright impossible. However, some relevant recent experience suggests that this might not be the case and that there would be enough investors who would be willing to take equity positions with limited rights and opportunities to reshape a development oriented MFI.

6　Back to Basics? – Yes and No

The question in the subtitle of this paper[37] is whether the recent events suggest returning to "Basics". I interpret this as meaning a possible return to the former values and their role in MF, SBF and related fields within the broader context of development finance. For space considerations, I cannot extensively address the more general questions whether and to what extent a more general "back to basics" might be required. However, a few sentences on this may still be appropriate, even if this mainly serves the purpose of pointing out a difference. As far as most features of MF in the style of the early 1990s are concerned, the idea of going "back to these basics" would be highly undesirable. This refers most of all to

- the very limited scope of services formerly provided by MFIs – credit only;

- the older methodology of lending – predominantly group lending;

- the predominant institutional form of MFIs – NGOs rather than corporations;

- the status of credit-granting NGOs as unregulated financial institutions;

- the low efficiency and the high costs of providing MF services[38];

---

[37]　Title and subtitle of the paper were assigned to me by the organizers of the conference.

[38]　See Schmidt/Zeitinger (1996) for empirical evidence.

- the very limited scale and outreach of MF operations and, finally

- the complete dependence of MFIs on the "generosity" of donors.

Even though the MFIs of the early 1990s may have appeared more exotic and more romantic to journalists, politicians and other outside observers than the small business banks of today that look almost like any other bank, a return to these "basics" would go at the expense of those millions of clients who would not be able to obtain financial services if the MF industry were again transformed into the amateurish cottage industry of 20 years ago. There has been progress in MF, and this is good for the large number of clients of most MFIs who now have much better access to financing. Many MFIs are now "universal banks" offering various kinds of credit, savings accounts, money transfer and many other services. Group lending has been replaced by individual lending in most cases. Several MFIs have been transformed into corporations and have become regulated and supervised financial intermediaries. In most cases, MFIs have greatly expanded the scale of their operations, a factor that made the cost of intermediation fall below 20%, a rate that appeared utopian only 20 years ago. Finally, many MFIs are no longer dependent on donor financing or have at least reduced their dependence considerably.

Is "Back to Basics" recommendable as far as the importance of values, especially Value 2, is concerned? Here my answer is unambiguously Yes. There are certainly many more cases of MFIs than those which Hugh Sinclair describes in his book in which Value 2-orientation is completely missing. But even apart from such extreme cases, there might be a tendency in a number of MFIs to rely less on a commitment to moral values than it used to be the case 20 years ago. Optimists would probably say that the general financial crisis and the microfinance crisis in India and a few other countries have ushered in a renaissance of value orientation. In a growing number of MFIs and in networks of MFIs, for instance that of the ProCredit Banks, efforts are made to strengthen the awareness among staff members that development finance aiming at poorer people and small businesses has a social, developmental and thus ultimately also immensely political role. Pertinent elements now play an increasing role in their staff training programs.

Of course, one should not ignore that thousands of MFI managers and tens of thousands of staff members have always had a clear ethical orientation in spite of the doubts that some observers have expressed with respect to MFIs from the commercial camp.

But there are also important differences between the situation of 20 years ago and that of today. The necessity to adopt a clear commercial orientation and the stronger connections that have developed between MFIs and the "normal" financial system have given Value 2 a more important role than it had in the past. These relatively new features of MF are a threat to the value orientation of MF, and this creates the need to take precautions that the Value 2-orientation does not get lost.

Today it is necessary to integrate a strong role for Value 2 into the corporate culture, the organizational structure and the governance and ownership structure of complex MFIs and MFI networks. Ways must be found and corresponding rules must be implemented that protect MFIs and their managers and staff from the temptation to disregard or even completely forget their ethical commitment in the face of growing day-to-day pressures. It is not enough to leave sufficient room for value-driven conduct, but there must also be firmer commitments that values remain important. What I have described above when I discussed the problems of MFIs going public is just one example of this kind of commitment.

So, at a structural level, we cannot go back to basics and to the former role of values. Today, good intentions and the right attitude and personality are no longer enough. There must be institutional features in MFIs and their governance and ownership structures that assure a strong role for ethics and Value 2. Even though this might make the access to capital markets more difficult, a responsible MFI must by all means be restrictive concerning to whom they sell their shares. In almost any legal systems, there are ways of doing this, for instance by including relevant clauses in the contracts they conclude with the investment banks that are involved in the IPO process.

References

Adams, D., Graham, D., Von Pischke, J.D. (eds.) (1984) Undermining Rural Development with Cheap Credit. Boulder: Westview Press.

Bateman, M. (2010) Why Doesn't Microfinance Work? London: Zed Books.

Besley, T. (1994) How Do Market Failures Justify Interventions in Rural Credit Markets. World Bank Research Observer 9:27–47.

Business Week (2007) The ugly side of microlending, Dec. 24, 2007 (US edition).

Chen, G., Rasmussen, S., Reille, X., Rozas, D. (2010) Indian Microfinance Goes Public: The SKS Initial Public Offering. In: CGAP FocusNote No. 65, Washington D.C.

FAZ (2011) Alternativen zur Mikrofinanz gesucht. Frankfurter Allgemeine Zeitung, June 17, 2011.

Financial Times of India (2012) Private Equity Firms Woo Indian Microfinance Institutions (published Oct. 5, 2012 and downloaded from the homepage of Symbiotics, Oct 20, 2012).

Fisher, I. (1904) The Nature of Capital and Income. New York: Macmillan.

Friedman, M. (1970) The social responsibility of business is to increase its profits, New York Times Magazine, September 13, 1970.

Furubotn, E., Richter, R. (2002) Institutions and Economic Theory: The Contribution of the New Institutional Economics, Ann Arbor: MichUniv Press.

Gonzalez-Vega, C. (1998) Do financial institutions have a role in assisting the poor? In: M.S. Kimenyi et al., Strategic Issues in Microfinance. Aldershot: Ashgate, pp. 11–26.

Hart, O. (1995) Firms, Contracts and Financial Structure. Oxford: OUP.

Hulme, D., Mosley, P. (1996) Finance Against Poverty. London-New York: Routledge.

Kant, I. (1788) Kritik der praktischen Vernunft. Riga, reprinted Erlangen 1984.

Kohl, H. (1990) Kants Gesinnungsethik. Berlin: de Gruyter.

Krauss, N., Walter, I. (2009) Can Microfinance Reduce Portfolio Volatility? Economic Development and Cultural Change 58:85–110.

Levine, R. (2005) Finance and Growth: Theory and Evidence. In: Aghion, P., Durlauf, S. (eds.) Handbook of Economic Growth. Amsterdam.

Levitsky, J. (ed.) (1989) Microenterprises in Developing Countries. London: ITDG.

Nair, A., Von Pischke, J.D. (2007) Commercial Banks and Financial Access. In: Barr M.S., et al. (eds.) Building Inclusive Financial Systems: A Framework for Financial Access. Washington: Brookings, pp. 89–116.

North, D. (1991) Institutions, Journal of Economic Perspectives 5:97–112.

ProCredit Holding KGaA (2012) Annual Report 2011, Frankfurt.

Roodman, D. (2011) Due Diligence: An Impertinent Inquiry into Microfinance. Washington: Center for Global Development.

Rosenberg, R. (2007) CGAP Reflections on the Compartamos Initial Public Offering: A Case Study on Microfinance Interest Rates and Profits. CGAP Focus Note 42, Washington, D.C.

Schmidt, R.H. (2010) Microfinance, commercialization and Ethics. Poverty and Public Policy 2(1):99–137.

Schmidt, R.H., Zeitinger, C.P. (1996) The efficiency of credit granting NGOs. Savings and Development 20:353–385.

Sinclair H. (2012a): The Dark Side of Microfinance, A conversation with Hugh Sinclair, Knowledge at Wharton: Finance and Investment, July 18, 2012.

Sinclair, H. (2012) Confessions of a Microfinance Heretic: How Microfinance Lost its Way and Betrayed the Poor. San Francisco: Berrett-Köhler.

Stiglitz, J.E., Weiss A. (1981), Credit Rationing in Markets with Imperfect Information, American Economic Review 71:393–410.

Tirole, J. (2008) The Theory of Corporate Finance. Princeton: Princeton Univ. Press.

Tschach, I. (2002) The Theory of Development Finance – How Microcredit Programmes Alleviate Credit and Labour Market Segmentation. Frankfurt: Peter Lang-Verlag.

Wagner, C. (2012).: From Boom to Bust: How different has microfinance been from traditional banking? Development Policy Review 30:187–210.

Weber, M. (1919) Politik als Beruf. Berlin: Duncker und Humblodt.

Woller, G., Dunford, C., Woodworth, W. (1999) Where to Microfinance? International Journal of Economic Development 1(1).

World Bank (2001) Finance and Growth: Policy Choices in a Volatile World. Oxford: Oxford University Press.

CHAPTER 4

Microcredit Interest Rates and Their Determinants: 2004–2011[*]

Richard Rosenberg[**], Scott Gaul[***], William Ford[****], and Olga Tomilova[*****]

From the beginning of modern microcredit,[1] its most controversial dimension has been the interest rates charged by microlenders—often referred to as microfinance institutions (MFIs).[2] These rates are higher, often much higher, than normal bank rates, mainly because it inevitably costs more to lend and collect a given amount through thousands of tiny loans than to lend and collect the same amount in a few large loans. Higher administrative costs have to be covered by higher interest rates. But how much higher? Many people worry that poor borrowers are being exploited by excessive interest rates, given that those borrowers have little bargaining power, and that an ever-larger proportion of microcredit is moving into for-profit organizations where higher interest rates could, as the story goes, mean higher returns for the shareholders.

Several years ago CGAP reviewed 2003–2006 financial data from hundreds of MFIs collected by the Microfinance Information Exchange (MIX), looking at inter-

---

[*] This paper and the research behind it have been jointly produced by Microfinance Information Exchange (MIX), KfW and Consultative Group to Assist the Poor (CGAP).

[**] Independent Consultant.

[***] Director of Analysis, Microfinance information eXchange (MIX).

[****] Market Intelligence Lead, Microfinance information eXchange (MIX).

[*****] Microfinance Specialist, Consultative Group to Assist the Poor (CGAP).

[1] In this paper, "microcredit" refers to very small, shorter-term, usually uncollateralized loans made to low-income microentrepreneurs and their households, using unconventional techniques such as group liability, frequent repayment periods, escalating loan sizes, forced savings schemes, etc.

[2] MFIs are financial providers that focus, sometimes exclusively, on delivery of financial services targeted at low-income clients whose income sources are typically informal, rather than wages from registered employers. Among these financial services, microcredit predominates in most MFIs today, but savings, insurance, payments, and other money transfers are being added to the mix, as well as more varied and flexible forms of credit. MFIs take many forms, for instance, informal village banks, not-for-profit lending agencies, savings and loan cooperatives, for-profit finance companies, licensed specialized banks, specialized departments in universal commercial banks, and government programs and institutions.

est rates and the costs and profits that drive those interest rates. The main purpose of that paper (Rosenberg, Gonzalez, and Narain 2009) was to assemble empirical data that would help frame the question of the reasonableness of microcredit interest rates, allowing a discussion based more on facts and less on ideology.

In this paper, we review a better and fuller set of MIX data that runs from 2004 to 2011. Though we defer most discussion of methodology until the Annex, one point is worth making here at the beginning. The earlier CGAP paper used data from a consistent panel: that is, trend analysis was based on 175 profitable microlenders that had reported their data each year from 2003 through 2006. This approach gave a picture of what happened to *a typical set of microlenders* over time.

This paper, by contrast, mainly uses data from MFIs that reported at any time from 2004 through 2011.[3] Thus, for example, a microlender that entered the market in 2005, or one that closed down in 2009, would be included in the data for the years when they provided reports. We feel this approach gives a better picture of the evolution of the whole market, and thereby better approximates the situation of a typical *set of clients* over time. The drawback is that trend lines in this paper cannot be mapped against trend lines in the previous paper, because the sample of MFIs was selected on a different basis. (We did calculate panel data for a consistent set of 456 MFIs that reported from 2007 through 2011; we used this data mainly to check trends that we report from the full 2004–2011 data set.)

The data set and the methodology used to generate our results are discussed further in this paper's Annex. Our main purpose here is to survey market developments over the period; there will not be much discussion of the "appropriateness" of interest rates, costs, or profits. A major new feature of this paper is that it is complemented by an online database, described later in the paper, that readers can use to dig more deeply into the underlying MIX data—and in particular, to look at the dynamics of individual country markets.

---

[3]   For readers interested in the composition of this group, we can summarize the distribution of the more than 6000 annual observations from 2004 through 2011. Note that this is the distribution of MFIs, not of customers served. Category definitions can be found in the Annex:

Region: SSA 14%, EAP 13%, ECA 18%, LAC 34%, MENA 5%, S. Asia 16%

Profit status: For-profit 39%, nonprofit 59%, n/a 2%. (Note that for-profit MFIs serve the majority of borrowers, because they tend to be larger than nonprofit MFIs.)

Prudentially regulated by financial authorities? yes 57%, no 41%, n/a 2%

Legal form: bank 9%, regulated nonbank financial institution 32%, credit union/co-op 13%, NGO 38%, rural bank 6%, other or n/a 2%

Target market: low micro 42%, broad micro 49%, high micro 5%, small business 4%

Financial intermediation (voluntary savings): >1/5 of assets 39%, up to 1/5 of assets 17%, none 44%

Age: 1–4 years 10%, 5–8 years 19%, >8 years 69%, n/a 2%

Borrowers: <10k 48%, 10k–30k 23%, >30k 29%

Not surprisingly, five more years of data reveal some important changes in the industry. For instance,

- Globally, interest rates declined substantially through 2007, but then leveled off. This is partly due to the behavior of operating (i.e., staff and administrative) costs, whose long-term decline was interrupted in 2008 and 2011. Another factor has been a rise in microlenders' cost of funds, as they expanded beyond subsidized resources and drew increasingly on commercial borrowings.

- Average returns on equity have been falling, and the percentage of borrowers' loan payments that go to profits has dropped dramatically. This is good news for those who are worried about exploitation of poor borrowers, but may be more ambiguous for those concerned about the financial performance of the industry.

- For the subset of lenders who focus on a low-end (i.e., poorer) clientele, interest rates have risen, along with operating expenses and cost of funds. On the other hand, low-end lenders are considerably more profitable on average than other lenders (except in 2011, when the profitability of the group was depressed by a repayment crisis in the Indian state of Andhra Pradesh).

As in the 2009 paper, we will look not just at interest rates but also at their components—that is, the main factors that determine how high interest rates will be. Lenders use their interest income to cover costs, and the difference between income and costs is profit (or loss). A simplified version of the relevant formula is

Income from loans = Cost of funds + Loan loss expense + Operating Expense + Profit[4,5]

In other words, interest income—the amount of loan charges that microlenders collect from their customers—moves up or down only if one or more of the components on the right side of the equation moves up or down.

That formula provides the structure of this paper:

- Section 1 looks at the level and trend of microlenders' **interest rates** worldwide, and breaks them out among different types of institutions (peer groups).

- Section 2 examines the **cost of funds** that microlenders borrow to fund their loan portfolio.

- Section 3 reports on **loan losses**, including worrisome recent developments in two large markets.

---

[4] "Operating expense" is the term MIX uses to describe personnel and administrative costs, such as salaries, depreciation, maintenance, etc.

[5] A fuller formula is:

Income from loans + Other income = Cost of funds + Loan loss expense + Operating expense + Tax + Profit.

- Section 4 presents trends in **operating expenses**, and touches on the closely related issue of **loan size.**

- Section 5, looks at microlenders' **profits,** the most controversial component of microcredit interest rates.

- A reader without time to read the whole paper may wish to skip to Section 6 (page 96), which provides a graphic overview of the movement of interest rates and their components over the period and a **summary** of the main findings.

- The Annex describes our **database and methodology,** including the reasons for dropping four large microlenders[6] from the analysis.

A dense forest of data lies behind this paper. To avoid unreasonable demands on the reader's patience, we have limited ourselves to the tops of some of the more important trees. But MIX has posted our data files on its website, including Excel pivot tables where readers can slice the data any way they like (http://microfinance-business-solution.mixmarket.org/rs/microfinance/images/Interest Rate Paper Supporting Data.zip). The pivot tables allow a user to select among 14 financial indicators and display 2004–2001 adjusted or unadjusted results (weighted averages and quartiles) broken out in any of nine different peer groupings, including individual countries.

In choosing which groupings of these data to include in the paper, we have had to select among more than 800 different data cuts that were available. Most of the information presented here is in the form of global cuts, often broken out by peer groups, such as region, for-profit status, loan methodology, etc. **But for many readers, the most relevant peer grouping will consist of the microlenders operating in a particular country.** We strongly encourage these readers to use the online pivot tables to customize an analysis of what has been happening in any specific country.

1   Level and Trend of Interest Rates

1.1   How to Measure Microcredit Interest

Before presenting data and findings, we need to discuss two different ways to measure interest rates on microloans: interest yield and annual percentage rate (APR). Understanding the distinction between these two is crucial for a proper interpretation of the interest rate data we present in this section.

From a client standpoint, a typical way to state interest rates is to calculate an APR on the client's particular loan product. APR takes into account the amount and timing of all the cash flows associated with the loan, including not only things

---

[6]   BRI (Indonesia), Harbin Bank (China), Postal Savings Bank of China, and Vietnam Bank for Social Policy.

that are explicitly designated as "interest" and "principal," but also any other expected fees or charges, as well as compulsory deposits that are a condition of the loan. This APR indicator is a good representation of the effective cost of a loan for borrowers who pay as agreed. APR can be substantially different from (usually higher than) the stated interest rate in the loan contract.

MicroFinance Transparency (MF Transparency) is building a database with careful APR information on some or all of the significant microlenders in a growing range of countries. Collection of these data is labor-intensive and depends on the willing cooperation of microlenders who might occasionally find the publication of these pricing specifics embarrassing. As of this writing, the MF Transparency website displays data from 17 countries.[7]

In contrast, the MIX database we draw from in this paper cannot generate APRs. What MIX provides is "interest yield," which expresses the total of all income from loans (interest, fees, other loan charges) as a percentage of the lender's average annual gross loan portfolio (GLP). From the vantage point of the lender, interest yield is clearly meaningful. But as an indication of what individual microborrowers are really paying, interest yield is inferior to APR in important ways. For instance,

- In 2011, about a third of microborrowers were served by lenders that use compulsory savings—that is, they require borrowers to maintain a percentage of their loan on deposit with the lender. This practice raises the effective interest rate, because the deposit requirement reduces the net loan disbursement that the borrower can actually use, while the borrower pays interest on the full loan amount. APR incorporates this effect, while interest yield does not.

- MIX's calculation of interest yield lumps the lender's entire portfolio together, even though that portfolio may contain loan products with quite different terms, and may even include products that are better characterized as small business loans rather than microloans.

- The denominator of the MIX interest yield ratio is GLP—the total amount of all outstanding loans that has neither been repaid nor written off. But some of those loans are delinquent—the borrowers are behind on payments. The effect of this difference can be illustrated simply. Suppose that total interest income is 200, and GLP is 1000, producing an interest yield of 20 percent that the "average" borrower is paying. But if the portion of the loans that is actually performing is only 800, then the average borrowers are really paying 25 percent.[8]

---

[7]   http://data.mftransparency.org/data/countries/

[8]   MIX is building better information about compulsory deposits, and makes adjustments that attempt to represent net portfolio more accurately, but we found that these MIX data were not yet consistent enough to produce reliable results at present. A very rough analysis of these data suggests that compulsory deposits in some MFIs might add something like 3 percent to the worldwide average APR. The average impact of adjusting for nonperforming loans is harder to decipher.

An internal MIX analysis in 2011, based on seven countries for which MF Transparency also had data, found that the MIX interest yield understated the MF Transparency APR by an average of about 6 percentage points. However, the sample was too small to allow for much generalization of this result.

Given the limitations of the MIX interest yield measure, why are we using it in this paper? One reason is that the MIX's much broader coverage provides a better sample of the worldwide microcredit market: over 105 countries for 2011, compared to MF Transparency's 17. An even more important reason is that MIX, having started collecting data long before MF Transparency, has many more years of data, allowing trend analysis that is not yet possible for the latter. We think it highly likely that interest yield trends and APR trends would move approximately in parallel over a span of years. A detailed discussion of this point will be posted along with our underlying data (http://microfinance-business-solution.mixmarket. org/rs/microfinance/images/Interest Rate Paper Supporting Data.zip).

How, then, should the reader regard the meaningfulness of interest yield data? Here is our view:

1. *Actual effective rates paid for specific loan products at a point in time.* Interest yield probably understates these by varying and often substantial amounts.

2. *Peer group differences* (for instance, how do rates at for-profit and non-profit microlenders compare on average?). We think that substantial differences in interest yield among peer groups are very likely a meaningful indication of a difference among the groups in what their average borrowers pay. However, some caution is appropriate here, because the gap between interest yield and true APR can vary from one peer group to another.[9]

3. *Time-series trends.* Trends in interest yields (the main focus of this section) are probably quite a good indicator of trends in what typical borrowers are actually paying, on the plausible assumption that the gap between interest yield and APR stays relatively stable on average from one year to the next.

Finally, we emphasize that the issue discussed above applies only to data about interest rates. It poses no problem for the majority of our analysis, which deals with the *determinants* of interest rates, namely cost of funds, loan losses, operating expenses, and profit.

---

[9] This is particularly true when comparing MFIs that focus on smaller loans to poorer clients, as against MFIs with a broad suite of loan products, some of which serve clients that might not fit one's particular definition of "micro."

1.2   Level of Interest Yields in 2011

Figure 1 shows a global median interest yield of about 27 percent. Distribution graphs like this one remind us that there is wide variation in microcredit rates, so any statement about a median (or average) rate is a composite summary that veils a great deal of underlying diversity. The regional distribution indicates that rates vary more widely in Africa and Latin America than in other regions. Also, we notice that rates are substantially lower in South Asia than elsewhere: the relative cost of hiring staff tends to be lower there, and—at least in Bangladesh—the political climate and the strong social orientation of the industry have probably led managers to focus more on keeping rates low.[10]

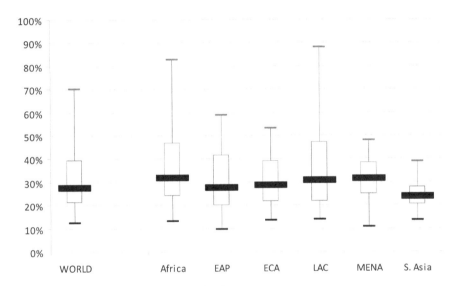

Fig. 1. MFI Interest Yield Distribution, 2011

Note: Interest and fee income from loan portfolio as % of average GLP, 866 MFIs reporting to MIX. The thick horizontal bars represent medians; the top and bottom of the white boxes represent the 75th and 25th percentiles, respectively; and the high and low short bars represent the 95th and 5th percentiles, respectively. So, for example, 95 percent of the MFIs in the sample are collecting an interest yield below about 70 percent. Data here are unweighted: each MFI counts the same regardless of size. EAP = East Asia and Pacific, ECA = Europe and Central Asia, LAC = Latin America and the Caribbean, MENA = Middle East and North Africa.

---

[10] Figure 1 and subsequent figures showing percentile distributions are unweighted; in other words, each MFI counts the same regardless of its size. Not surprisingly, the median in such a distribution may be different from the weighted average (e.g., Figure 3) where large MFIs count for proportionally more than small MFIs. However, in the particular case of the 2011 global interest yield, the weighted average (see Figure 2) and the median are very close, about 27 percent.

1.3 Global Average Interest Rates Have Stopped Declining in Recent Years

Figure 2 shows a drop in average global microcredit rates through 2007, but not thereafter. (Inflation-adjusted rates fell in 2008 because few microlenders raised their rates enough to compensate for the spike in worldwide inflation that year.)[11] The analysis of interest rate determinants later in the paper suggests that the main reason world average rates didn't drop after 2007 is that operating (i.e., staff and administrative) costs stayed level.[12]

On the assumption that the microcredit market is getting more saturated and competitive in quite a few countries, we might have expected a different result. Analysis of individual countries where the market is thought to be more competitive shows continued interest rate decline post-2006 in some (e.g., Bolivia, Nicaragua, Cambodia) but not in others (e.g., Mexico, Bosnia/Herzegovina, Indonesia). Sorting out the evidence on the effects of competition would require more detailed country analysis than we were able to do for this paper.

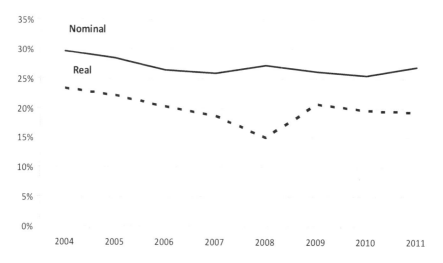

Fig. 2. Global Interest Yield Trends, 2004–2011

Note: Global interest and fee income from loans/average total GLP, weighted by GLP, both nominal and net of inflation.

---

[11] The same effects show up in panel analysis where we tracked the 456 MFIs that reported consistently to MIX every year from 2007 to 2011.

[12] As we will see later (compare Figures 3 and 13), the correlation between interest yield and operating cost shows up at the regional level: AFR and EAP, the two regions with interest rate declines since 2006, also had lower operating costs.

1.4 Peer Group Patterns

The regional breakout in Figure 3 shows that over the full 2004–2011 period, Latin America is the only region with no significant decline in average interest yield. However, there is important regional variation since 2006: Africa and East Asia/Pacific show substantial continued declines—perhaps because they were the least developed markets in 2006. At any rate, these two regions are the ones that

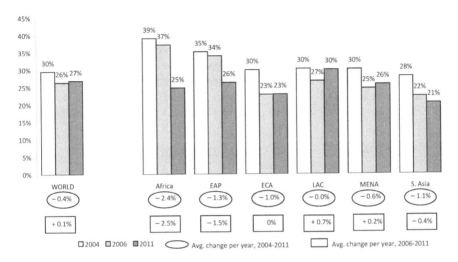

Fig. 3. Interest Yield Changes 2004–2011

Note: Interest and fee income from loans as percentage of average GLP for the period, weighted by GLP. The Africa series begins in 2005 rather than 2004.

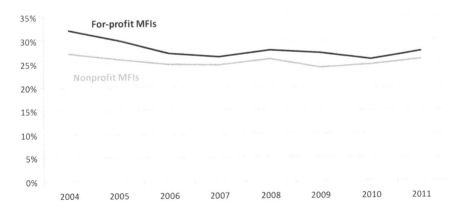

Fig. 4. For-Profit vs. Nonprofit Interest Yields, 2004–2011

Note: Total interest and fee income/average total GLP, weighted by GLP. MFIs are assigned to the "for-profit" or "nonprofit" depending on their legal status in 2011.

substantially improved their operating expenses since 2006 (see Figure 13). But reported average rates actually went back up in Latin America, the most commercialized of the regions.

Figure 4 illustrates the unremarkable finding that for-profit microlenders collect higher average interest yields than nonprofit microlenders. However, for-profit interest rates have dropped more than nonprofit interest rates: the average difference between the two peer groups dropped from 5 percentage points in 2004 down to 1.7 percentage points by 2011. By way of illustration, on a $1000 loan in 2011, the annual difference between the for-profit and nonprofit interest charges would amount on average to $17, or less than $1.50 per month.

When we separate microlenders by the target market they serve (Figure 5), we find that in institutions focused on the low-end market (smaller average loan sizes, and thus presumably poorer borrowers) interest rates are actually higher in 2011 than they were in 2004.[13]

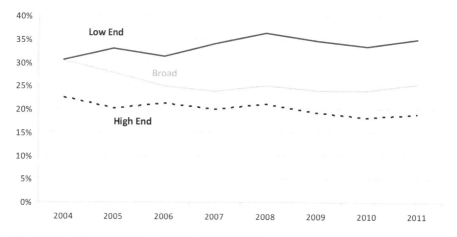

Fig. 5. Interest Yields by Target Market, 2004–2011

Note: Total interest and fee income/average total GLP, weighted by GLP, nominal. MFIs are grouped by "depth"—average loan balance per borrower as % of per capita gross national income. For the "low lnd" market, depth is <20% or average loan balance < US$150. For "broad," depth is between 20% and 149%. For "high end," depth is between 150% and 250%. For the "small business" market, which is not included in this graph, depth is over 250%.

---

[13] Loan sizes here are measured as a percentage of countries' per capita national income. People with wide on-the-ground experience of many MFIs agree that their average loan sizes bear some rough relation to client poverty—poorer clients tending to take smaller loans—but the relationship is very far from perfect. See, for instance, Schreiner, Matul, Pawlak, and Kline (2006) and Hoepner, Liu, and Wilson (2011).

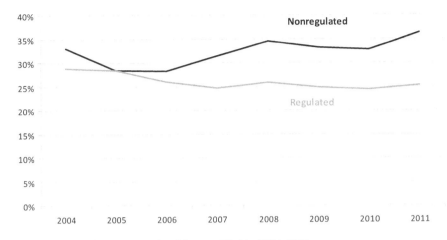

Fig. 6. Regulated vs. Nonregulated Interest Yields, 2004–2011

Note: Total interest and fee income/average total GLP, weighted by GLP.

Figure 6, comparing regulated and nonregulated microlenders,[14] seems to point in the same direction. Regulation refers here to licensing and/or prudential supervision by the country's banking authorities. Most of the regulated microcredit portfolio is in banks, and most of these are for-profit. The regulated lenders tend to have lower rates: they tend to offer larger loans, while the nonregulated MFIs tend to make smaller loans that require higher operating costs per dollar lent. Rates among nonregulated microlenders have been rising substantially since 2006.

The two preceding figures show higher rates for lenders that tend to focus on smaller borrowers. At first blush, this looks like bad news for low-end clients. However, the trend probably reflects some shifting of low-end clientele: if banks and broad-market microlenders have been capturing more of the easier-to-serve portion of poor borrowers, then the unregulated and low-end microlenders would be left with a somewhat tougher segment of clients, and their rising interest rates might simply reflect the higher expenses of serving this segment.[15] Another factor

---

[14] "Regulated" refers to banks and other finance companies that are subject to prudential regulation and supervision by the county's banking and financial authorities. The rest of the MFIs are categorized as "nonregulated": like any other business, they are subject to some regulation (e.g., consumer protection) but not to prudential regulation whose objective is to guard the financial health of an institution taking deposits from the public. MFIs are categorized based on their status in 2011.

[15] If this conjecture is true, we might expect to see average loan sizes decreasing in both broad-market and low-end MFIs, as well as in both regulated and nonregulated MFIs. This is indeed what has happened—average loan sizes have declined by roughly five percentage points among all these groups since 2006. And operating expense ratios have been rising for MFIs aimed at the low-end clientele.

is that funding costs for low-end lenders have been rising, as we will see below (Figure 8).

The fact that costs and thus interest rates are rising for microlenders who focus on poorer clients has a bearing on the perennial argument over whether to protect the poor by imposing interest rate caps. As costs rise for low-end microlenders, a given fixed-interest rate cap would put (or keep) more and more of them out of business as the years go by.

Having sketched a few important patterns and trends in interest rates, we now turn to the principal elements that determine (or "drive") those rates. To repeat, the simplified description of this relationship is

Income from loans = Cost of funds + Loan loss expense + Operating expense + Profit

After looking at these determinants individually, we will put them back together again in Section 6 to show how the trends in these elements combine to produce the trends in interest yields.

2   Cost of Funds

Microlenders fund their loans with some combination of equity (their own money) and debt (money borrowed from depositors or outside lenders). In a sense, the equity is free, at least for a not-for-profit lender that has no shareholder owners who collect dividends. But borrowed funds entail a cost in the form of interest expense.

Funding Costs Have Been Rising. Figure 7 shows a slow, steady climb in the nominal costs at which microlenders can borrow money to fund their loan portfolios. This climb is both less pronounced but more jumpy when we look at the real (i.e., net of inflation) cost of funds.[16] The most probable explanation of the rise in borrowing costs is that as microlenders expand, they can fund less of their portfolio from the limited amounts of heavily subsidized liabilities from development agencies, and they have to turn increasingly toward more expensive commercial and quasi-commercial debt from local and international markets.

Some people hope that funding costs will decline substantially as more and more microlenders mobilize voluntary deposits, but such a result is far from guaranteed. Over the time span of our study, average funding costs actually look slightly higher for lenders that rely heavily on voluntary savings than for lenders that take no such savings.[17] Also note that any decrease in funding cost produced by savings mobilization can be offset by increases in operating costs to administer the savings function, especially for small-sized liquid deposits that are aimed at the microclientele.

---

[16]   The sharp changes in real rates in 2008 and 2009 probably reflect the time it took for interest contracts to reprice following the world inflation spike in 2008.

[17]   The difference, about 0.1 percentage points, is probably not statistically significant.

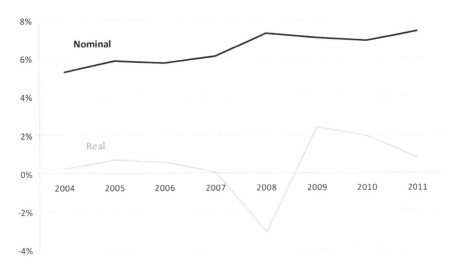

Fig. 7. Cost of Funds, Nominal and Real, 2004–2011

Note: Financial expense as % of liabilities, weighted by liabilities, both nominal and adjusted for each country's inflation.

2.1 Peer Group Analysis

Figure 8 shows another piece of bad news for microlenders focused on low-end borrowers: the average cost of funds is growing faster for this peer group than for others. Funding costs for microlenders that focus on high-end borrowers have stayed fairly level, while funding costs have climbed substantially for broad-market

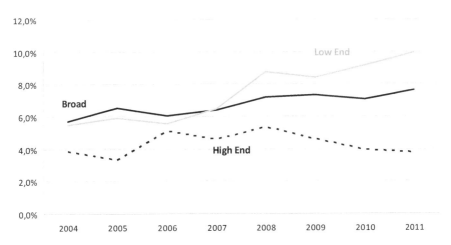

Fig. 8. Cost of Funds (Nominal) by Target Market 2004–2011

Note: Financial expense as % of liabilities, weighted by liabilities.

microlenders and especially for low-end microlenders.[18] This rise in funding costs is part of the reason that average worldwide interest yields paid by microborrowers have not been declining in the past few years, and interest yields paid by customers of low-end lenders have actually grown, as we saw in Section 1.

Not surprisingly, regulated institutions like banks and licensed finance companies have been able to borrow money an average of 1.5 percentage points cheaper than nonregulated lenders. Most of the regulated microlenders can take savings, and interest cost for their savings is lower than for large commercial borrowings.[19] Regulated institutions have some cost advantage even on large commercial loans: lenders see them as safer because they are licensed and supervised by the banking authorities. Also, regulated microlenders on average can absorb larger borrowings, which can reduce their interest and transaction costs.

3   Loan Loss Expense

Most microloans are backed by no collateral, or by collateral that is unlikely to cover a defaulted loan amount once collection expenses are taken into account. As a result, outbreaks of late payment or default are especially dangerous for a microlender, because they can spin out of control quickly.

When a borrower falls several payments behind on a loan, or something else happens that puts eventual collection of the loan in doubt, the sound accounting practice is to book a "loan loss provision expense" that reflects the loan's loss in value—i.e., the lowered likelihood it will be collected in full. This practice recognizes probable loan losses promptly rather than waiting for the full term of the loan to expire and collection efforts to fail before booking the loss. If the lender books a provision expense for a loan, but the loan is later recovered in full, then the provision expense is simply reversed at that point. In this section, we look at the quality (i.e., collectability) of microloan portfolios through the lens of net loan loss provision expense. We stress that this indicator approximates actual loan losses over the years, not just levels of delinquency (late payment).

Loan losses have recently been climbing fast in India and Mexico, but the average for the rest of the world has been fairly stable. The spike in India is due mainly to the recent collapse of microcredit repayment in Andhra Pradesh.[20] The apparently serious problem in Mexico has been longer in the making. But in the rest of the world, average loan loss has declined from a worrisome level of almost 4 percent in 2009 back toward a safer level a bit above 2 percent in 2011.

The loan levels in Figure 9 are calculated from microlenders' reports to MIX, usually but not always based on externally audited financial statements. However,

---

[18] For definitions of the three target market designations, see the note below Figure 5.

[19] At first blush, this may seem inconsistent with the preceding finding that MFIs who take voluntary deposits have higher funding costs that those who do not. The explanation is that funding costs have been particularly high for unregulated deposit-takers.

[20] See, for example CGAP (2010) on Andhra Pradesh.

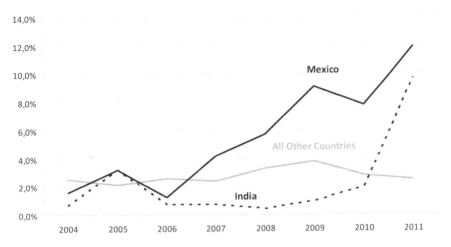

Fig. 9. Loan Loss Provision 2004–2011

Note: Net annual provision expenses for loan impairment as % of average GLP, weighted by GLP.

microlenders, especially the unregulated ones, use many different accounting policies for recognizing and reporting problem loans. Microlenders (like other lenders!) often err in estimating their credit risk. Their errors are seldom on the high side, and many external auditors are remarkably generous when it comes to allowing optimistic approaches to loan loss accounting. MIX makes an analytical adjustment to reported loan losses, in effect applying a uniform accounting policy to recognition of those losses.[21] The point of this adjustment is uniformity, not fine-tuning to the particular circumstances of a given lender; thus the MIX loan loss adjustment might not accurately reflect the risk of each institution's portfolio. However, we have no doubt that when looking at broad groups of microlenders, the MIX adjustments generate a picture that is closer to reality than the financial statement figures submitted by the institutions.

As shown in Table 1, MIX's adjustment has only a small effect on Mexican loan loss rates, suggesting that the Mexican loan loss accounting may be fairly close to realistic. However, the adjustment almost triples India's average 2011 loan loss from a self-reported 9.7 percent to an adjusted figure of almost 29 percent. The authors have not gone back to review the individual financial statements of the Indian microlenders in MIX, but the *prima facie* hypothesis would be that there might be a massive overhang of under-reported loan losses that will continue to depress overall Indian profitability in subsequent years.[22]

---

[21]   MIX's loan loss adjustment protocol is described in the Annex.

[22]   We understand that India's central bank has relaxed some loan-loss accounting rules for MFIs in 2011. The probable motive is to let Indian commercial banks reduce the losses they have to recognize on loans they have made to the MFIs.

Table 1. Effect of MIX Adjustments on 2011 Loan Loss Expense

	Unadjusted	Adjusted
MEXICO	11.9 %	12.1 %
INDIA	9.7 %	28.9 %

3.1 Peer Group Analysis

The only clear pattern we've noticed in the peer group breakouts for this indicator is that on average for-profit microlenders have had higher loan losses than non-profits do (Figure 10), this would seem to be a *prima facie* indication of a tendency toward riskier lending and collection practice among for-profit MFIs on average. However, the gap seems to be narrowing, except for the for-profit spike in 2011, which is almost entirely due to loan losses of Indian for-profits.

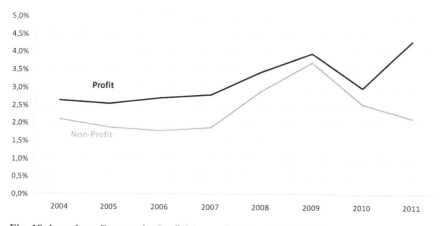

Fig. 10. Loan Loss Expense by Profit/Nonprofit Status, 2004–2011

Note: Net Loan loss expense (unadjusted) as % of GLP, weighted by GLP.

4   Operating Expenses (and Loan Size)

Operating expenses include the costs of implementing the loan activities—personnel compensation, supplies, travel, depreciation of fixed assets, etc. Operating expenses consume the majority of the income of most microlenders' loan portfolios, so this component is the largest determinant of the rate the borrowers end up paying.

Declines in operating expenses (i.e., improvements in efficiency) have slowed recently. Much of the hope for lower interest rates is based on an expectation that as microlenders acquire more experience they learn to lend more efficiently. Standard economic theory tells us that, in young industries, one normally expects to see cost improvements as firms (or the whole industry in a given market) acquire more experience. Eventually, though, the most powerful efficiency lessons have been learned, and the learning curve flattens out: at this point efficiency improves slowly if at all in the absence of technological breakthroughs.[23] In addition to the learning curve, there is hope that the pressure of competition will force lenders to find more efficient delivery systems.

Figure 11 shows that global average operating costs for MIX microlenders fell substantially through 2007, but the downward trend was interrupted in 2008 and again in 2011. Are microcredit operating costs getting toward the bottom of their learning curve? Or are we seeing temporary bumps with further improvement in efficiency yet to come? No conclusion can be drawn at this point—certainly not on the basis of worldwide average behavior. Efficiency trends differ a lot from one region to another (Figure 12). Since 2006, operating efficiency has improved substantially in relatively immature markets like Africa and EAP, but has been flat or even increased in the other regions. A further complication, the impact of loan sizes, is discussed later in this section.

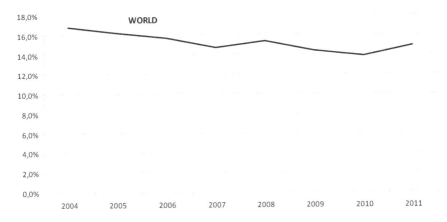

Fig. 11. Operating Expense Ratio, 2004–2011

Note: Operating (i.e., staff and administrative) expense as % of average GLP, weighted by GLP.

---

[23] This is especially the case with microfinance, where there are relatively few economies of scale after MFIs grow past 5,000 or 10,000 clients.

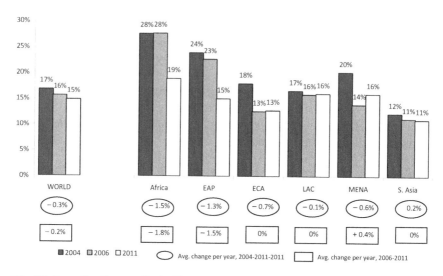

Fig. 12. Operating Expense Ratio Changes, 2004–2011

Note: Total operating expense/average GLP, weighted by GLP, nominal. The Africa series begins with 2005 rather than 2004.

4.1 Peer Group Analysis of Operating Costs, Including the Impact of Loan Sizes

Thus far, the measure of administrative efficiency that we have used is operating expense as a percentage of average outstanding GLP. This ratio can be thought of as the operating cost per dollar outstanding. It is meaningful for many purposes,

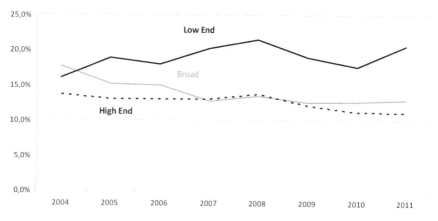

Fig. 13. Operating Expense Ratio 2004–2011, by Target Market

Note: Operating (staff and administrative) expenses/average GLP. (For definitions of the three target market designations, see the note below Figure 5.)

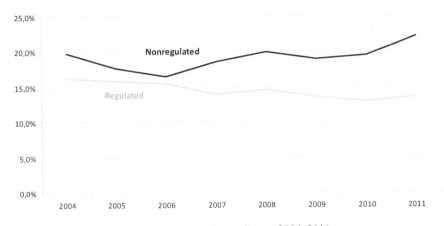

Fig. 14. Operating Expense Ratio by Regulatory Status, 2004–2011

Note: Operating (staff and administrative) expenses/average GLP

but using it to compare the "efficiency" of different microlenders can be problematic. We will illustrate this important and widely overlooked point at some length, using as examples a comparison among lenders serving different target markets, and a comparison between regulated and unregulated lenders.

Figures 13 and 14 seem to show not only that both low-end lenders and unregulated lenders are less efficient than others (i.e., have higher average operating costs per dollar of portfolio lent), but also that they are losing efficiency over time.

It is common to equate this kind of "efficiency" with the quality of management. But this can be seriously misleading, especially in comparing different kinds of microlenders. Managers at the low-end microlenders and the unregulated microlenders lend and collect much smaller loans,[24] which tend to cost more to administer than large loans do, when measured per dollar lent, even with the best possible management.

Figure 15 is uses Philippine data to illustrate two points. The main point is that operating cost per dollar lent (the lower plotted curve) does in fact tend to be higher for tiny loans. The secondary point is that interest yield (the upper plotted curve) parallels the operating cost curve: as we said, operating cost is typically the most important determinant of the interest that borrowers pay.[25]

The cost per dollar lent, which we have used so far an as efficiency indicator, penalizes lenders making smaller loans, because their operating costs will always tend to be higher as a percentage of each dollar outstanding. However, we can compensate (to some extent) for the effect of loan size by changing our indicator

---

[24] See Figure 19.

[25] The Philippines plot was selected because it was a particularly clean and striking illustration of the points being made here. The relationships are quite a bit looser in most countries, and occasionally even run in the other direction. Nevertheless these points are true as statements of general tendency, and the correlations are substantial.

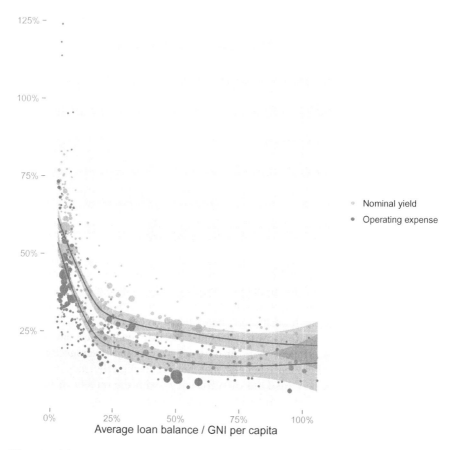

Fig. 15. Pricing and Cost Curves for the Philippines

from cost per dollar lent to cost per loan outstanding—in other words, we divide operating costs not by the amount of the average outstanding loan portfolio, but rather by the average number of active loans outstanding over the year, regardless of how large those loans are.

Table 2 illustrates the difference in these indicators with two hypothetical lenders that have the same size loan portfolio but very different administrative costs. We posit that both institutions are managed with the lowest possible operating cost given their loan sizes and other circumstances.

Using the standard efficiency measure, cost per dollar outstanding (5), the low-end lender looks bad by comparison, but this is a meaningless result given the difference in loan sizes. The low-end lender's efficiency looks better when presented as (6) cost per loan outstanding.[26]

---

[26] The dynamic would be the same if cost per borrower were used instead of cost per loan.

Table 2. Two measures of efficiency

	Low-End MFI	High-End MFI
1. Avg number of active loans	100,000	10,000
2. Avg outstanding loan size	$200	$2,000
3. Avg loan portfolio [(1) x (2)]	$20 million	$20 million
4. Operating expense	$4 million	$2 million
5. Cost per dollar o/s[(4) ÷ (3)]	20%	10%
6. Cost per loan o/s [(4) ÷ (1)]	$40	$100

But using this latter measure makes the high-end lender look worse. Are its managers really less efficient? No: making a *single* large loan does tend to cost more than making a *single* small loan—for instance, the larger loan may require additional analysis or a more skilled loan officer. The point is that as loan size increases, operating cost per loan also increases *but at a less than proportional rate.* This leaves us with the same statement that we made at the beginning of the paper: it usually costs more to lend and collect *a given amount of money* in many small loans than in fewer big loans.

Now let us return to our efficiency comparison between regulated and unregulated microlenders. The cost-per-dollar measure we used in Table 2 made it look as if the unregulated lenders were less efficient, and that their efficiency was actually getting worse. But if efficiency is taken as a measure of management quality, the comparison is unfair, because unregulated loan sizes average roughly half of regulated loan sizes, and are getting smaller over time.[27] Figure 16 uses cost per loan, which can be a more useful measure of the evolution of efficiency over time. This presentation suggests a probability that cost management in the unregulated microlenders is actually improving.[28]

Turning back to target market peer groups (Figure 17), we see that by a cost per loan metric, low-end lenders no longer look relatively inefficient, and their average cost levels have been quite stable in relation to per capita income. At the other end of the spectrum, high-end lenders show improved efficiency since 2005 (though some of this is probably a result of their declining average loan sizes).

Some readers may have found this discussion of efficiency measures annoyingly convoluted. By way of apology, we offer instead a simple take-home message: be

---

[27]   See Figure 20.

[28]   How can unregulated MFIs' operating cost be improving in relation to the number of loans, while at the same time it is getting worse in relation to the amount of the loan portfolio? Both of these can happen because loan sizes in the unregulated MFIs have been dropping.

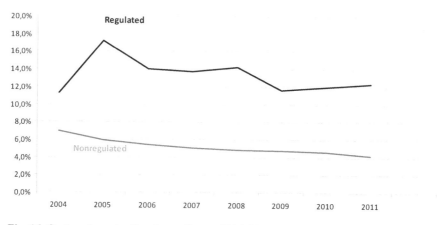

Fig. 16. Cost per Loan by Regulatory Status, 2004–2011

Note: Operating costs/number of active loans averaged over the year and expressed as % of per capita gross national income.

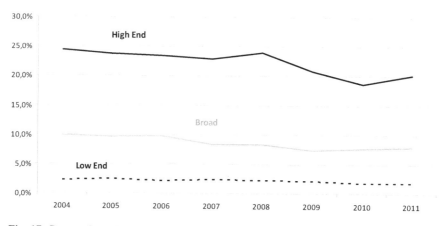

Fig. 17. Cost per Loan by Target Market, 2004–2011

Note: Operating costs/number of active loans averaged over the year and expressed as % of per capita gross national income.

very cautious when using either efficiency measure—cost per dollar or cost per loan—to compare the cost-control skills of managers of different institutions.

4.2 Mission Drift; Savings Mobilization

As more and more of the microcredit portfolio moves into regulated banks and other for-profit institutions, a common concern is that these commercialized microlenders will lose their focus on poor customers and gradually shift to larger (and supposedly more profitable) loans. However, it is hard to find support for this

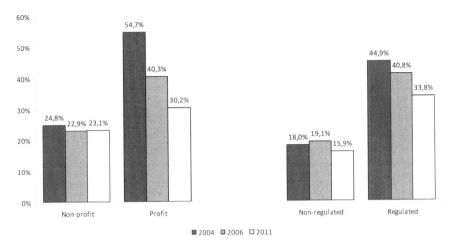

Fig. 18. Average Loan Size 2004–2011, by Regulated and For-Profit Status

Note: Annual average of loan portfolio divided by annual average of numbers of active loans, expressed as % of per capita gross national income, weighted by loan portfolio.

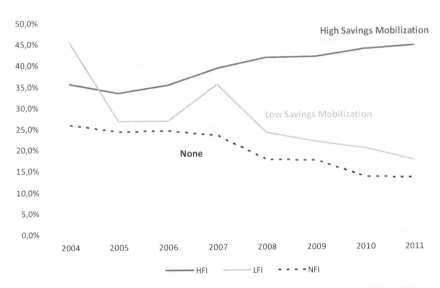

Fig. 19. Average Loan Size by Degree of Voluntary Savings Mobilization, 2004–2011

Note: Annual average of loan portfolio divided by annual average of numbers of active loans, expressed as % of per capita gross national income, weighted by loan portfolio. "High" means voluntary savings >20 % of total assets, "low" means <20 %, "none" means 0 %.

concern in the MIX data. To begin with, the assumption that larger loans will tend to be more profitable doesn't appear to be true, as we will see in the following section when we discuss lenders' profits. In fact, the average loan size in for-profit and regulated MFIs has been dropping steadily since 2004 (Figure 18).[29],[30] This doesn't necessarily mean that concerns about mission drift are unfounded. But if commercialization is producing mission drift, that mission drift does not seem to be playing itself out in any widespread shift to larger loans.

Not surprisingly, smaller (and presumably poorer) borrowers tend to have less access to deposit services from their microlenders. Figure 19 shows that loan sizes are much higher in institutions that offer significant voluntary savings services than in institutions that offer little or no voluntary savings. What is more, loan size is climbing in the former but shrinking in the latter.[31]

5   Profits

Profit is a residual: the difference between income and expense. In financial institutions, net profit is often measured as a percentage of assets employed or as a percentage of the shareholder's equity investment.

5.1   Profits in Perspective

Before looking at level and trend of MFI profits, we first clarify profit's impact on the borrower. Microcredit profits are so controversial that it can be easy to overestimate how much they affect the interest rates that borrowers pay. Figure 20 shows how much microcredit interest rates would drop if all lenders chose to forgo any return on their owner's investment—an extreme supposition indeed. The impact of profits is not insignificant, but rates would still be very high even without them. Of course, this figure presents average results: there are many microlenders whose profits constitute a larger percentage of the interest that they charge.

Notably, the impact of profit on interest rates is falling. Profit as a percentage of interest income declined fairly steadily from about 20 percent in 2004 to about 10 percent in 2011.

---

[29]   The same pattern shows up in data using a consistent panel of MFIs, so this result is not driven by entry of new MFIs into the for-profit or regulated peer groups.

[30]   We repeat here our earlier warning that the correlation between loan size and client poverty is very rough, especially when applied to changes over time in an MFI.

[31]   Alert readers may note that the two findings in this subsection (**Mission drift; savings mobilization**) don't have much to do with operating costs, or indeed with any aspect of interest rates. But we thought they were interesting anyway.

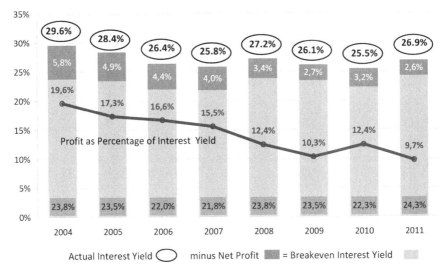

Fig. 20. Impact of Profit on Global Interest Rates, 2004–2011

Note: Profit (net income – taxes) is calculated as a % of GLP; all results weighted by GLP.

5.2 Level and Trend of Microlender Profits

Profit levels in the industry vary widely (Figure 21). In 2011, about a quarter of microlenders earned annual returns greater than 20 percent on shareholders' investment. About 5 percent produced profits higher than 40 percent. In 2011, out of a total sample of 879 MFIs, 44 had returns on equity higher than 40 percent, and only seven of those were significant lenders with over 100,000 clients.

At the other end of the spectrum, plenty of microlenders lost money, especially in Africa and in South Asia (where some lenders working in Andhra Pradesh had a very bad year).

Of the various components of interest rates, profits are the most controversial. Some think that a microlender has no right to claim it is pursuing a "social" mission if it is extracting profit, or anything beyond a very modest profit, from its services to poor clients. Others argue that high profits will encourage innovation and faster expansion of services, and that competition will eventually squeeze out excesses. It is very hard to parlay empirical data into a quantification of a "reasonable" profit level for microcredit, and we will not attempt to do so here.[32] We limit ourselves to comparing the average profitability of microlenders with that of commercial banks (Figure 22).

---

[32]   The Social Performance Task Force has tried to address standards of reasonableness for microfinance profits, but does not seem close to being able to define any quantitative benchmarks for evaluating appropriate returns, even for organizations that profess to have a "double bottom line." See, e.g., http://sptf.info/sp-task-force/annual-meetings

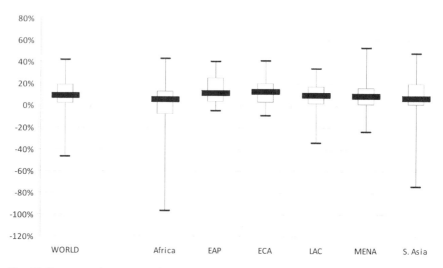

Fig. 21. Return on Average Equity 2011, World and Regions

Note: After-tax net profit as % of average shareholders' equity or nonprofit net worth, un-weighted. The thick horizontal bars represent medians; the top and bottom of the white boxes represent the 75th and 25th percentiles, respectively; and the high and low short bars represent the 95th and 5th percentiles, respectively.

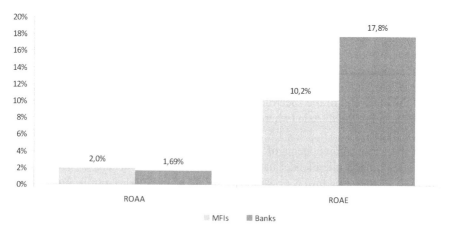

Fig. 22. 2011 Profits—MFI vs Commercial Bank, Returns on Average Assets and Equity

Note: MFI data from MIX. Bank data from BankScope, including only those countries where MIX MFIs are present. Country-by-country results weighted by MFI GLP.

When measured against assets, profit is slightly higher on average for microlenders than for banks in the same countries. But compared with microlenders, commercial banks have more scope to leverage their capital structure: that is, they fund more of their assets with other people's money—deposits and borrowings—

rather than with their own equity. As a result, microlenders, despite their higher returns on assets, tend to do markedly less well than banks in producing returns on their owners' equity investments.

When we look at overall trends in MFI profitability, it is useful to disaggregate India (Figure 23), a huge market where some institutions had disastrous years in 2010 and especially 2011, due to the crisis in Andhra Pradesh. If India is included, average profits show a pronounced decline from 2004 to 2011. If India is excluded, the average level of profits is much lower, but the rate of decline is less.

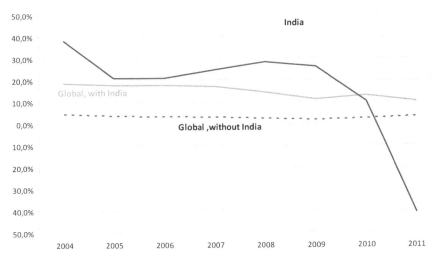

Fig. 23. Global Return on Average Equity, with and without India, 2004–2011

Note: After-tax net profit as % of average shareholder's equity, weighted by equity.

International investment funds that funnel commercial and quasi-commercial money to microlenders have not generated impressive results: annual returns peaked at about 6 percent in 2008 but have languished between 2 percent and 3 percent in 2009–2011 (Lützenkirchen 2012). Returns have been well below what the funds could have earned by investing, for instance, in commercial banks.

5.3 Peer Group Analysis

Unremarkably, for-profit microlenders produce higher returns on equity than non-profit MFIs, except for 2010–2011, when the performance of Indian for-profits dragged the group down (Figure 24).

More surprisingly (to some, at least), low-end lenders on average have been distinctly more profitable than broad-market or high-end lenders, except for 2011, when most of the Indian institutions that took a beating were ones that served low-end markets.

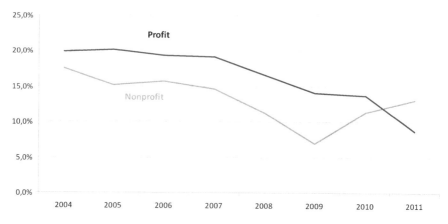

Fig. 24. Return on Equity by For-Profit Status, 2004–2011

Note: Return on average shareholders' equity, weighted by equity.

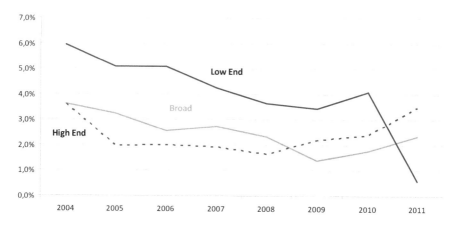

Fig. 25. Profitability of Assets by Market Segments, 2004–2011

Note: Return on average assets, weighted by assets.

6   Overview and Summary

Having broken interest yield into its main components, we now reassemble them in Figure 26, which presents their evolution from 2004 to 2011.[33] What happened over the period, *on average*, is that

---

[33]   In both years, the components add up to slightly more than the interest income from the loan portfolio. The discrepancy is the result of taxes as well as other income not from the loan portfolio, neither of which are represented among the components. The dis-

- Operating expenses declined as microlenders became more efficient,

- Financial expenses grew significantly as microlenders took on more commercial funding,

- Loan losses increased (probably by more than the unadjusted amount shown here), and

- Profits dropped, with the result that

- Interest yield dropped by 2.7 percentage points over the period.

We saw earlier (Figures 3 and 12) that most of the decline in operating costs and interest yields occurred early in the period.

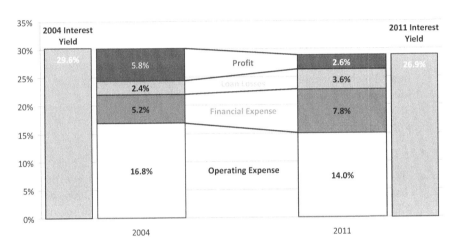

Fig. 26. Drivers of Interest Yields, as % of Yield, 2004–2011
Note: All data as percentage of average GLP, weighted by GLP.

Here by way of review are some of the other main conclusions of this paper:

Interest Rates

- MFIs' nominal interest yield averaged about 27 percent in 2011, having declined in 2004–2007, but not in 2007–2011.

- Rates have been rising for microlenders focused on low-end borrowers.

- Rates have dropped for banks and other regulated microlenders, but risen for NGOs and other unregulated microlenders.

crepancy is bigger in 2011 mainly because MFIs were earning more nonportfolio income then, from investments and from other financial services.

Cost of Funds

- Funding costs have climbed substantially as microlenders fund more of their portfolio from commercial borrowing.

- Funding costs have risen most for microlenders serving the low-end clientele.

- So far at least, voluntary savings mobilization has not necessarily lowered funding costs.

Loan Losses

- Two large markets, India and Mexico, have seen sharp rises in bad loans in recent years; but average loan losses for the rest of the world have been fairly steady.

- Analytical loan loss adjustments by MIX suggest that the 2011 financial statements of some Indian microlenders may have substantially underestimated their probable loan losses, creating an overhang that may continue to depress their profitability in subsequent years.

Operating Expenses

- Operating cost is the largest determinant of interest rate levels.

- The decline of average operating expense (i.e., improvement in efficiency) has slowed recently, though trends differ by region. Since 2006, cost per dollar outstanding has dropped rapidly in Africa and EAP, but stagnated or risen in the other regions.

- It remains to be seen whether the plateau in operating costs over the past few years will be followed by further declines, or whether this plateau represents the bottoming out of the learning curve effect.

- Cost per dollar outstanding is the prevalent measure of operating efficiency, but it can be very misleading if used to compare different microlenders in terms of management's effectiveness at controlling costs.

- Average loan size trends do not support a hypothesis of mission drift in commercialized microlenders: over the period, average loan sizes dropped much more among for-profit microlenders and regulated microlenderss than among nonprofit and unregulated microlenders.

- Not surprisingly, low-end microborrowers have considerably less access to savings services than high-end microborrowers.

Profits

- The percentage of borrowers' interest payments that went to microlender profits dropped from about one-fifth in 2004 to less than one-tenth in 2011.

- Microlenders' returns on assets average slightly higher than commercial bank returns, but microlenders average much lower than commercial banks in producing returns on shareholders' investment.

- Microlender returns to shareholders' equity dropped substantially over the period; much but not all of this drop is due to severe recent problems in the Indian state of Andhra Pradesh.

- Low-end markets were substantially more profitable than others during the period, except for 2011 where low-end microlender profits were depressed by the Andhra Pradesh crisis.

References

CGAP (2010) Andhra Pradesh 2010: Global Implications of the Crisis in Indian Microfinance. Focus Note 67. Washington: CGAP. http://www.cgap.org/sites/default/files/CGAP-Focus-Note-Andhra-Pradesh-2010-Global-Implications-of-the-Crisis-in-Indian-Microfinance-Nov-2010.pdf.

Hoepner, Andreas G.F., Liu, Hong, Wilson, John O.S. (2011) The Outreach Measurement Debate in Microfinance: Does Average Loan Size Relate to Client Poverty? http://papers.ssrn.com/sol3/papers.cfm?abstract_id=1956569.

Lützenkirchen, C., Weistroffer, C. (2012) Microfinance in evolution: An Industry between crisis and advancement. Deutsche Bank, September 13, 2012.

Rosenberg, R., Gonzalez, A., Narain, S. (2009) The New Moneylenders: Are the Poor Being Exploited by High Microcredit Interest Rates? Occasional Paper 15. Washington: CGAP. http://www.cgap.org/sites/default/files/CGAP-Occasional-Paper-The-New-Moneylenders-Are-the-Poor-Being-Exploited-by-High-Microcredit-Interest-Rates-Feb-2009.pdf.

Schreiner, M., Matul, M., Pawlak, E., Kline, S. (2006) Poverty Scorecards: Lessons from a Microlender in Bosnia-Herzegovina. http://www.microfinance.com/English/Papers/Scoring_Poverty_in_BiH_Short.pdf.

Acknowledgments: The authors are grateful to KfW for financial support, to MIX for data and data processing, and to CGAP for analytical models and publication services. We thank Matthias Adler, Gregory Chen, Alexia Latortue, and Kate McKee for insightful comments. Of course, it is the authors, not the commentators or sponsoring agencies, who are responsible for the conclusions and views expressed here.

Annex: Data and Methodology

By Scott Gaul

What Data Did We Use?

Data for this analysis was drawn from the MIX Market database for the years 2004–2011. Yield data is not widely available before 2004 in the database. Institutions were dropped from the analysis if data were not available for all of the indicators used in the analysis, to ensure that differences in indicators are not due to differences in the samples for those indicators.

In total, the dataset consists of 6043 observations for 48 variables for 2004–2011 (including descriptive information about the institution—name, country, legal status). The full data set includes any institution that provided data in a given year, subject to some exclusions described below. Consequently, this dataset reflects both changes in the market—from the entry and exit of participants—as well as changes in the voluntary reporting of data to MIX Market. For summary statistics, we feel that this dataset still provides an accurate read on the relative levels of interest rates in a given market at a given point in time, as well as the changes over time.

In addition, a balanced panel data set is also used for some analysis. In the balanced panel, only institutions that provide data for all years of the period are included. Thus, changes in indicators for the panel data are due to changes at those institutions, not changes in the composition of a peer group or market. The longer the period used for the panel dataset, the fewer institutions make the cut. We chose a five-year panel, covering 2007–2011, which let us use 456 institutions. We used the panel data mainly as a cross-check against results from the full data set.

We tried to focus as much as possible on microlenders whose mission included financial sustainability, because we are exploring links between interest charges and the cost components that largely determine those charges. Those links are weakened in lenders that have access to large continuing subsidies.[34] This focus, along with data availability issues, led us to exclude a few large lenders from the dataset.

- BRI. We left Bank Rakyat Indonesia (BRI) out of the analysis because it blends microcredit with a significant portfolio of commercial lending activity, but does not provide the disaggregated revenue and expense data that would be necessary for the analysis in this paper.

---

[34] One problem with large subsidies is that they can substantially distort the operational picture presented by a lender's financial statements if—as is common—the subsidies are not correctly segregated as nonoperating income. More generally, we wanted this paper to focus mainly on the vast majority of MFIs that have to respond to market conditions and costs.

- Harbin Bank. Harbin is a large Chinese bank with a massive microcredit portfolio (in 2011 Harbin alone had 19 percent of global portfolio in MIX's dataset). MIX Market has only two years of data for Harbin Bank. Given the potential distortion of trend data, as well as uncertainty about its activities and mission, we did not include Harbin in the final dataset.

- PSBC. Postal Savings Bank of China (PSBC) is a large microlender in China. As with Harbin Bank, the scale of its activities (GLP of US$14 billion in 2011) has a significant influence on global figures and any peer groups in which it is included, but MIX has no data on PSBC before 2010, and the data have only a one-star quality ranking. In addition, the government linkage increases the likelihood of subsidized pricing.

- VBSP. Vietnam Bank for Social Policy (VBSP) is a large state bank that receives substantial government subsidies. Interest rates at VBSP are well below what would be needed to cover costs, so we also dropped it given its influence on global and regional results.[35]

We also excluded a few other institutions whose interest income, as well as substantial continuing losses, strongly suggested a policy of subsidized pricing and absence of an intent to reach financial sustainability. These institutions are so small that their treatment does not materially affect our results.

MIX applies a set of standard adjustments to MFI data.[36] By default, data used in the paper are unadjusted. Since the adjustments require several data points as inputs, the sample for unadjusted data is larger than for adjusted data (covering 4389 observations, in this case). In addition, adjusted data are not disclosed for individual MFIs on the MIX Market site, while unadjusted data are. Thus, the analysis from this paper can be largely replicated by users of the MIX Market site for unadjusted data. When adjusted data are used in the paper, they are explicitly referenced as such.

Peer groups were calculated from MIX Market data based on the definitions below. For each peer group, the count (number of observations), median, minimum, maximum, simple average, and weighted average are reported. Weighted averages are computed using the denominator of the ratio, unless indicated otherwise. For instance, return on (average) equity is weighted by the average equity when aggregated. Medians and weighted averages are the most frequently used metrics in the paper. Informally, medians describe the "typical MFI" since they report data

---

[35] One problem with large subsidies is that they can substantially distort the operational picture presented by a lender's financial statements if—as is common—the subsidies are not correctly segregated as nonoperating income. More generally, we wanted this paper to focus mainly on the vast majority of MFIs that have to respond to market conditions and costs.

[36] For description of MIX's adjustments, see http://www.themix.org/sites/default/files/Methodology%20for%20Benchmarks%20and%20Trendlines.pdf

on the MFI at the 50th percentile of the distribution. Weighted averages describe something closer to what is "typical" for clients since larger institutions serve more clients and also receive more weight in the results. Calculations for both match the methods used on MIX Market.

The data files on which the paper is based can be found at http://microfinance-business-solution.mixmarket.org/rs/microfinance/images/Interest Rate Paper Supporting Data.zip. Most of the data re displayed in Excel pivot tables, which make it easy to conduct detailed analysis of individual country markets as well as any other peer group of interest.

Definitions of Indicators, Peer Groups, and Loan Loss Provision Adjustments

Indicator	Derivation
Average loan size	Average gross loan portfolio / average number of active loans
Cost of funds	Financial expense / liabilities
Cost per loan	Operating cost / average number of active loans
Gross loan portfolio	Total outstanding balance on all active loans
Interest yield (nominal)	All interest and fee revenue from loans / average gross loan portfolio
Interest yield (real)	Nominal interest yield adjusted for inflation
Loan loss expense	Net annual provision expense for loan impairment / average gross loan portfolio
Operating expense ratio	Total operating (i.e., personnel and administrative) expense / average gross loan portfolio
Return on average assets	(Net operating income – taxes) / average assets
Return on average equity	(Net operating income – taxes) / average equity

MIX Peer Groups

Group	Categories	Criteria
Age	New	1 to 4 years
	Young	5 to 8 years
	Mature	More than 8 years
Charter Type	Bank	
	Credit Union	
	NBFI	
	NGO	
	Rural Bank	

Group	Categories	Criteria
Financial Intermediation (FI)	Non FI	No voluntary savings
	Low FI	Voluntary savings < 20 % of total assets
	High FI	Voluntary savings > 20 % of total assets
Lending Methodology	Individual	
	Solidary Group	
	Individual/Solidarity	
	Village Banking	
Outreach	Large	Number of borrowers > 30.000
	Medium	Number of borrowers 10,000 to 30.000
	Small	Number of borrowers < 10,000
Profit Status	For Profit	Registered as a for profit institution
	Not for Profit	Registered in a non-profit status
Region	Africa	Sub-Saharan Africa
	Asia	South Asia and East Asia and the Pacific
	ECA	Eastern Europe and Central Asia
	LAC	Latin America
	MENA	Middle East and North Africa
Scale (Gross Loan Portfolio in USD)	Large	Africa, Asia, ECA, MENA: > 8 million; LAC: >15 million
	Medium	Africa, Asia, ECA, MENA: 2 million – 8 million LAC: 4 million – 15 million
	Small	Africa, Asia, ECA. MENA: < 2 million LAC: < 4 million
Sustainability	Non-FSS	Financial Self-sufficiency < 100 %
	FSS	Financial Self-sufficiency = 100 %
Target Market (Depth = Avg. Loan Balance per Borrower/GNI per Capita)	Low end	Depth < 20 % OR average loan size < USD 150
	Broad	Depth between 20 % and 149 %
	High end	Depth between 150 % and 250 %
	Small business	Depth over 250 %

Loan Loss Adjustments

MIX's policy on analytical adjustment of loan loss provisioning is found at http://www.themix.org/sites/default/files/Methodology%20for%20Benchmarks%20and%20Trendlines.pdf:

"Finally, we apply standardized policies for loan loss provisioning and write-offs. MFIs vary tremendously in accounting for loan delinquency. Some count the entire loan balance as overdue the day a payment is missed. Others do not consider a loan delinquent until its full term has expired. Some MFIs write off bad debt within one year of the initial delinquency, while others never write off bad loans, thus carrying forward a defaulted loan that they have little chance of ever recovering.

We classify as 'at risk' any loan with a payment over 90 days late. We provision 50 percent of the outstanding balance for loans between 90 and 180 days late, and 100 percent for loans over 180 days late. Some institutions also renegotiate (refinance or reschedule) delinquent loans. As these loans present a higher probability of default, we provision all renegotiated balances at 50 percent. Where ever we have adequate information, we adjust to assure that all loans are fully written off within one year of their becoming delinquent. (Note: We apply these provisioning and write-off policies for benchmarking purposes only. We do not recommend that all MFIs use exactly the same policies.) In most cases, these adjustments are a rough approximation of risk. They are intended only to create an even playing field, at the most minimal of levels, for cross institutional comparison and benchmarking. Nevertheless, most participating MFIs have high-quality loan portfolios, so loan loss provision expense is not an important contributor to their overall cost structure. If we felt that a program did not fairly represent its general level of delinquency, and we were unable to adjust it accordingly, we would simply exclude it from the peer group."

CHAPTER 5

Financial Services That Clients Need: The 3.0 Business Models, Reconciling Outreach with Sustainability

*Robert Peck Christen**

1 Introduction

Formal financial services hold the potential to improve the lives of the general population, including low-income families, as well as contribute to general economic progress. The development of the finance function in an economy is linked to overall economic growth.[1] Countries with more private lending to private enterprises and liquid stock exchanges grow faster than countries with less developed banking systems.[2] Well functioning financial systems ease financial constraints that hold back development of industries and productive sectors.[3]

Lendol Calder argues convincingly that the development of the consumer finance industry in the twentieth century has shaped the behavior of the North American middle class. Entering into credit arrangements means borrower typically forgo some present consumption to repay installment credit, become more disciplined with respect to which consumables they purchase, and end up working harder to achieve their material satisfaction.[4] Consumer credit has become an important driver of economic growth and governments take great pains during economic recessions to keep the cost of credit low for consumers and home purchasers.

Globally, microfinance has contributed to the lives of poor families by supporting their income generating opportunities, smoothing their consumption, and help-

---

* President, Boulder Institute of Microfinance; Professor of Practice, Maxwell School of Citizenship and Public Affairs, Syracuse University.

[1] Gurley, J.G. and Shaw, E.S. "Financial Aspects of Economic Development." American Economic Review 45, pp. 515-538. 1955

[2] Levine, R. Loayza, N. and Beck, T. "Financial Intermediation and Growth: Causality and Causes." Journal of Monetary Economics 46, 31-77. 2000

[3] Demirguc-Kunt, A. and Levine, R. "Finance, Financial Sector Policies, and Long Run Growth." Policy Research Working Paper 4469. The World Bank Group. January 2008

[4] Calder, L. Financing the American Dream: A cultural History of consumer credit. Princeton University Press. 1999

ing them meet important family goals like education, shelter, and old-age income security.[5] In a number of countries, the progress of microfinance has contributed to financial deepening and overall economic progress; this has been clearly documented in Bolivia where private micro-credit is now worth 11 percent of GNP, and one third of total private bank credit in the economy.[6]

While the early development finance literature blamed the lack of credit on unwilling bankers and immoral, ignorant poor clients, the fact has always been that providing formal financial services to low-income families is a hard business. Banks have not known how to provide these services, and as a result don't imagine how they can be provided profitably. Poor families look at the current offering of banking services and don't see how they make sense for their own circumstances. This reinforces the perception in the traditional retail banking community that the poor don't save and are high credit risks; that they are not a profitable market segment.

Transaction costs are, and always will be a significantly higher proportion of the value of a financial service for the poor. The math is clear. Whether it costs a bank one dollar to have a client withdraw cash at a teller window, or 35 cents for that same client go to an ATM, or ultimately, 15 cents to transact over a mobile money network – those costs are proportionately higher for smaller transactions.[7] Until now, the poor have lived further from connection points of the national financial system than their middle class compatriots. Even with the advent of agent-banking, which will undoubtedly bring connection points far closer to the poor, they will also bring many more points closer to the emerging salaried middle class that is expected to be their primary beneficiary. It is likely that the poor will always experience higher costs to get to and transact on any system, especially as a proportion of the amount they are moving. They will still need to pay or take a longer time to get to the connection point, and they will have to pay the fees these connection points will charge to handle cash. We are still a long way from a fully digitalized economy where those costs might be rendered irrelevant.[8]

The riskiness of lives led by the poor provides an extra challenge to any provider of formal financial services. Their income is highly variable, their overall financial situation can change quite quickly and dramatically, and, as a result, they have a relatively short planning horizon. A large number of poor pull themselves out of poverty in any given year, and yet, the loss of a job, a health crisis, or some other catastrophic event pushes a significant number of otherso below the poverty line. While access to basic formal financial services can help families cope with

---

[5]   Sebstad, J and Cohen, M. "Microfinance, Risk Management and Poverty." Pact Publications, 2001.

[6]   Gonzalez Vega, C.

[7]   Westley, G. "Is there a case for small savers?" CGAP. 2011.

[8]   CGAP "Branchless Banking Agents in Brazil Building Viable Networks" 2010.

this variability, the variability makes it harder for the financial institution to design and deliver products that contribute to the bottom line.[9]

On the credit side, variability of income complicates the work of a lender. Due to the asymmetry of information about household income and cash flows and the extent to which a potential client fulfills his or her financial obligations, the lender has a difficult time assessing credit-worthiness. And, once a credit relationship is established, the variability in income and cash flows over the course of their agreement can create moments where repayment is threatened.[10]

On the savings side, the variability of income and cash flows can make it difficult to accumulate significant balances in accounts. It is both difficult to get funds into the account on a regular basis, given the inability to make direct electronic deposits of a salary (for example), and, it can be difficult to sustain balances in the face of sudden demands in the household.

On the insurance side, while higher levels of risk faced by poor families would seem to make them ideal targets for micro-insurance, they are generally unwilling to purchase the intangible 'benefit' of a payout at some distant, unpredictable future, for an uncertain (though somewhat likely, event). Large numbers of poor families have not yet been able to experience the concrete benefit of micro-insurance.

For those who support a financial inclusion agenda, these basic challenges inherent in the nature of their poor and their transactions must also be set in the broader context of the set of other opportunities in retail banking. Especially where there is a significant emerging middle (salaried) class, consumer finance, automobile and housing finance, bill payments, and currency operations can all generate more profits, more quickly, without the deep institutional transformation that is necessary to successfully serve the poor. The opportunity cost for entering into the low-income markets can be quite steep, unless they are an extension of services that are already provided to salaried workers in those same communities. This seems to be particularly true for those middle and lower middle-income countries where salaried wage earners compose a significant portion of the population.

Present micro-lending techniques require the hiring of a very large number of specialized loan officers that can quickly become an important portion of the total number of staff in a retail bank. Given the power of banking labor unions in many environments, senior managers are reluctant to get into this labor intensive line of products. Bank staff is also relatively well paid. There is often a problem when absorbing less well-paid micro-lending loan officers into the bank in terms of internal equity. Often microcredit loan officers are paid with a much higher proportion of variable incentive-based pay than bank officers, further complicating the absorption of the microcredit model into commercial financial institutions.

---

[9]   Sebsted & Cohen. 2000.

[10] Stiglitz, J. and Weiss, A. Asymetric Information in "Credit Markets and Its Impoications for Macro-economics" Oxford Economic Paper, New Series, Vol 44, No 4. Special Issue on Financial Markets, Institutions and Policy (October, 1992), 694-724.

As financial markets develop, and especially if local capital markets grow, microfinance organizations can access funds more easily. Often, it seems they can obtain funds more easily from national and international capital markets than if they were to try and capture savings in the communities where they make their loans. The up-front infrastructure cost of setting up the deposit mobilizing branch or agent network is substantial.

Micro-insurance has had mixed results. Credit-life insurance is broadly accepted and has been sold on the back of microcredit arrangements; it is viewed by many MFIs as a major revenue generator. Yet the idea of insurance has not caught on much with clients. Perhaps, too few clients have experienced the benefits of holding an insurance policy and therefore do not perceive this financial serve as one that provides concrete value, especially if they are being asked to pay monthly premiums. Perhaps, the current suite of products so not really meet important client needs, and rather, are simply an extension of products that were developed for other, quite different market segments. Early experience with micro-insurance products suggests that we have a long way to go before the poor consider them to be a standard component of their portfolio.

2   Re-focus on the Clients – Is There Real Need and Opportunity?

By 1985, the principle loan products and delivery methods of microcredit were set. Individual loans, solidarity group lending and village banking were all being replicated in numerous relatively small organizations around the globe. Some years later, village savings and loans groups were developed independently in Asia and then in Africa. The four approaches are all highly standardized in their operational mechanisms and target fairly well defined client segments. Organizations that use 'village banking' or 'savings and loans groups' approaches generally target the poorest clients, while those using 'individual loans' approaches target the less poor. Since the late 1980s, the organizations that have focused on the original three lending methods have concentrated on building stronger institutions that have the greatest potential to grow to scale and include hundreds of thousands and even, millions of microcredit clients. After twenty years of robust growth, a series of questions that have been raised about the effectiveness of micro-credit to lift the poor out of poverty (which many in the general public thought it was promising to do). And a series of events such as the IPOs, competitive behavior, and even, occasional predatory practices, that have revealed the commercial nature of specific organizations. As a result, we are now seeing a desire to re-focus on clients.

For many, this means introducing elements into the conversation about the qualitative nature of the financial services being offered. They are raising questions as to whether the loans are good for clients, whether they are being given in an ethical manner, and whether interest rates, solidarity methods, and collections procedures follow the principles of 'responsible finance'. These issues are NOT the subject of this chapter; though the author views these as necessary conversations in a fast developing field and as a particularly useful way for the organizations that are supported by the development community to differentiate themselves from consumer finance more generally in the minds of the general public.

Instead, this paper postulates that it is time to re-focus our efforts on providing a more complete suite of formal financial services that are easier to use, safer, and more affordable for poor clients. Can we address the core, eternal challenges we have always faced and only partly solved, for serving the poor? Can we figure out new delivery channels, products, and business models that produce step-changes in the supply of financial alternatives to informal finance? Are there client segments that we could reach, but do not? Are there life-cycle events in families that we could design products for that would keep families from dropping into poverty.

These are the questions that should concern anyone who believes that financial inclusion is an important part of the development of national banking systems. These are the questions that will drive the quest for the innovation that will be required to reach the hundreds of millions of unbanked in lower income countries. These are the questions that drive the remainder of this chapter.

Market Segments: There are a significant number of segments of families that live on less than a dollar a day (per capita) that are not well served by micro-credit, and even less well by other, non-credit financial services. In a survey of the market for formal financial services done by Oliver Wyman for the Bill and Melinda Gates Foundation in 2008 and 2009, the significant majority of these poor earned their wages primarily in farming and in casual (day) labor or as low-income salaried workers (domestics, and labor in small and microenterprises). Most micro-credit programs do not explicitly target, these groups, though some individuals are certainly incorporated into solidarity groups in many countries.[11] Microcredit remains biased toward those members of the informal sector that carry out 'urban-based' independent economic activities (even if these occur in small towns in rural areas), and NOT toward the educational, health, shelter, and consumption needs of farmers, low level salaried workers, and casual labor who actually dominate the informal workforce of most low income countries.

Too Poor for Credit: In many countries, even poorer informal sector workers are not attended to by mainstream microfinance. The incomes earned by the bottom quintile of the income distribution are too variable to support credit relationships and are potentially better served with some sort of approach like BRAC's "ultra-poor" graduation program that combines in-kind income support with a savings product that, over time, builds the capacity to repay tiny loans through newly developed income earning activities.

In recent years, many middle income countries are putting conditional cash transfer programs in place to support the poorest families, and increasingly, think-

---

[11]   (Oliver Wyman 2008, 2009)

ing about how to channel these cash flows into bank accounts. This connects these families with the national financial system and to transactions networks that allow them to benefit from other government and financial services. These programs may have a more direct poverty alleviation effect than microfinance, especially for those families that do not operate a microenterprises.

Regional Disparities: Some areas, like Latin America, and South Asia have achieved significant market penetration in the traditional 'targeted' client base. Other regions have lagged, though there are exceptions in certain countries where microfinance has had a long and strong tradition such as Morocco, Bosnia, Uganda, Ghana, and Indonesia. Microfinance has yet to 'take off' in Sub-Saharan Africa like it has in either of the pioneering regions. Programs across South Asia have had a 'rural' bias, concentrating their loans in small towns and villages while in Latin America, micro-credit has largely been an urban and peri-urban phenomenon.

Classes of Clients: That said, even in the countries with the strongest market penetration, there are significant relatively poor populations that are not well attended. For example the Bangladeshi equivalent of the Latin American microenterprise (a small scale furniture maker) was never the objective of the myriad solidarity group programs of Grameen, BRAC, ASA, Proshika, or others. And, with notable exceptions such as Mexican clients of Compartamos and the Bolivian clients of Crecer and Promujer, the very poor, female inhabitant of rural areas of Latin America, are relatively less-extensively served.

SMEs: Recently, a great concern has arisen about a gap in the financing of small enterprises that are important engines of employment generation and of economic progress the world over. The IFC recently estimated that the about half of SMEs do not have a loan or overdraft line-of-credit that it needs for business purposes.[12] They catalogued the barriers to SME finance as a higher degree of default risk due to asymmetry of information, lack of credit bureaus, poor loan origination capability (analytical techniques), poor legal frameworks for enforcing loan contracts, lack of policy support, and high transactions cost, among other causes. These barriers are particularly more significant for small, as compared with medium-sized businesses. Small businesses are generally family run; they still mix personal with businesses finances. They are less formal, especially with respect to how completely financial transactions are accounted for in bookkeeping and financial statements, which for the basis of bank credit. They are less consolidated and more exposed to business risk related to the principal owner/operators. The IFC has identified over 150 models for making loans to SMEs and it is currently in the process of figuring out how to coordinate the efforts of development finance institutions in this area through the G20's Global Partnership for Financial Inclusion (GPFI).

---

[12]   IFC. "Scaling Up SME Access for Financial Services in the Developing World." 2010

Small Farmers: The single largest group in the Oliver Wyman study of under-served clients living on less than 2 dollars a day was composed of 600 million farmers. Greater access to financial services and appropriately designed products can have a pronounced effect not only on poor rural households, but also on over-all growth in poorer countries. A 1 % growth in GDP associated with agriculture, for example, increase the expenditures of the poorest 30 % of the population ap-proximately 2.5 times more than growth initiated in any other sector. Similarly, estimates suggest that growth in agriculture is approximately 3.2 times more effec-tive at reducing the poverty of people living on less than USD 1 per day than non-agricultural growth.[13] From a gender perspective, research suggests that if women in developing countries had the same access to productive agricultural resources as men, then farm yields would increase an estimated 20–30 %, and would in turn boost national agricultural output by 2.5–4.0 %.[14] Yet rural households report very little access to formal financial services of any sort.[15]

Casual Laborers and Low-Wage Salaried Workers: The second largest group in the Oliver Wyman study of underserved clients were not microenterprises, but rather, day laborers and low-wage employees. There are almost as many individu-als living on less than 2 dollars a day in these two categories as small farmers. And, they are not the subject of most microlending operations; their income is ei-ther very irregular, or, they have salaries. Most of these workers are the employees of micro and small businesses, domestics working in homes, and day laborers on farms or construction sites. Except for remittances, they do not have access to formal financial services. The chief barrier to their access is the irregularity of their incomes, either because it varies day to day or season to season (casual la-borers) or because of job instability (employees).

Life-Cycle Events: While there are a number of client segments that are not cur-rently well served with a full set of formal financial services, even those who do have some access usually have access to only one, very rigid and highly standard-ized product that primarily serves as an additional source of general finance into the household. In order to build sustainable, scalable financial institutions to serve the poor, organizations concentrated on attaining volume as quickly as possible. This meant a one-size-fits-all approach to products. Yet, all of us, the poor in-cluded, require different financial products and services at different points in our life to accomplish our multiple family goals.

Young families need financing to get married, set up a household or business, and to take on the medical costs associated with bringing young children into the world. Later on, they need to save for children's education, marriage, and provide

[13] Ibid.

[14] UN Women (2011).

[15] Christen, R. and Anderson, J. "Financing Agriculturally Dependent Households." CGAP Forthcoming

for their own later years when they will not be as productive. Toward the end of their lives, they often need to rely on funds they receive from their children, rents from properties they own, payments from government, and their own savings. At life's end, funeral expenses can be substantial.

Along the way, low-income families have a variety of specific financial needs that may not be well served with current microfinance products that were designed to finance working capital for productive and trading activities. While both loan and savings products are useful for general short term purposes they may not be particularly well suited to the cash flows associated with some of the longer term activities poor households manage. Neither are they flexible enough to match the precise cash flows associated with household financial goals. Borrowers find themselves borrowing from other sources to repay microcredit because their repayment schedules to not match household cash flows.

Investments in Productive Assets: Often families must purchase major assets such as a water buffalo, an over-lock machine, or a freezer whose repayment schedule would most beneficially be drawn out for a far longer period than is common in microcredit. While these assets contribute to the family's income, they do at a slow rate. When MFIs force repayment in 4–6 months, as is often the case, servicing this loan would use up the entire household's repayment capacity, driving out any other financing for other needs like education, working capital, or to meet an emergency.

Emergencies and/or Catastrophic Events: All families have sudden emergencies. Someone loses a job, gets sick, or there is a death in the family. There are also any number of smaller, less dramatic events that strain a family's budget and require immediate attention. Many "savings and loans" groups and village banks do have an emergency loan feature, but with some exceptions, most MFIs do not make funds available immediately upon request to attend to such emergencies. Very few MFIs can take deposits; these could be available for emergencies, and at a far lower cost to the client than borrowing.

And, on occasion, families suffer from catastrophic weather, civil, or events that can wipe out the entire family asset base. At present, the principal micro-insurance that is widely available is 'credit-life' which covers the outstanding balance of the loan, and in many cases enough to cover part of the cost of the borrower's funeral. Index-based insurance that would protect assets in the case of weather related loss has not yet gained a strong track record, in part due to the poor condition of weather stations and their historic data.

Home Improvements: Most poor families must accumulate building materials little by little to add to or to improve their homes. This sort of saving is best accomplished when families 'have a little extra' they can set aside. The purchase of building supplies is a way to turn cash into a less liquid asset that keeps its value. These materials are exposed to theft, loss, and degrading due to weather conditions – increasing the cost of building wealth.

Education, Weddings, and Other Major Expenditures: All families have particular moments when major expenditures completely overwhelm month to month budgets; so they require funds from outside the normal flows. Classic cases are saving for annual holiday/festival celebrations, coming of age festivities, funerals, school fees, planned surgery, means of transportation, or marriage. Normally, the timing of these major expenditures does not align with the highly structured microfinance products that may be available in the community. And, most microfinance continues to be in the form of loans, when most of these goals could be met with programmed commitment savings accounts at a far lower cost to the poor, if these were available.

There are a large number of client segments and major life cycle events that happen in families that drive a potential demand for well-designed and delivered financial services that is not currently being met. An effort to re-focus on clients should be built around a suite of products that are safe, affordable, and easy to use that addresses a significantly broader range of goals, cash flows, and behavioral considerations. Perhaps the most interesting area for further exploration is related to the design elements that help poor families balance:

- their preference for illiquidity (to encourage accumulation of savings);
- for immediate availability (to address emergency situations),

with

- the need for disciplining mechanisms (to both save and repay loans – as a means for accumulating large assets),
- the need to make deposit services available at the moment and place where extra cash occurs (to both keep costs down and to help resist the temptation to spend elsewhere).

If we can overcome these design challenges, we can help low-income families better achieve their most important goals, and bring them more fully into the formal economy. Further understanding clients, their goals, and their financial requirements is the key to building and deploying higher impact products and services that make sense for their providers, and to full financial inclusion.

3   Client Centered Innovations That Build on Core Products and Delivery Channels

Rather than talking in abstract terms about designing products and services that are more tailored to client's financial lives, we should try and see just how these might be different than is what is available today. After all, it's clear that the poor use current products for a full range of goals and situations; so what's so special that results from re-focusing on clients?

The following section relates a number of innovative products or services that represent Version 3.0 of microfinance, as we are defining it here in this chapter. They use the lessons we have learned about what works for the poor and adds in special features that tailor the relationship around behavioral characteristics that help in the achievement of family goals and that take into account family cash flows. These products have been chosen for their illustrative capability, not because they have been wildly successful. Time will tell whether these particular innovations will last and be useful. Together, they suggest the nature of future developments that are more client-centric.

Specialized Micro-credit: Agricultural microfinance is an example of a particularly important adaptation of micro-credit principles to a new target group that requires products that respond to a quite different cash flow. Traditional micro-lenders in Latin America have adapted their techniques in order to make loans in direct support of agricultural production activities. AgroAmigo, PRODEM, Caja Los Andes, and PROCREDIT El Salvador have all hired loan officers with agronomic training who make loans to farmers with terms and conditions that have been adapted to the crop cycle. For example, loans are made with balloon payments due at harvest time and disbursements that are staggered to accommodate major moments in the investment cycle around soil preparation and planting.

A number of urban MFIs have used a value chain approach to lend to specific groups of microentrepreneurs. But one of the most interesting examples of a client driven approach to product design was CEMEX's "Patrimonio Hoy initiative" in Mexico. CEMEX is a Mexican company that sells cement and other building materials throughout urban areas. As Prahalad describes in his book, The Fortune at the Bottom of the Pyramid, Patrimonio Hoy staff spent many months with slum dwellers to understand their lives, their construction patterns, and their interactions with the distributor of building materials. As a result they developed a solidarity group based lending model that allowed clients to accumulate savings toward building materials, and ultimately, borrow a little to finish their small projects. The savings and credit groups were managed by neighborhood staff, and the local distributors were worked into the model in a way that increased their sales.

Savings Mobilization: Perhaps the most fruitful area for further design and delivery innovation is deposit mobilization. There would seem to be ample opportunity to design products around specific family goals such as meeting annual school fees or planting expenditures and around specific cash flow such as harvest payments or the daily profits from a microenterprise.

The usefulness of this approach was tested in a field experiment with the Opportunity International Bank of Malawi. In this (randomized control trial) exercise, smallholder cash crop farmers were offered either an ordinary savings account or a commitment savings account where they voluntarily 'froze' their accounts until a specified date immediately prior to planting season so the funds would be available for farm inputs. Those relatively few farmers that did take up the commitment products san an increase in land under cultivation (9.8%), use of agricultural inputs (26 %), crop output in the subsequent harvest (22 %), and household expenditures in the months immediately after harvest (17.4 %). Commitment accounts also allowed farmers to 'credibly claim' that their funds were tied up when faced with demand from their social networks.[16]

Micro-insurance: Micro-insurance is in its infancy when compared with micro-credit and deposit mobilization. We simply don't know which products beyond credit-life work very well for the poor. And, in fact, credit life mostly is a good deal for the MFIs that offer it. The key challenge with micro-insurance is to ensure that it offers good value for the poor.

One example of a creative approach to insurance is the "Caregiver" insurance product offered by the Micro Fund for Women in Jordan. Initially, the organization had focused on developing a traditional health insurance product that would ensure its clients could obtain access to the health care they needed – by charging a premium that would then cover charges at the doctors' office or the hospital. After studying their clients' needs, as related to health events, they came to understand that the women had access to health services, but were not taking advantage of them due to the ancillary costs of hospitalization. So they developed the Caregiver policy that covers per diem for each night in the hospital, costs of hospitalization, lost income when not working, travel costs, and other costs associated with not working while sick. By covering the gaps in the costs associated with a health event, the product was well received by clients. After a year, the product reported achieving full sustainability, even after paying out 300 claims on a client base of 13,500 women. And, women are getting treated more frequently than before.

But there is more to understanding clients than just figuring out a new market niche to fill. The work of the MicroInsurance Centre' MicroInsurance Learning and Knowledge Project (MILK) is drilling down far more deeply than any other effort in an attempt to look at individual insurance products from the perspective of the business case for the insurer, and at whether these products represent good value for clients. The later, "Doing the Math" efforts compare premium payouts to the alternative ways that the low-income families would normally pay for the cost of risks covered by the insurance to see whether their investment in premiums are a good bet. While they are not RCTs or impact studies, they do represent a critical step in how we need to be engaging with clients in coming years of micro-financial product design!

4   Improvements in delivery channels that may benefit clients

From the perspective of potential clients, the transformation that is occurring in the access to national payments system may be the most important development in the financial services industry in many decades. We have yet to see, but the possi-

---

[16]   Burne, Gine Goldberg, Yang, "Commitments to Save: A field experiment in Rural Malawi", May 2011.

bility may exist to drive transactions costs down to historically low levels which could permit the inclusion of exponentially greater numbers of lower income members of the general public. While initially, these transactional systems were built on networks of retail to clear banking halls of bill payments, they are increasingly channeling conditional cash transfers and other government payments, tax payments, and to send money (remittances) between private citizens. It is these two later functions that have the potential to include hundreds of millions of poor who live on less than 2 dollars a day – and maybe, providing one of the key ingredients in any national financial inclusion plan.

Payments Systems: Over the past decade, a number of countries have invested in the development of their national payments systems. Some countries have moved to create transactional platforms that associate non-banking (retail) infrastructure with the financial system in order to create access to the financial system in neighborhoods and villages where there are no bank branches. National governments are seeing the advantages of these 'agent' banking systems to channel government conditional cash transfers, salary and other payments, and even, private remittances. This reduces costs to governments for making these payments and increases their degree of control over money flows as cash emerges from the informal and travels into the formal financial system.

Brazil is a world leader in agent-banking. Within a few short years after their creation in the late 1990s the four large banks that manage most of the agents had covered virtually every single one of 5,564 municipalities in the country. Today they have around 150,000 agents that handle well over one billion dollars a year in small transactions. According to CGAP, bill payments compose almost 90 percent of transactions in urban areas, while deposits and withdrawals and loan repayments and others composed 60 percent of rural transactions. Profits are stronger in rural areas due to the present fee structure, even though there are fewer and smaller transactions every day. Consumer lending has increased 500%, in significant measure due to the existence of agent-banking. At least 12 million 'simplified' saving accounts were opened.

The Brazilian agent-banking system has faced difficulties, which are certainly a harbinger of challenges most other newer systems will face in coming years. Agents complain of security risk, 41% have been robbed with an average loss of $8,100 for which they are responsible for the first $540. Almost 30% report having money stolen by their own workers. And 16% have had clients engage in fraud, mostly with counterfeit bills. Cash management time is substantial and most agents go to the bank twice a day to clear their accounts. Poor connectivity reduces the profit margins in many areas from 10% ($124) a month to 2.6% ($27) a month. Most agents do not make enough money from fees to consider it a driver for the model, they do not really even know how much they are making.[17] For most agents, their profits amount to an insignificant 5 dollars a day. Banking agents have seen a strong uptick in their other business due to higher foot-traffic through their shops, which seems to

---

[17]   CGAP, "Branchless Banking in Brazil; Building viable networks", February 2010.

be their primary motive for continuing to participate. And yet, agent-banking plays a vital role for increasing financial inclusion in rural areas.

Mobile Money: One extremely exciting variant of agent-banking is mobile money. Mobile money allows people to send money over their cell phones through a vast network of agents, mostly airtime resellers. These resellers are spread across the country and especially in poorer neighborhoods and rural villages that are often net recipients of remittances from family working in the cities. The hope is that transaction costs for basic financial services can be driven down very low, perhaps as low as us$0.15. Airtime resellers and other agents are mostly very local businesses who pay their employees a small fraction of what a teller would make at a bank.

The most significant experience to date with mobile money is M-Pesa in Kenya where since 2007, 15 million Kenyans have used the system to send money to someone else. In a month, more transactions flow through M-Pesa than globally, through all of Western Union. The mobile money service is a significant profit center for its Telcom parent (Safaricom), and it continues to grow. Families that use M-Pesa have dramatically reduced their transaction costs from 3 dollars a payment to less than 50 cents.[18] A study has shown that clients who use M-Pesa can keep a better pattern of consumption, and in particular, a better food consumption patter when facing negative income shocks, like losing a job, cattle death, crop or business failure or health shocks.[19] This is because M-Pesa's efficiency as a money transfer system turbo-charges social networks that respond at a time of crisis.

At present, M-Pesa is being used:

1. to transfer money into savings accounts and make loan payments (M-kesho product with Equity Bank and other such relationships),

2. to sell index-based micro-insurance to farmers (Kilimo Salama with Syngenta Foundation),

3. to channel the transactions of tiny SACCOs who don't have their own back office operations,

4. to offer a pre-paid VISA Card,

5. to offer a pre-paid smart card (Changamaka) that allow members to receive medical treatment at designated hospitals for at a low per-visit cost,

6. to help farmers acquire irrigation pumps (Kickstart), and to channel conditional cash transfers to the very poor to help buy food (Concern Worldwide),

7. and, to provide safe drinking water through a fee-for-service model (Grundfos LIFELINK).

---

[18]   Michael Ferguson, "Notes From the Field: The Emerging effects of M-Pesa's rural outreach at the household level," February 2010, Microfinance Opportunities.

[19]   Jack, William G. and Suri, Tavneet, Mobile Money: The Economics of M-Pesa (January 2011). NBER Working Paper No. w16721. Available at SSRN: http://ssrn.com/ abstract=1749882

Without doubt, the development of this mobile money network is spurring tremendous innovation in financial and other services to the poor that are based on a steady stream of very small transactions.

Early on, journalists commented on the fact that the extension of banking agents into a couple of previously unserved areas of the Amazon River of Brazil had led to higher levels of enterprise growth and consequently, municipal tax revenue. Instead of having to go down-river several hours to transact, local families were able to receive their remittances, salary checks and other payments locally, and spend them locally too. This impact on local communities and ultimately, national economies is just beginning to be explored. A recent study of M-Pesa concluded that it had four local effects:[20]

- **Local economic expansion:** In essence, the team found that, M-Pesa facilitated increased money circulation which had an effect of increasing local consumption. This meant more business for local store owners and others. In addition new business and employment opportunities arose out of the establishment of M-Pesa agents; existing store owners could also diversify their offering by including this service that is now in much demand

- **Security:** Other than physical security (i.e. muggers realizing that few people carry liquid cash) the study found that M-Pesa contributed to money security, that is by enabling people to safely store funds in their mobile money account

- **Capital accumulation:** Being able to save money instead of spend it enabled wage earners to accumulate financial resources on their phone safely even without having to have a bank account or resort to a less secure mechanism such as keeping cash under the mattress

- **Business environment:** "M-PESA reduces the overall transaction cost of moving capital along a network and increases the flow of capital. While the amount of money M-PESA moves is relatively small among formal financial systems in Kenya, the number of transactions and volume of flow is increasing and covers larger segments of Kenya's population in terms of income, age and depth and breadth of access (Jack and Suri, 2009)"

Furthermore, in perhaps one of the few more negative externalities of M-Pesa, a recent AfDB brief outlines why it thinks that M-Pesa may be contributing to Kenyan inflation as the velocity of its transactions are three or four times higher than other components of money.[21]

---

[20] "Megan G. Plyler, Sherri Haas and Geetvea Nagara "Community-Level Economic Effects of M-PESA in Kenya: Initial Findings"," IRIS Center, University of Maryland.

[21] AfDB Brief, "Inflation Dynamics in Select East African Countries: Ethiopia, Kenya, Tanzania, Uganda;" 2011.

From the perspective of the clients, the challenge of all agent-banking systems is whether they can drive transaction costs down sufficiently to enable traditional financial products to become more attractive, or to support the development of new types of services. As yet, the experiences are new and the fee structures are not yet settled. For example, today, M-Pesa fee structures favor small savers. Deposits into the system are free and only withdrawals are charged. That would favor small savers who would drop off money each day but only withdraw occasionally – a pattern development finance groups would like to encourage. But already, M-Pesa agents are agitating for fees on all transactions – which could rapidly reverse this 'favorable' bias toward individuals who save small amounts frequently. Until fees structures settle, there is no way to know whether the poor will incur lower costs as a percent of the total transaction. It will be interesting to see whether mobile money can spread more rapidly than at present. Right now, in a number of countries, it's being held back by banks.

Another challenge will be to push (non-mobile money based) agent-banking models out into poorer neighborhoods and villages in poorer countries. Thus far, agent-banking models have grown quickest in middle income countries where there is a substantial "bill-paying" middle class whose transactional volume is sufficient to float the system. In poorer countries, efforts are being made to float new systems on the back of remittances and conditional cash transfers. It's clear that these volumes are not sufficient to float the more complete banking agents of the "Brazilian" type.

But most importantly, from a client perspective, the development of agent-banking transactional platforms does not guarantee the development of client centric, higher value, financial products that respond better to family goals, cash flows, and vulnerabilities. Just because a poor person in a village receives a remittance from a family member in the city or a conditional cash transfer from the government, they should not be considered to be 'included''. The most basic level of financial inclusion should be based on whether an individual has an account into which he or she can deposit funds for an indeterminate purpose and indeterminate time. And then, we should concern ourselves with whether these accounts are useful on the basis of the number of transactions in them. Only then, can we understand whether the spread of agent-banking represents the most significant pro-poor disruptive 'technology' in the modern history of retail banking.

5   The Importance of Strong Institutions

Strong institutions are key to reaching clients with a fuller range of more sophisticated financial services that are safe, affordable and easy to use. Only institutions that have achieved sustained profitability, a strong equity base, secure access to capital from financial markets, and extensive outreach can invest the necessary financial and human capital in next generation products. The economics of these next generation financial services will require them to be offered at very large scale at a very low price point that can only come from that scale. The more individualized credit products, low-balance deposit accounts, and a wider variety of micro-insurance will all require significantly lower transaction costs. Many of these products will grow out of new business models that pair microfinance institutions with operators of national payments systems, insurance and re-insurance companies, national retail chains, and potentially, mobile phone operators.

Fortunately, the microfinance sector has become highly concentrated in most countries where the top five MFIs reach more than 80% of all clients.[22] The top 200 MFIs all have several millions or tens of millions of dollars in equity and can undertake the large investments in back office MIS, branch and agent networks, market studies, and additional staff that will be required. They operate on a national level, serve hundreds of thousands, or millions of clients, and have often already entered into major corporate partnerships to generate new opportunities for clients.

That said, there are still many countries where no MFIs have achieved the necessary scale to enter into the arrangements that underlie Version 3.0 business models that will better serve clients needs. Support organizations, microfinance investment vehicles, and donors will still need to provide technical assistance, access to international capital markets, and support to create the necessary supporting infrastructure in those countries. Governments will need to put in place appropriate regulation and supervision schemes, non-bank financial institution frameworks, payments/transactions networks, and coordinate among a variety of agencies to seamlessly promote the partnerships that will form the new business models for full financial inclusion.

Two very important steps in the right direction have been the creation of the Alliance for Financial Inclusion that brings together the top regulators and financial authorities from almost 80 countries and the Global Partnership for Financial Inclusion of the G20. Both initiatives have built a growing consensus around the importance of incorporating the bulk of the population into the formal financial system as a means to encourage economic growth, food security, and to combat financial crimes. These organizations have been amply supported by global technical organizations like CGAP, UNCDF and the UN Special Advocate for Financial Inclusion, the IFC, and others who have contributed their expertise.

6   Conclusions

The recent push to put the focus back on clients is welcome and relevant. The community that has believed in the usefulness of microcredit, and more broadly, microfinance, has built a significant number of well performing financial institutions that serve the poor. It took the better part of twenty years to demonstrate that microfinance could become a legitimate part of the banking system, that institutions that serve the poor can be profitable, can become publicly owned companies,

---

[22]   MIX Market, 2012.

and can reach scale that is relevant on a national level. These are tremendous achievements, not replicated in many other fields of development.

Nevertheless, the provision of financial services to the poor is characterized by an extremely limited variety of loan products, some, but not sufficient deposit services, and very little insurance beyond credit-life. There is great enthusiasm for the role of payments systems in reaching the poor, but it's not yet clear that these systems will be viable in low-income neighborhoods and rural villages. It's time to move to the next stage in a general strategy to provide financial services to the poor; figuring out what services are most useful to the poor that we can provide profitably. To accomplish this, we need to keep the following in mind:

The present conversation around responsible finance is useful, even necessary. It can also become a distraction from the overall goal of full financial inclusion if it becomes our principal client-facing objective. Responsible finance does not push the field forward, does not lay out a series of ideas for how more and a more diverse set of clients can be served with a full range of useful products. It focuses too much on 'do no harm' and not enough on 'do good'.

The only reason we can re-focus on clients is that we have sustainable, scalable, and strong financial institutions that have a double bottom line objective; they care about reaching down market. We must strengthen our resolve to support the growth of the field. There are a significant number of market segments that are not well served and the appropriate institutional structures still need to be put in place.

It is more critical than ever for governments to build the necessary infrastructure that can provide the single most important drop in transaction cost of the past 40 years. In some cases they will need to make its infrastructure available, will need to push its transactional volume through payments systems to ensure their viability, and may need to use some financial institutions to directly offer financial services. In all cases, governments will need to set financial inclusion goals and engage in appropriate financial regulation and supervision.

This paper has identified the opportunities that remain to better serve clients. There are clients who engage in agriculture, small business, day and casual labor, fisheries and forestry that are not well served with present suite of microloan products. There are relatively few men in the lowest income brackets who are served. There are countries and regions of the world where microfinance has only stared and the institutional structures remain weak.

There are a wide variety of financial needs that could be better addressed with more attention to the financial goals, cash flows and vulnerabilities of the poor. It's clear that the greatest challenge of all is to develop savings accounts that are capable of receiving small amounts on a daily basis, and secure them against the daily pressures to spend. While we have gained a number of insights into the financial behavior of the poor but have not yet turned them into products that work better for millions of families.

The lasting legacy of micro-credit may well be that the poor are a worthy economic segment, are engaged in their own progress, and if given basic tools like finance, can pull themselves up into a better situation. Let's hope that the current debate about clients doesn't truncate the drive to serve them with a full range of useful products offered by strong, market driven institutions that have a profit motive front and center in their mission statement. Version 3.0 of microfinance should return clients to the center of our attention; insisting that it is time to design a next generation of a more complete range of financial services that are based on a more thorough understanding of clients' financial goals and capabilities, that work for the organizations that provide them.

CHAPTER 6

"Microfinance 3.0" – Perspectives for Sustainable Financial Service Delivery

Matthias Adler* and Sophie Waldschmidt**

1 Introduction

Over the last three decades, microfinance has matured into a sustainable and scalable development finance approach. By the end of the last decade, microfinance had developed towards full financial self-sufficiency, which was considered a breakthrough for mainly NGO-type institutions, serving millions of clients already at that time.

The real take-off, however, was observed in the 1990s and the first ten years of this century when commercialization played an increasingly decisive role. We see unprecedented growth of client outreach and microcredit organizations transforming into full-fledged and licensed microfinance institutions (MFIs), with Latin American institutions such as Banco Sol or Mibanco leading the way. Over the last ten years, a dynamic proliferation of microfinance in Eastern Europe and the former Soviet Union could be observed, as well as the emergence of young MFIs, albeit at a significantly lower level, in Sub-Saharan-Africa. More specifically, the last five years were characterized by an increased integration of microfinance into financial markets and the emergence of private commercial lenders and professional networks with some of them being under the institutional umbrella of microfinance groups, such as ProCredit Holding. Apart from this, equity capital providers and a growing number of microfinance investment vehicles entered the sector. As some of them were successful structured funds, the crowding in of risk-averse but socially-oriented private investors was made possible.

And yet, a history of impressive growth in client outreach and a success story of an industry building process based on a social rationale had never been seen before, which clashed with the bad news on irresponsible practices, overheating competition, lack of adequate control systems, and inappropriate regulatory environments, all of which fuelled by research results denying microfinance to have had any tangible poverty impact. It seems that microfinance could not meet the high expectations from many believers that it would be a silver bullet for the way

---

* Principal Economist, KfW.
** Junior Consultant.

out of poverty. Many voices that had praised microfinance so high have now condemned it as "another" failure of development ideas. Consequently, at this point in time, the question arises whether microfinance stands (again) at a crossroads.

Mindful of helping to shape the future of microfinance against the backdrop of increased risks, sustainability doubts, and, of course, the nearly 3 billion people hitherto not having access to reliable and affordable financial services, KfW organised at the end of 2012 a symposium on the future of microfinance. This event aimed at revisiting the successes of microfinance, addressing bad practices and doubts about its impact potential, and raising the question of how the next generation of microfinance – called "Microfinance 3.0" could look. "Microfinance 3.0" should demonstrate that it is not only possible to reconcile financial and social goals but that the two are intertwined in the sense that financial viability is a precondition to permanently delivering the development mission. Both goals, however, need to be balanced in a fair and responsible way.

This paper reflects some of the discussions held at the KfW symposium and tries to raise some of the important questions that undoubtedly need further discussions as the microfinance landscape continues to develop. After a short look at the achievements and challenges of today's microfinance landscape, this paper will depict a new vision for the industry called "Microfinance 3.0." This vision consists of professional, sustainable, deposit-taking institutions (3.1), good corporate governance (3.2), financial services diversity (3.3), fairness and transparency (3.4), sound financial infrastructure and conducive regulation (3.5) as well as responsible funders (3.6). In a fourth part, we will illustrate the role of funders by summarising KfW's microfinance strategy which tries to respond to the "Microfinance 3.0" elements.

2   A Look at Microfinance Today

After nearly four decades of impressive expansion, today 150 million poor clients have been reached, with a current outstanding aggregate loan portfolio of approximately 45–60 billion USD. Microfinance works in more than 100 countries in the developing world, and among several development finance models it has proven to be one of the most effective and sustainable.

It has not only reached out to this impressive number of clients and their family members, but it has also strengthened the ownership and capacities of institutions to make changes happen for the benefit of their clients. Fifteen years ago, there were strong debates on financial versus social sustainability, and over the years, a number of institutions showed that it is actually possible to reconcile the two. Part of the success story is the evidence that financial sustainability is needed in order to serve more clients with better products now and in the foreseeable future. Without the commercialization of microfinance, this outreach would not have been even thinkable. So there is a clear promise for a further scale-up of microfinance in the future:

- Efficiency is improving, albeit modestly translating into a gradual lowering of microfinance interest rates. This has been achieved as well by a growing yet overall sound competition in the market;

- Asset quality is still quite high which is an indicator of microfinance markets' overall robustness, even in stormy times;

- At aggregate level, there was no major justification to speak about a universal crisis of microfinance. Besides overall healthy loan portfolio quality, there were no signs of large-scale mission drift, neither in terms of client outreach nor in terms of "exploitative" interest rates, not in terms of irresponsible returns. The part of MFI yields that went to profits has rather moved slightly downwards[1];

- The microfinance "world" is not just an MFI serving clients but has developed, in some countries, into an ecosystem encompassing, inter alia, non-financial service providers, such as telecommunication platforms;

- Technology innovations have permitted lower transaction costs and reaching out to the rural population, so far lagging behind with access to finance. Branchless banking has been one of the top issues of new delivery models, allowing the overcoming of time and geographical barriers thus helping to reduce transaction costs for clients. While promising, these innovations still raise a number of questions that need to be discussed (inter alia, sustainable business models and regulatory issues);

- On the funding side, we see an ongoing interest of private sector actors for microfinance, understanding how MFIs "tick" and what they need. There is room to believe that private sources of funding will rather grow than decrease. Given the financing needs, this is at the same time necessary but also highly desirable.

And yet, there are a number of challenges, suggesting that microfinance, while just having reached its cruising altitude, still has a long way to go:

1. The core values of microfinance need further strengthening. The impressive achievements of microfinance take place at a time of an unprecedented allegation of failure and lack of impact, expressed by some media and academia. Symptoms of manifest reputation and repayment crises in some particular markets in very different regions, culminating in the late 2010 Andhra Pradesh events, have triggered a debate on core values of microfinance. This also raised concerns about its complete future altogether. "The party is over," "Suicide of a great idea" and the like were the headlines in the press, and some of the critics have had a great time selling their books.

---

[1]   See Rosenberg et al, (2013): Microcredit Interest Rates and Their Determinants: 2004-2011, Washington D.C.

The notion of failure was predominant, yet the question of too high expectations was not raised as much. The old question of whether it is good to make profits with poor people's money is re-emerging on the surface. The 2012 Banana Skins report highlighted the rise of the (perceived) over-indebtedness risk for clients and providers. The challenge is to restore confidence and to ensure good practice standards are being observed in the industry. Sustainable microfinance in this context requires both transparent and fair treatment to clients and a strong commitment from microfinance funders of the public and private sector. While all evidence suggests there is no worldwide microfinance crisis, the critics are right to point at some of those bad practices we have seen, and these need not only to be taken seriously but also to be firmly addressed.

2. Different kinds of clients – from smallholder farmers to small businesses – are yet to be served. There are still many people in need of financial services; according to CGAP estimates, more than 2.7 billion people living on less than 2 USD per day lack access to finance. And these people have tangible yet different needs to improve their living conditions. This raises the question of how these needs translate into an effective demand for financial services, and how this demand can be served by adequate financial products in an appropriate way. The challenge is to go beyond the classical microcredit and offer other credit services as well as non-credit financial services. Other credit products include loans tailored to the needs of small businesses that sometimes have been graduating out of the "microenterprise world." Many of them have proven to attract the attention of a growing number of MFIs, partly to tap an important business and development impact potential (employment generation) but also as a response strategy to overheated "classical" microcredit markets. On the other hand, the need for social and financial protection translates into different financial services, including credit, savings, and insurance. This must be accompanied by sound regulation (see more in detail in section 3.5), which has seen progress but is far from being accomplished.

3. We need to get clear about what microfinance can achieve and what impact and outreach it can have for promoting development and poverty reduction. Related to this is the allegation that microfinance has not delivered on the widespread promise to lift people out of poverty. However, we know many stories which prove that millions of people have been better off with microfinance services. Yet, the questions of "how do we know" and "what impact are we talking about" are legitimate. The challenge is to find a consensus on the appropriate methodology to measure impact, while stripping off the "panacea myth," and to be clear about the dimensions of impact. "Knowing your client" and understanding the "poor economics" are promising paths to get a balanced view on microfinance impact. Rather than asking to what degree clients have been lifted out of poverty the question should be how

well an institution serves its clients and how well poor clients can benefit from access to financial services in order to improve their living conditions.

4. The vision of sound, local financial systems is still valid and, consequently, so is financial systems development. It is a sound financial system that not only provides stability but also, and in many developing countries even more importantly, provides more access to finance and more diversified and better services to a growing part of the population. In short, in contrast to recent perceptions that financial sectors are at best not harmful to people, the financial system development claim remains that it has a development function so that also the population including poor people should and can benefit from it. The validity of the financial systems development paradigm rests on the ground that access to financial services is essential to improve the lives of people in developing countries (and elsewhere as well, of course).

Given the high promise, there remains much to do and many challenges to address. Putting the recent hefty critics into the context of a success story of microfinance, the industry may indeed well be, in some way, at a crossroads. Taking microfinance to the next generation, making full – and responsible – use of technology, the outreach and the sustainability promise will be a key success factor for this emerging phase. This would be the ambition of "Microfinance 3.0."

3   Key Elements of "Microfinance 3.0"

The discussions have shown so far that more focus should be put on clients and their needs. This is something only sustainable institutions and a sound, conducive financial system are able to provide. In order to approach this topic more in depth, let's try to distil some lessons learnt about what could be a vision to move towards an ideal "Microfinance 3.0" world.

A Vision for "Microfinance 3.0"

"Microfinance 3.0" is a system where professionally managed, well governed, and financially sustainable financial institutions offer as part of a sound financial ecosystem a broad array of financial services beyond the classical microcredit that are tailored to clients needs, including the use of technology as a means to serve clients. They treat their clients in a fair and transparent way, are relentless on mobilizing local funding sources, ensure adequate staff training, and reduce transaction costs while maintaining a close relationship with their clients. Regulators are rigorous promoters, and funders help to foster good standards and innovation.

Let's look at some of the details of this vision:

3.1 Professional, Sustainable, Deposit-Taking Institutions

There are different client segments with different needs. In order to serve these (better), strong institutions are needed. They should be professionally managed because this is a key prerequisite for strong performance in terms of outreach and financial sustainability. They should be sustainable in order to meet the demand of growing, more diverse populations. Further, they should be deposit taking because financial intermediation is vital in a sound financial system that is to serve poor people; deposits benefit poor people in numerous ways, e.g. for "predictable" shocks such as schooling, marriage, or old age.

Professional institutions need some kind of license but also the appropriate equity capital to get this license, sound internal control systems, and good management and staff quality. These institutions require a lot of good quality staff; therefore, training and professional human resource management is crucial since in many countries, a number of challenges are associated with staff recruitment, training, and retention. Regarding internal controls, professional institutions need adequate IT and management information (MIS) systems. These include sound risk management and internal audit and should be integrated into the product manuals, particularly the credit approval mechanism.

3.2 Good Corporate Governance

Good corporate governance is key for the promotion of responsible practices, professional performance, and ultimately the accomplishment of the development mission. Important prerequisites are well functioning boards providing clear strategic oversight in accordance with the mission, support management delivering its duties, and always acting in the best interest of the MFI. Good corporate governance draws a clear line of responsibilities between shareholders, board, and management. In a broader sense, it includes the right internal control systems in order to guide management's work towards achieving its goals in a transparent, responsible way.

Not surprisingly, good corporate governance is far from being achieved at broad scale[2], and much work is yet to be done. This will also help ensure a sound expectation management, e.g. regarding growth and return expectations of the board in order to drive the institution away from what is responsibly achievable. In a growingly diversifying investor landscape, good corporate governance practices help to create a level playing field among investors – it is the common denominator of behaviour among quite different types of funders.

---

[2] In the 2012 Banana Skins Report, (lack of) good corporate governance was ranked as the second most important risk the MFI industry is facing. It was ranked 2 notches higher than in the 2011 report.

3.3   Diversity of Financial Services Offered

"Microfinance 3.0" does not imply a complete change in business models. For instance, serving existing clients with new products such as education finance services can be a promising shift. When it is true that the classical microcredit should not be the only service offered because of the fact that for a number of financial needs, it is not the best answer, this does not mean to renounce or to scale down credit products altogether. The challenge is rather to innovate credit products aiming at specific client needs:

- **Agriculture loans:** There is growing attention to support the income generation through access to loans for smallholder households. The new CGAP strategy is explicitly focusing on this target group, representing a large share of the world's population without access to finance.

- **Small business loans:** For many MFIs it makes sense to offer credit also to small businesses. Some of them – although limited in number[3] – are former micro-entrepreneurs who now are able and willing to take larger loans. They would simply drop out as clients if the MFI strictly capped the loan size at the usual microloan average. Why should a good MFI want to lose these good clients? But there is also a potential to get new clients. This does not necessarily mean a mission drift since small businesses can hire staff such as unskilled workers and hence include the very poor in the economic and financial system. Moreover, small business loans increase the MFIs' efficiency which would balance the higher transaction cost of reaching out to clients in poorer segments or more remote areas. Furthermore, small business loans can play the role of a transmission belt to the formal economy, due to the importance of small businesses for the local labour market.

- **Energy efficiency loans:** Much has been said and written about "green microfinance," and its potential is great. In the meantime, there is a growing number of approaches to either fund the use of renewable energy directly through microloans or provide energy efficiency loans for micro and small enterprises, but also for private households, such as the exchange of window panes (many examples in South East Europe) or biogas schemes for private households in Asia[4].

- **Education loans:** There is a particularly high demand for education loans in developing countries, i.e. in Africa, where even the poorer segments of the population are making a lot of sacrifices to pay school fees for their children

---

[3]   Recent estimates published by CGAP are in the range of 10–20 % of micro-entrepreneurs qualifying for small business loans for further business expansion due to their track record, their dynamics, and the development of their business.

[4]   See the biogas "window" (subcomponent) of the Microfinance (Debt) Fund for Asia (MIFA), a joint initiative by KfW and IFC.

and are particularly lacking financial resources during the time of the beginning of the new school year in August/September. Access to financial services can smoothen severe financial constraints for many households and give a perspective for human development through access to professional/ higher education. Of course, adequate savings products are needed as well. Education loans can also mean loans to education institutions which a number of African MFIs are already serving as clients. Education finance is one of the most innovative fields of financial services; the development is only starting off and experiences are not manifold. However, it is an area which merits a lot of support from DFIs or institutional investors.

Among non-credit innovations, of course the most pressing demand is for *savings*. The challenge is to continue to support enough strong MFIs that are not only licensed to mobilize deposits but also capable of doing so at a large scale. It is good news that a large part of MFIs' funding already comes form local savings, but still too many MFIs still do not have a deposit-taking license. So clearly the 3.0 microfinance landscape would have to be one with microcredit-only institutions diminishing or fading out over time.

Along with the outreach dimension, also called financial deepening and broadening, it has been part of the new development finance paradigm that MFI funding does not have to be necessarily cross-border funding but rather should, to a growing extent, come from local sources. Deposits are not only important to serve clients (better), but for the MFI itself it is of vital interest to become more independent from foreign (currency) funding sources. So the question is how the industry can succeed in bringing more and more local funding on the liabilities side of MFIs' balance sheets, the most prominent of them being local savings but also, as a future perspective, bond holders and other sources of private capital. Where this is not yet feasible, external funders are increasingly thinking of providing at least part of their cross-border funding in local currency through initiatives such as the TCX Fund.

Concerning *branchless banking*, expectations are very high that financial services, particularly money transactions provided through mobile phone devices, could revolutionize client outreach especially in rural areas. It is true that one of the challenges MFIs are facing is high transaction costs compared to banks, leading to higher microcredit interest rates than banks would charge. If this transaction could be lowered to a significant degree, payment services could be offered much more cheaply and/or people in remote areas could be reached. There is also a potential for linking government payments, both social transfers and payments to civil servants through "access to finance channels," which can be helpful to integrate large parts of the unbanked population.

However, the service providers often are not financial institutions but mobile phone operators and the like. Which role can they play in financial system development, and how should the system adapt to them? Here again, a level playing field is needed which includes adequate regulation. Payment service innovations based on technology are not only relevant in terms of reducing transaction costs from an MFI perspective. They can become extremely important when their potential to reduce clients' transaction costs is factored in, a dimension that is often given too little attention. Transaction costs from a client's perspective, for example, consist of visiting a financial institution in the next district capital just for making loan repayments or withdrawing money from a savings account – this cost can be quite substantial. For many people, this also includes the opportunity costs of income foregone during the time of visiting the MFI.

Micro-insurance has also attracted a lot of attention, yet many services still refer to one single type of insurance, the life insurance, of which the bulk of insurance schemes are compulsory when taking a loan. Only part of these insurance contracts – albeit a growing part – are made on a voluntary basis to get insured against a sudden loss of the family earner and its financial consequences. In turn, compulsory life insurance should rather be seen as part of the credit technology and is used by MFIs as a means to reduce the credit risk. The demand is rising in the more difficult fields of insurance for the bottom of the pyramid segments of the population: livestock insurance, weather insurance, and, ultimately, health insurance. However, many dimensions in the life of poor people such as natural disasters would require insurance services rather than other financial services.

3.4   Fair and Transparent Client Treatment, Including Pricing

Responsible practices are the basis of any MFI-client relationship: fair and transparent treatment, avoiding over-indebtedness, sound collection practices, and promoting financial literacy. When institutions act in a professional way, there should not be necessarily a trade-off between a good financial performance and responsible service delivery. In turn, irresponsible practices are not conducive to a sustainable development of the institution. In "Microfinance 3.0," practices such as flat interest rate charges and other intransparent standards would gradually disappear, whereas responsible credit approval schemes, accompanied by good incentive systems for MFI staff, would become a mainstream development. Overall, responsible finance goes beyond consumer protection and also beyond microfinance; it is an integral part of sound financial systems development.

3.5   Sound Financial Infrastructure and Conducive Regulation

A healthy environment remains vital for good MFI performance although the bulk of what can go wrong seems to lie within the institutions themselves, as the 2012 Banana Skins report has shown[5]. "Microfinance 3.0" is a "marketplace" with ef-

---

[5]   Out of the top 12 risks mentioned, about two-thirds are related to MFI management/governance and about one-third to rather exogenous factors such as political interference and inappropriate regulation.

fective credit bureaus and a microfinance regulation in place that is adapted to MFIs' needs, i.e. that is conducive to their development. Sometimes there may be a tension between the macroeconomic goal of stable financial sectors and the objective to increase access to finance for the lower income segments of the population, but this tension seems to be overestimated in many countries. On the contrary, some regulators also begin to see the risks of financial exclusion for the well-being of the financial sector.

As some of the indebtedness patterns have shown, responsible regulation has been among the deficits in some markets. Perhaps you can call this the forgotten – or at least neglected – half of responsible finance. While the overall regulatory environment seems to be improving, there have been a number of inappropriate regulatory moves which gave raise to concerns. It is unclear if there is necessarily a causal relationship between the events of the overheating of the microfinance market and client over-indebtedness, but at least there is a clear time context. Do regulators yield to political pressure generated by those crises and throw the baby out with the bath water by imposing, with good intentions to contain bad practices, inadequate regulatory constraints? Some problematic issues include:

- Inadequate, sometimes prohibitive minimum capital requirements;

- (Re)introduction of interest rate caps that can endanger MFI sustainability;

- Poor over-indebtedness avoidance and debt crisis management;

- Restrictive loans to deposits ratios, i.e. restricting the lending activities by linking the loan portfolio to the volume of savings mobilized which can be counter-productive for newly deposit-taking institutions if no waivers are being granted.

These tendencies clearly show that much more dialogue with regulators is needed. Regulators should take a view of helping to build an industry rather than slowing it down. Besides an industry-promoting, level playing field oriented regulation, the priority should go to setting up effective credit bureaus. Effective credit bureaus are characterized, inter alia, by the following:

- It is compulsory for all financial institutions to report to the credit bureau;

- The credit bureau provides consistent, reliable, and comprehensive information in a timely manner;

- The credit bureau provides not only negative but also positive information (i.e. a positive track record of the client).

3.6   The Role of Funders

Microfinance funders need to be complementary, integrative, and additional to the rest of the industry. The funding landscape is rapidly changing. Starting with donor grants, one of the main funding sources has come from Development Finance Institutions (DFIs) who actually account for 60 % of overall cross-border funding. DFIs have paved the way for commercial funders to join in. DFIs have set up MFI greenfield banks as reference models for good practices and funds that also supported the emergence of 100–200 top performing, fully licensed MFIs that actually account for the bulk of the client outreach in developing countries. They were active in countries where private sector actors would not have gone and showed that microfinance can work sustainably even in difficult countries.

And yet, DFIs, while playing a role as long-term, patient investors, face the challenge of "responsible exits." Will they succeed in bringing in new investors that stick to good standards and will not drop out in stormy times? Will debt funders understand the risk of overheating in some markets, and will equity funders understand the need to adopt a buy and hold attitude rather than (just) expecting (quick) returns? And finally, how do all these questions relate to the issue of future microfinance Initial Public Offerings (IPOs)?

4   The Funder Perspective – KfW's Approach

KfW has been supporting microfinance almost since its inception. It is today one of the most important funders, along with other DFIs. With a portfolio of more than 2 billion euros of outstanding commitments, KfW has been playing an active role not only as a funder in microfinance but also with regard to a conducive market environment. It has been promoting responsible microfinance since 2007, long before the outbreak of the financial crisis. KfW's vision is to develop a healthy microfinance sector including a number of full-fledged regulated, deposit-taking MFIs.

KfW's vision is to create and enhance the sustainable access of un(der)served groups of the population to credit, savings, and other financial services (e.g. payment services or money transfers, and microinsurance). In order to achieve this goal, KfW has steadily invested in its growing microfinance portfolio for more than ten years.

4.1 KfW's Microfinance Strategy

Based on KfW's long and extensive experiences in the sector, its microfinance strategy consists of six main elements:

1. **Responsible selectivity and sound institution building:** KfW focuses on the selection of professional and responsible partner institutions operating in a favourable environment and promoting institution building. For a sound market development, the successful institutions are most needed to make changes happen. Although a growing number of institutions have achieved an impressive track record, much is to be done to further strengthen these

institutions and also support the next tier of high potential but not yet mature institutions.

2. **Network approach:** This approach means promoting best practices through investments in microfinance funds and holdings and the use of KfW's large know-how regarding (structured) funds/Microfinance Investment Vehicles (MIVs). Networks often have standardized systems and procedures which makes institution building even more efficient. Working with networks implies the support of global and regional initiatives instead of just focusing on single country projects.

3. **Focus on income generating loans for MSME clients:** Micro, small and medium enterprises (MSMEs) have been the primary target group. They contribute significantly to employment and income creation in developing countries – especially for the low-income groups of the population. These enterprises lack access to financial services which excludes them from many economic opportunities. However, KfW would not support pure consumer lenders.

4. **"Microfinance plus": Extension to other credit products (e.g. rural finance, "small business loans," energy efficiency, education finance) and also savings:** KfW promotes the diversification of credit products as well as the development of financial services other than credit. The former includes energy efficiency, agriculture, and education loans. The latter consists of savings, but also money transaction and insurance products.

5. **Promotion of responsible finance:** KfW stands for responsible finance. This includes, in a narrow sense, the way a financial institution treats its clients, and it should do so in a fair and transparent way, including an effective credit technology. In a broader sense, it also includes "good quality funding" and sound regulation and supervision.

6. **Diversity of instruments:** KfW has a broad array of different instruments adapted to the respective sectoral environment and the funding needs of its professional partner institutions. KfW mainly provides its partners with mezzanine and senior loans, guarantees, and TA grants, and holds equity participations (funds, holdings) as well as direct participations (MFI networks).

4.2 KfW's Microfinance Portfolio

In 2012, the microfinance portfolio amounted to 2.1 billion euros and hence represented the biggest share (39%) of the total financial sector portfolio. The majority of this volume came from KfW funds (62%) while 31% were provided through German federal budget funds and 7% by other investors. As part of the German budget funds, 2% of the microfinance portfolio was allocated for technical assistance measures. KfW promotes microfinance in five different approaches: greenfielding, upgrading, downscaling, linking, and structured funds.

New (*greenfield*) MFIs need equity capital and capacity building. KfW has supported the foundation of various MFIs, usually belonging to network holdings such as ProCredit, ACCESS, ADVANS, and Finca Microfinance Holdings.

In a similar way, KfW accompanies small non-governmental financial organizations and unlicensed microfinance institutions in transforming into licensed, deposit-taking financial institutions (*upgrading*). An impressive example is the Cambodian ACLEDA Bank, which was established as a national NGO for micro and small enterprise development and credit in January of 1993. Ten years later, ACLEDA Bank became licensed as a commercial bank after having tripled its capital to 13 million USD. Today, another decade later, the issued and paid-up capital amounts to more than 100 million USD, and ACLEDA Bank itself is establishing own affiliates in Laos and Myanmar.

KfW also promotes *downscaling* approaches by assisting commercial banks in offering microfinance products. Long established partners include the Small Industries Development Bank of India (SIDBI) or Corporación Financiera de Desarrollo (COFIDE) in Peru, or Seker Bank in Turkey.

Finally, KfW has promoted initiatives in *structured finance* helping to stabilize and enhance good performing MFIs' access to private sector capital. Among these are some flagship initiatives such as the European Fund for Southeast Europe (EFSE) or the Microfinance Enhancement Facility (MEF).

5   Conclusions

The global financial crisis did not stop at microfinance institutions and their customers. As the effects of the crisis have begun to affect customers directly, credit risks have increased. In this environment, many MFIs have proven to be able to manage the crisis period reasonably well. There was evidence that the industry has been robust and there is trust that it would emerge from the crisis (even) stronger. On the other hand, there were signs of "unhealthy" competition and over-indebtedness in a number of countries. Against this backdrop, the following conclusions can be drawn from the ongoing debate:

1. The current challenge is to strengthen MFI and build a sound market environment. Institution building is not only relevant with regard to their financial and social performance but also with a view to making them (more) resilient to crisis impact and unhealthy competition. Crisis resilience will be a decisive factor to further attract private capital for MFIs and ensure sustainable access to finance for the un(der)served population in developing and transition countries. Without such strong institutions, there can be no sound market development.

2. Responsible finance and commercial microfinance are not necessarily contradictory to each other. It is true that some practices went badly wrong, and criticism has to be taken seriously. There is a lot to be learned from unfair client treatment, wrong incentives, and lack of oversight. And having a good value compass is a prerequisite to do microfinance business.

3. Clients' needs matter, and sound, professionally managed – and governed – institutions remain at the center, because only these can deliver on the financial inclusion claim. In this context, a lot still needs to be done to promote savings. A good infrastructure is key as well. Technology can be seen as an important element but is not an end in itself.

4. DFIs should be clear about their roles, and these are manifold: standard setter for good corporate governance, promoters of funding structures attractive to private investors, product innovator and financier of a sound financial infrastructure.

5. On the impact of microfinance, there is consensus about the impressive achievements in terms of industry building. Regarding the well-being of clients, the need for better impact measurement tools is however highlighted. A closer look should be taken at how well an MFI serves its clients, rather than looking at personal "success stories."

6. The end-game is still to push the financial frontier to underserved regions, people, and markets. The underlying rationale should be two-fold:

   • People in developing countries need – and can make good use of – financial services to improve their living conditions;

   • Financial services do benefit people so financial institutions can deliver on this claim.

Overall, there is room to believe that the next generation of microfinance, highlighted as "Microfinance 3.0," will see more financial inclusion, guided by strong institutional professionalism, a strong commitment to offer innovative products tailored to clients' needs, a conducive regulation, and a set of values ensuring that responsible finance practices become more sustainably anchored in the microfinance industry.

References

Ardic, O.P., Chen, G., Latortue, A. (2012) Financial Access 2011. Access to Finance Forum No. 5. Washington: CGAP.

CGAP (2013) Strategic Directions FY2014 – FY2018. Advancing Financial Inclusion to Improve the Lives of the Poor. Washington DC.

Christen, R.P. (2013) Financial Services that Clients Need: The 3.0 Business Models, reconciling outreach with sustainability. Berlin.

Chu, M. (2011) Microfinance. Today and Tomorrow, Presentation at Microfinance: Inclusion & Sustainable Business – IE Business School, 22 February 2011.

Ehrbeck, T. (2012) The Hidden Champions of Low-Income Banking. Blog on www.huffingtonpost.com.

Glisovic, J., Martinez, M. (2012) Financing Small Enterprises. CGAP Focus Note 81, Washington DC.

Lahaye, E., Rizvanolli, R. (2012) Current Trends in Cross Border Funding for Microfinance. Washington: CGAP Brief.

Lascelles, D., Mendelson, S. (2012) Microfinance Banana Skins 2012 – Staying Relevant. New York: Centre for the Study of Financial Innovation.

Maurer, K. (2013) The Role of DFIs in the emerging 3.0 Responsible Funding Landscape – Responsible Corporate Governance and beyond, Berlin.

McKee, K (2012) Voting the Double Bottom Line, CGAP Focus Note 79, Washington DC.

McKee, K., Lahaye, E., Koning, A. (2011) Responsible Finance: Putting Principles to Work. CGAP Focus Note 73, Washington DC.

Roodman, D. (2012) Due Diligence: An Impertinent Inquiry into Microfinance. Washington: Center for Global Development.

Roodman, D. (2013) Armageddon or Adolescence? Making Sense of Microfinance's Recent Travails. Berlin.

Rosenberg, R., Gaul, S., Ford, W., Tomilova, O. (2013) Microcredit Interest Rates and Their Determinants: 2004–2011. CGAP Forum Paper,Washington DC.

Schmidt, R.H. (2008) Microfinance, Kommerzialisierung und Ethik, University of Frankfurt.

Schmidt, R.H. (2012) Core Values of Microfinance under Scrutiny: Back to Basics? Berlin.

Terberger, E. (2012) The Microfinance Approach: Does it Deliver on its Promise? In: Terberger, Eva (ed.) Die Unternehmung, 4/2012. Baden-Baden: Nomos.

CHAPTER 7

Microfinance Beyond the Standard? Evaluating Adequacy and Performance of Agricultural Microcredit[*]

Ron Weber[**]

Abstract

Microfinance was successful in increasing access to credit for micro, small and medium enterprises in developing countries, particularly in urban areas. The offer of installment loans as the standard credit product for new and very small customers has been indentified as one of the keys that enabled microfinance institutions to reach out to formerly unbanked entrepreneurs. However, these standard loans always were considered as inadequate for agricultural entrepreneurs with seasonal production cycles. For this reason, this paper investigates the effects of providing flexible agricultural microfinance loans (flex loans) to farmers as an alternative to standard installment loans. The study was carried out in cooperation with two banks of the AccessHolding Microfinance AG in Tanzania and Madagascar. A mixed-methods approach was applied relying on observations during field visits and in-depth portfolio analyses.

Our results reveal that the combination of standard and flex loans enables the investigated microfinance institution to address a wide range of agricultural producers. Based on our results it seems very unlikely that seasonal agricultural producers would have had credit access without flex loans. Standard loans are only adequate to address non-seasonal agricultural producers. We also find that non-seasonal agricultural producers repay their loans with delinquency rates similar or even better than those of non-farmers. For seasonal agricultural producers a redis-

---

[*] The views expressed in this paper are entirely those of the author and do not necessarily represent those of KfW. The authors are grateful to Access Microfinance Holding AG and LFS Financial Systems GmbH in Berlin, Germany, for the provision of data, in particular Stephan Hödtke and his colleagues from the LFS IT department. Furthermore, we would like to thank all colleagues from AccèsBanque Madagascar for their great support during the field visits in Madagascar and for contributing their expertise; Claudia Schmerler is also acknowledged for her helpful comments.

[**] Project Manager, KfW.

tribution of principal payments from periods with low agricultural returns (grace periods) to periods when agricultural returns are high is necessary to keep their delinquency rates at the level of non-farmers. Furthermore, we find that flex loans can be offered sustainably and that agricultural lending has become a strategic focus of the Access Bank in Madagascar.

1   Introduction

The impacts of microfinance on developing countries are currently discussed controversially. Microfinance has achieved the financial inclusion of millions of micro, small, and medium entrepreneurs that had no access to financial services before (Love and Peria, 2012). Merely thirty years have passed since the foundation of the Grameen Bank, and already there are signs of microcredit oversupply and even borrower over-indebtedness, particularly in emerging countries (Taylor, 2011; Vogelgesang, 2003). However, the contribution of microfinance to investment stimulation, employment generation, and economic development is less controversial (Duvendack *et al.*, 2011; Pande *et al.*, 2012).

Lending techniques applied by microfinance institutions (MFIs) are adequate to reflect the business conditions of many micro, small, and medium enterprises (MSMEs). Loan sizes are adapted to the borrowers' incomes based on intensive client assessments, relationships are established by carefully increasing loan amounts for good borrowers, and loan products are standardized by offering mainly installment loans (standard loans) with loan repayment starting immediately after loan disbursement. Product standardization is even considered as one of the main reasons for the high repayment rates and, hence, the success of microfinance (Armendáriz de Aghion and Morduch, 2000; Jain and Mansuri, 2003). However, product standardization also has several drawbacks.

When repayment schedules cannot be harmonized with investment returns, the number of potential projects that can be realized is limited. For a project to be financed with a short-term installment loan, fast turnovers and regular cash flows of nearly the same level are required. Longer-term projects need time to mature though before they generate returns sufficiently high to repay the loan balance. In consequence, profitable investments might not even be realized due to mismatches between cash flow and repayment obligations (Field *et al.*, 2011). Most MFI clients are, hence, traders, using their loans to finance working capital, and the share of loans for long-term projects remains low (Dalla Pellegrina, 2011).

Moreover, while microfinance has reached many urban entrepreneurs, it still needs to accomplish its mission for MSMEs in rural areas, particularly for entrepreneurs in the agricultural sector (Hermes *et al.*, 2011; Llanto, 2007). Most agricultural production types are characterized by a high level of seasonality leading to mismatches between expenditures during planting season and revenues at the time of harvest (Binswanger and Rosenzweig, 1986). Particularly here, standard loans, which cannot account for seasonal cash-flow patterns of agricultural producers, seem to fall behind.

The provisioning of microfinance loans with flexible repayment schedules (flex loans) is, hence, stipulated by the literature (e.g., Llanto, 2007; Meyer, 2002; Dalla Pellegrina, 2011; Field *et al.*, 2011). Yet, despite the potential of flex loans to increase the outreach of MFIs, at present only few MFIs are willing to make repayment schedules more flexible.

Based on field visits and data of the management information systems of two banks of the AccessHolding Microfinance AG in Tanzania and Madagascar, this paper provides a mixed-methods evaluation of product adequacy and the effects of providing standard and flex loans to agricultural firms. The rest of this report is organized as follows: In the second part, we will provide a brief discussion why standard loans are mainly applied in microfinance and how this determines the type of MSMEs financed by MFIs. In the third part, the analyzed MFIs will be briefly presented. Based on this background, we will present four evaluation questions and the evaluation methodology. In the fourth part, we will assess agricultural lending in both banks along these evaluation questions.

2   Lending Principles in Microfinance

Driven by negative experiences of the supply-led development finance period in the 1960s and 1970s and the failure of state-owned development banks in the 1980s (Adams and Graham, 1981; Maurer, 2011), governments and central banks in many developing countries have started to improve the regulatory and operating environment in the financial sector. These improvements were important preconditions for the successful development of the commercial microfinance industry, which is driven by various attempts such as developing regular banks to better serve MSMEs and professionalizing existing and creating new MFIs (Krahnen and Schmidt, 1994; Maurer, 2011). For MFIs, informal MSMEs have represented the typical target clients as informal MSMEs are normally neglected by regular banks. Rather than applying the conventional, collateral-based lending approach followed by regular banks or the joint liability principle of group lending mostly applied by non-commercial MFIs, commercial MFIs typically use income based individual (liability) lending techniques instead. Thereby the family and the business income, i.e., the total household income, determines the repayment capacity of a loan applicant and is the basis for the decision of the MFI whether a loan is granted and how much credit will be disbursed. As reliable income statements or balance sheet data are hardly available in the informal MSME sector, MFIs themselves carry out detailed assessments of loan applicants to evaluate their repayment capacities[1]. Driven by the support of donors, development finance institutions, and commercial banks, individual lending MFIs can today be found all over the world, although mainly in urban areas (Llanto, 2007).

---

[1]   For further information on the principles of microfinance the reader is referred to Armendáriz de Aghion and Morduch (2010) and Kong and Turvey (2008).

One of the main reasons for the success of MFIs is the provisioning of standard loans. Standard loans are also widely applied by individual lending MFIs. Despite the fact that installments of standard loans are adapted to the income of the borrower, including the cash flow of the financed project and other income sources of the borrower's household (Armendáriz de Aghion and Morduch, 2010), repayment schedules of standard loans cannot be harmonized with the cash-flow occurrence of the borrower. Thus, standard loans might be adequate for businesses generating fast returns on a regular basis, e.g., petty traders (Llanto, 2007). However, for longer-term projects with irregular and uncertain return patterns, standard loans seem counterintuitive as such projects need time to mature before first returns are realized. The project can only be financed if an entrepreneur is able to smooth temporary cash-flow shortfalls of the financed project by other income sources. In consequence, profitable projects cannot be realized at all or only with higher repayment risks when cash flow and repayment obligations do not match (Field *et al.*, 2011). Hence, product standardization might reduce default risks for clients with continuous cash flows but limits the focus of MFIs to projects fulfilling the product requirements (Weber and Musshoff, 2012). Unsurprisingly, most MFI clients are traders with fast turnovers, using their loans to finance mainly working capital. The share of long-term loans offered by MFIs and especially loans to entrepreneurs with seasonal returns typically found in the agricultural sector, however, remains low (Dalla Pellegrina, 2011).

Agricultural production is often characterized by a high level of seasonality which frequently leads to periodical imbalances between expenditures in the planting and revenues in the harvesting seasons (Binswanger and Rosenzweig, 1986). For this reason, loans with flexible loan repayment schedules harmonized with agricultural production cycles are often stipulated in the agricultural economics literature (Meyer, 2002; Dalla Pellegrina, 2011). In this context, Meyer (2002) argues that firms in Bangladesh with significant agricultural income would be better served with loan repayment schedules matching expected cash flows and shifting principal repayment to the time of harvest. Furthermore, Dalla Pellegrina (2011) states that compared to (flexible) loans of informal money lenders and conventional banks, standard loans of MFIs are less suitable to finance agricultural projects. The absence of adequate loan products for agricultural firms is, hence, considered to be one reason why the penetration of agricultural clients by MFIs is still low (Christen and Pearce, 2005; Llanto, 2007).

In addition to inadequate loan products, the outreach of MFIs to rural areas where most of the agricultural production takes place is constrained by higher operational costs when compared to urban areas. The reason is that distances are longer and population densities are lower, making it more time and fuel consuming for banks to approach and to monitor borrowers (Armendáriz de Aghion and Morduch, 2010; Caudill *et al.*, 2009). Collection costs are considered to be one of the largest operational cost components in microfinance (Shankar, 2007). Here, grace periods increase the time period that loan amounts are outstanding and, hence, lead to higher interest returns for the MFI, contributing to compensate for higher operational costs.

Despite the potential of flexible repayment schedules to increase the outreach of MFIs to rural areas, most MFIs are still reluctant to make repayment schedules more flexible. They might fear that more flexibility reduces repayment rates. However, there is no empirical evidence that could support this concern. However, most research focusing on the effects of flexible repayment schedules on loan repayment is based on experiments, with mixed results that need to be proven in reality yet. In a field experiment in India, Field and Pande (2008) randomly assigned microfinance loans to borrowing groups of a MFI with either monthly or weekly repayment installments. They find that different repayment schedules have no significant influence on loan delinquencies. In a later experiment with the same MFI, Field et al. (2011) complement their first investigations by analyzing the effect of a two-month grace period[2] on loan delinquencies of borrowers. They find higher loan delinquencies for loans with grace periods. However, despite their randomization, the granting of grace periods was arbitrary and did not depend on the underlying cash-flow patterns of the borrowers. Hence, they were not able to control whether the investigated borrowers needed the grace period to compensate cash-flow induced liquidity shortfalls. In a similar experiment with randomly assigned loans to borrowing groups in India, Czura et al. (2011) tried to extend the earlier research and implicitly addressed potential cash-flow shortfalls of the borrowers. To limit other sources of influence, they only focused on dairy farmers. All borrowers in their experiment used the loans to buy lactating dairy cows, i.e., cows that were giving milk at the time of purchase but that would stop giving milk for two months after the lactation phase. This event was expected to occur a certain time after loan disbursement, and, hence, the borrower would suffer a cash-flow shortfall at that moment. Czura et al. (2011) assigned different loan types to the borrowers: standard loans, loans with pre-defined grace periods, and loans with flexible grace periods where the borrower was allowed to postpone up to two repayment installments at any time three months after loan disbursement[3]. Their results show that loan delinquencies of loans with flexible grace periods were not higher than those of standard loans. Their experimental results showing that grace periods do not undermine repayment discipline are further supported by Godquin (2004), who investigates the loan repayment behavior of MFI borrowers in Bangladesh. She finds that loans with grace periods have significantly lower loan delinquencies than standard loans. These findings suggest that switching from standard loans to flex loans does not necessarily affect repayment quality. Moreover, these findings support the argument that decreasing the number of repay-

---

[2]   During a grace period the borrower only needs to partly fulfill his repayment obligations (principal, interests). The graced repayment obligations are postponed to the future, usually when returns occur.

[3]   Given the monthly repayment plans, the postponement of two installments is similar to a two-month grace period. Two months is the average resting phase of a dairy cow between two lactation periods. During the resting phase the cow produces no milk, and, hence, generates only costs and no returns.

ment installments bears potential to increase efficiency of MFIs as flex loans are not associated with higher loan defaults.

Hence, it is not surprising that a recent approach to enhance access to finance for agricultural MSMEs is driven by the commercial microfinance industry. Christen and Pearce (2005) have presented the principles of this new "Agricultural Microfinance Model" which adapts the general microfinance approach for agricultural MSMEs. In this attempt, the German AccessHolding Microfinance AG (represented through Access Banks in currently seven developing and emerging countries) was among the first institutions that introduced flex loans for agricultural MSMEs in Africa and in Madagascar in particular.

3   Institutions

The institutions investigated in our evaluation are AccessBank Tanzania (ABT) and AccèsBanque Madagascar (ABM). Currently only ABM has introduced and offers flex loans.

ABT is a commercial MFI with a special focus on MSMEs. The bank operates in Tanzania as a fully-fledged commercial bank and is owned by the five founders, the AccessHolding Microfinance AG, the Belgian Investment Company for Developing Countries, KfW (the German Development Bank), the International Finance Corporation (IFC), and the African Development Bank. During the first four years of operation from 2007 to 2011, the bank grew steadily and currently operates eight branch offices in the greater Dar es Salaam area. ABT disburses all loans in the local currency, Tanzania Shilling (TZS), and procedures of the bank are specially designed for and only allow for disbursing individual loans. Up to date (2013), the bank only offers standard loans in the micro segment, and loans to agricultural entrepreneurs are still granted under the standard loan procedures. Hence, they are not yet adapted to the agricultural production cycles and have fixed repayment schedules and maturities without grace periods.

ABM operates as a fully-fledged commercial MSME bank in Madagascar and is owned by its founders, the AccessHolding Microfinance AG, BFV-Société Générale, KfW, IFC, and the Triodos-Doen Fund. ABM offers its services through 17 branch offices. In contrast to ABT, the branch network of ABM reaches far beyond the capital Antananarivo where ABM began its business after foundation in 2007. Like ABT, ABM also disburses all loans only in local currency (Madagascar-Ariary, MGA) and only on an individual lending basis. At the moment, there are six different business loan products in the micro segment: standard loans, housing loans, emergency loans for unforeseen private expenditures (e.g., accidents), flex loans, warehouse receipt loans[4], and value chain loans in cooperation with an input

---

[4]   ABM owns the warehouses and takes stocks of crops (currently only rice) from farmers (at market prices) as loan collateral. During the loan repayment period, the stock can be reduced according to the changing collateral requirements. ABM charges the client with a stock depositing fee. Besides getting the stock as collateral accepted, the farmer benefits from increasing crop prices after the harvesting season.

supplier[5]. Besides loans, both banks offer various types of deposits, ATM services (only ABT), and money transfer services (Western Union, Money Gram).

The loan granting process of both banks is typical for commercial MFIs involved in individual lending and is similar to other banks of the AccessHolding

Table 1. Client Characteristics of AccessBank Tanzania and AccèsBanque Madagascar

| | | AccessBank Tanzania | | | | AccèsBanque Madagascar | | | | | |
| | | Farmer[1] Standard Loan | | Non-Farmer | | Farmer[3] Standard Loan | | Farmer[3] Flex Loan | | Non-Farmer | |
Variable	Unit	Mean	SD[2]	Mean	SD[2]	Mean	SD[2]	Mean	SD[2]	Mean	SD[2]
Household Income	CU[3]	986	1,084	1,040	1,232	1,944***	2,714	575***	853	3,620	6,755
Household Expenses	CU[3]	–	–	–	–	1,632***	1,511	357***	694	3,264	6,480
Age	years	44***	9.42	39	8.32	40.61***	10.26	41.67***	11.07	39.80	9.74
Gender (female)	%	71***	–	40	–	51***	–	26***	–	59	–
Family Members	number	5.29***	2.08	5.00	2.00	4.76***	1.89	5.55***	2.15	4.66	1.86
Marital Status (married)	number	–	–	–	–	88***	–	89***	–	85	–
Higher Education	%	30***	–	24	–	–	–	–	–	–	–
Work Experience	month	–	–	–	–	86.62***	65.70	165***	115	107.47	74.31
Repeat Client	%	39	–	37	–	35***	–	11***	–	37	–
Deposit	%	72	–	47	–	68***	–	71***	–	66	–
Number of Observations (total)	number	538		20,796		3,113		2,221		88,782	
Animal Producers	number	531		–		3,083		222		–	
Crop and Vegetable Producers	number	7		–		30		1,999		–	

[1] Farmer Standard Loan, agricultural firms with standard loan; Farmer Flex Loan, agricultural firm with flex loan; Non-Farmer, non-farmer with standard or flex loan; ***,**,* indicate a significant mean difference between farmers with standard loans and farmers with flex loans compared to non-farmers on a 1%, 5% and 10% level, respectively. Comprises only primary agricultural producers, i.e., livestock, crop as well as fruit and vegetable producers.

[2] SD, Standard Deviation.

[3] CU, Currency Unit in thousand Tanzania Shilling for AccessBank Tanzania and in thousand Malagasy-Ariary for AccèsBanque Madagascar.

[5] ABM cooperates with an input supplier for poultry production. If a loan applicant fulfills the requirements to raise a high-yield poultry breed, he will use the loan from ABM to buy a full package to raise these chickens from the input supplier (chicken, vaccination, feed). Thus, the farmer generates higher returns through a better chicken breed, and the bank reduces its risk that the client's business will work out unsuccessfully.

Microfinance AG (Weber and Musshoff, 2013). In addition to intensive on-site client assessments, this includes the verification of investigated information through cross-checks carried out by the loan officer and a decentralized loan decision at the branch office level through a credit committee.

Table 1 provides a characterization of non-agricultural and agricultural clients of ABT and ABM and even further classification of both animal and fruit and vegetable producers. Whether a client is classified as an agricultural entrepreneur is decided by the banks along the following two criteria: First, more than 50 % of the client's household income needs to be generated through agricultural production, i.e. crop, fruit and vegetable, or livestock production. Second, the client must use the loan for agricultural production purposes. This strict classification only covers primary agricultural producers. Clients with businesses only related to agricultural production (input supply for farmers, processing of agricultural produce) are not considered as agricultural clients. Based on the seasonality of a farmer's production type, he can be granted a standard loan or a flex loan.For Tanzania, table 1 reveals that farmers are mostly animal producers, are on average five years older, have a slightly larger family size, are mostly female, and are better educated than non-agricultural loan applicants. In Madagascar, household income and household expenses of farmers are lower than for non-farmers. There is a lower share of female clients in the group of farmers with flex loans compared to farmers with standard loans and non-farmers. Furthermore, farmers with flex loans are mostly crop and vegetable producers, and farmers with standard loans are mostly animal producers.

4   Evaluation Questions and Methodology

Taking into account the attributes of standard loans and flex loans and the existing experience with the effects of inflexible repayment schedules on credit access for firms with cyclical cash flows, we will assess the overall success of the introduction of flex loans along the following evaluation questions:

1. "Product":   Are lending principles and product characteristics of flex loans adapted to farmers' needs?

2. "Credit Access": How far can standard loans and flex loans achieve the financial inclusion of farmers?

3. "Loan Repayment": Does the financial inclusion of farmers increase the credit risk of the MFIs?

4. "Sustainability": Is agricultural lending a strategic field of business for ABM?

In order to answer our evaluation questions, we chose a mixed-method approach, consisting of (I) the investigation of the flex loan procedures in AccèsBanque

Madagascar, based on field visits to two branch offices in different regions of Madagascar and semi-structured interviews with the bank's staff and clients; and (II) an in-depth portfolio analysis of ABT and ABM.

For (II) we applied data-adjusted regression analyses to investigate (a) the probability that a loan applicant receives a loan when he applies for one, (b) when an applicant is granted a loan, how much of the amount he is asking for finally is approved (this approach corrects also for likely income differences), and (c) how many of the loan installments the borrower has to pay are not paid in time. In all of our analyses, clients with standard loans (without grace periods) serve as the reference group. This reference group is plausible for three reasons: First, it comprises the majority of all borrowers; second, this group can be observed since the MFIs were founded; and, third, this group is the benchmark for both banks' management to judge the success of any product modification.

The datasets we use for the portfolio analyses comprise all microloans both banks have disbursed since the first month of operation (ABT: November 2007, ABM: February 2007) until April 2011 (ABT) and May 2012 (ABM). Our data was extracted from the Management Information System (MIS) of the banks and include loan and respective client data. The loan data (e.g. number of installments, interest rate) are generated automatically by the MIS as soon as a loan is disbursed. The client data which is generated through the in-depth client assessments by the loan officers is entered manually into the MIS. Consequently, it was necessary to clean the client data for obvious data entering errors and outliers, which was jointly conducted with the staff of both banks. Furthermore, we excluded those loan applications that were withdrawn by the client before the bank had made a loan decision, loans that were still in the decision process, and loans with incomplete client or loan data.

The in-depth portfolio analyses summarize the key results of Weber and Musshoff (2012), Weber and Musshoff (2013), and Weber *et al.* (2013). The reader is referred to these articles for a detailed explanation of applied regression approaches and the regressions results.

5   Evaluation Results

5.1   Are Lending Principles and Product Characteristics of Flex Loans Adapted to Farmers' Needs?

This section is based on field visits to different branch offices of ABM in April 2013 and semi-structured interviews with the banks' staff and clients.

In Madagascar, about 70 % of the total population (most of it living in rural areas) is employed in the agricultural sector, and the mainly small scale agricultural sector contributes about 30 % to the country's GDP, after the (mainly informal) services and (mining) industries sectors. Hence, for ABM to successfully reach small entrepreneurs in rural areas it has to ultimately acknowledge agricultural production circumstances and simultaneously consider the local specifics in the microfinance sector. For this reason, ABM introduced flex loans four years after its foundation but only in selected branch offices in rural areas.

The difference between standard loans and flex loans is the consideration of future cash flows of the client to determine the client's repayment capacity, i.e., the amount the client is able to use for loan repayment per month as loans of ABM must be repaid on a monthly basis. For standard loans, typically the cash flows of the client during a given period before the loan application are expected to also occur in the future. The repayment capacity is calculated on the average monthly cash flow minus all the client's private expenditures reduced by 30 % to allow covering unforeseeable expenses (e.g., accidents). For flex loans, the transfer of past cash flows would be misleading as most farmers (despite the high seasonality of expenditures and returns) usually rotate crops year by year. Furthermore, commodity prices vary. Thus, the responsible loan officer has to structure a cash flow calendar by evaluating not only plantation and harvesting periods but also all related costs and returns of an agricultural activity on a monthly basis. Because most farmers' agricultural activities are diversified, this needs to be done for all agricultural activities of the farmer. As most farmers also have income from non-agricultural sources, these sources also need to be considered and might even have to be assessed with the procedures for standard loans. The higher the farmer is diversified, the less likely it is that he will c.p. face months with negative cash flows and, hence, negative repayment capacities. Nevertheless, flex loans allow for granting grace periods for months with negative cash flows. ABM grace periods are defined by months with loan repayments below the annuity that would be due with the application of a standard loan. There are also consecutive grace periods possible, and cash-flow analyses are verified by credit committee members for each loan on the branch level. One further difference to standard loans is the frequency and the purpose of visits to clients after loan disbursement. While with standard loans only one visit is foreseen to keep in contact with the client before the first repayment installment (for standard loans typically one month after disbursement), one additional visit takes place with flex loans. The purpose of visits is to verify that the loan was used to finance the intended activity. The reason for this verification is that for the cash-flow estimation the returns of the financed activity were considered, and a deviation (e.g., when the farmer plants another crop) increases the probability that the client runs into repayment problems.

Concluding, these flex loan procedures show that lending principles in ABM are designed to respond to the farmers' needs. They further demonstrate that loan officers in agricultural lending need special skills. They must be experienced with standard loan procedures and need to have a profound understanding of farming.

5.2 How Far Can Standard Loans and Flex Loans Achieve the Financial Inclusion of Farmers?

This section is based on mean comparison tests between agricultural and non-agricultural clients of ABT and ABM as well as regression analyses wherein the sector affiliation of the client was considered as an additional control variable.

Our results for Tanzania reveal that farmers applying for standard loans have a lower probability of receiving a loan than non-agricultural firms. Furthermore, the loan amounts for farmers with access to credit are not significantly different than those for other clients of ABT. Our results for Madagascar, however, are different. Here, farmers applying for standard loans have the same probability of receiving a loan as non-farmers. The results further show that farmers applying for flex loans have a higher probability of receiving a loan compared to non-farmers. For the loan amounts disbursed, we find that farmers with standard loans receive larger loan amounts than non-farmers. For farmers with flex loans, we find lower disbursed loan amounts compared to non-farmers. When comparing farmers with standard and flex loans, we find that farmers with flex loans have a higher probability of receiving a loan than farmers with standard loans. In contrast, we find a largely negative effect for the disbursed loan amounts, indicating that farmers with flex loans receive smaller loans than farmers with standard loans, a result which might be related to the cautious lending practice, i.e., the perceived credit risk of ABM for clients with flex loans. Of further importance for the interpretation of these results is the consideration of the loan distribution among agricultural production types financed through both loan products. Here our data reveal that almost all flex loans were granted to crop and vegetable producers whereas standard loans were mostly granted to animal producers.

We conclude that the better credit access probabilities for seasonal farmers indicate that providing flex loans helps to financially include farmers with seasonal production types. The loan distribution amongst production types for both banks further reveals that the client share of seasonal agricultural producers was rather low when flex loans were not accessible. This suggests that without providing flex loans, non-seasonal agricultural producers would be addressed by the banks, but it is unlikely that seasonal agricultural producers would be given credit access at all.

5.3 Does the Financial Inclusion of Farmers Increase the Credit Risk for the MFIs?

This section is solely based on regression analyses wherein the sector affiliation of the client was considered as an additional control variable.

Our findings for ABT indicate that agricultural clients with standard loans report lower delinquencies than non-agricultural clients. For ABM, our results reveal no significant delinquency differences between farmers and non-farmers with standard loans (both without grace periods). Taking into consideration that most farmers with standard loans are animal producers with continuous returns, this result does not seem surprising. In contrast, we find higher delinquencies for farmers of ABM with flex loans than for non-farmers with standard loans (both without grace periods). This suggests that while the provisioning of flex loans seems to be a prerequisite to creating credit access for farmers with seasonal production types, flex loans without grace periods cannot overcome seasonality related repayment risks of seasonal agricultural producers. However, this difference disappears for those farmers with flex loans that were granted a grace period. Hence, grace periods are crucial for flex loans to bridge the wedge between discontinuous returns and continuous repayment obligations.

To sum up, from a risk perspective our findings reveal that standard loans seem to be adequate for farmers with continuous returns and that grace periods are crucial for financially including farmers with seasonal production types without increasing delinquency levels. Moreover, our results confront the widespread wisdom that agricultural borrowers are generally riskier than non-agricultural borrowers when they are adequately addressed.

5.4   Is Agricultural Lending a Strategic Field of Business for ABM?

This section is based on field visits to different branch offices of ABM in April 2013 and on semi-structured interviews with the banks' staff and clients.

After two years of lending experience with flex loans and, hence, the agricultural sector, ABM began to further develop the agricultural lending business with products corresponding to the clients' needs (warehouse receipt loans, value chain loans). This seems especially plausible as the agricultural sector contributes about 30 % to the country's GDP. Considering at the same time the high share of people employed in agriculture, the challenge of agricultural finance in Madagascar is the fragmentation of the sector, resulting in high costs per disbursed loan. These higher costs have to be compensated by the interest rates charged. Thus, even if the efficiency of loan provisioning by ABM can be considered as high, agricultural lending is associated with higher lending costs when farm sizes remain small. The question is whether and how ABM can overcome this problem. Seeking for a further standardization of the flex loan lending principles seems to be a promising field of intervention. Yet, given the already high efficiency of ABM in agricultural lending, the cost reduction potential here is limited. The increase of the average farm size resulting in larger requested loan sizes could circumvent this dilemma; however, this is beyond the banks' influence (unless the bank would strategically focus on larger farmers, which is not the case) and will depend on the general economic development of Madagascar. If employment opportunities emerge, people will migrate to urban areas and, hence, sell or lease their property to others. During the field visits such tendencies could be observed although these observations cannot be generalized for the agricultural sector as a whole. However, looking at the profit margins of ABM's agricultural producers (both seasonal and non-seasonal), there is no reason to assume that farmers are unable to cover the (only slightly) higher interest rates charged by ABM for flex loans. Taking this into consideration we would like to state explicitly that we find no reason for political interventions in agricultural lending (e.g., interest subsidies, interest rate caps) in Madagascar. Given the sustainability of agricultural lending in ABM and the short time period of only two and a half years the bank has experience with flex loans, we even believe that any market distorting lending policy intervention would jeopardize the strategic focus of ABM towards agricultural lending. At the moment, however, there is no such intervention in sight. Furthermore, not only the costs of borrowing determine the decision whether and from which institution farmers borrow. We find that when farmers request loans, the money is needed at that time (and not a month later). The fast loan processing time (1–7 days from application to disbursement) can be considered as the most important competitive advantage for ABM generally and for the agricultural lending business in particular.

The sustainability of ABM's agricultural lending will also depend on how the bank will be able to manage the weather risk exposition and specifically covariate weather risks in its loan portfolio in the future. Here, the geological conditions of Madagascar which split the island into different ecological zones sensitive to different weather events guarantee a natural diversification to some extent. The same follows (with regional differences) from farmers' generally well diversified production schemes. However, extreme weather events (e.g., droughts in the western part or hurricanes in the eastern part of the island) can instantaneously affect all seasonal production types in one region. In order to avoid largely negative effects on the banks' performance, ABM can either continue to conservatively assess agricultural yields and commodity price developments or seek for risk transfer instruments (or both). The latter might be too early to consider as the bank currently has only 3.8 % of the total loan portfolio exposed in the primary agricultural sector. However, the bank seeks for an (primary) agricultural share of the total loan portfolio of up to 25 % which might be a different story.

In conclusion, we consider agricultural lending a strategic field of business of ABM. The positive experiences with flex loans have even led to further focusing the agricultural sector in Madagascar by the introduction of new products. Additionally, the positive experience of ABM has led to the launch of flex loans by ABT (and further banks of the AccessHolding Microfinance AG in Africa will follow). Moreover, the warehouse receipt loans which were only recently introduced by ABM already showed demonstration effects for one other MFI in Madagascar.

References

Adams, D.W., Graham, D.H. (1981) A critique of traditional agricultural credit projects and policies. Journal of Development Economics 8(3):347–366.

Armendáriz de Aghion, B., Morduch, J. (2000) Microfinance beyond group lending. Economics of Transition 8(2):401–420.

Armendáriz de Aghion, B., Morduch, J. (2010) The economics of microfinance, 2nd ed. Cambridge, London: The MIT Press.

Binswanger, H.P., Rosenzweig, M.R. (1986) Behavioural and material determinants of production relations in agriculture. Journal of Development Studies 22(3):503–539.

Caudill, S.B., Gropper, D.M., Hartaska, V. (2009) Which microfinance institutions are becoming more cost effective with time? Evidence from a mixture model. Journal of Money, Credit and Banking 41(4):651–672.

Christen, R.P., Pearce, D. (2005) Managing risks and designing products for agricultural microfinance: Features of an emerging model. CGAP Occasional Paper, No. 11.

Czura, K., Karlan, D., Mullainathan, S. (2011) Does flexibility in microfinance pay off? Evidence from a randomized evaluation in rural India. Paper presented at the Northeast Universities Development Consortium Conference 2011, Yale University.

Dalla Pellegrina, L. (2011) Microfinance and investment: A comparison with bank and informal lending. World Development 39(6):882–897.

Duvendack, M., Palmer-Jones, R., Copestake, J.G., Hooper, L., Looke, Y., Rao, N. (2011) What is the evidence of the impact of microfinance on the well-being of poor people? EPPI-Centre, Social Science Research Unit, Institute of Education, University of London, London.

Field, E., Pande, R. (2008) Repayment frequency and default in microfinance: Evidence from India. Journal of the European Economic Association 6(2–3): 501–509.

Field, E., Pande, R., Papp, J., Rigol, N. (2011) Debt structure, entrepreneurship and risk: Evidence from microfinance. Harvard Working Paper.

Godquin, M. (2004) Microfinance repayment performance in Bangladesh: How to improve the allocation of loans by MFIs. World Development 32(11):1909–1926.

Hermes, N., Lensink, R., Meesters, A. (2011) Outreach and efficiency of microfinance institutions. World Development 39(6):938–948.

Jain, S., Mansuri, G. (2003) A little at a time: the use of regularly scheduled repayments in microfinance programs. Journal of Development Economics 72(1): 253–279.

Kong, R., Turvey, C.G. (2008) Vulnerability, trust and microcredit: The case of China's rural poor. Research paper / UNU-WIDER, Vol (2008)52, UNU-WIDER, Helsinki.

Krahnen, J.P., Schmidt, R.H. (1994) Development finance as institution building. A new approach to poverty-oriented banking. Boulder: Westview Press Boulder.

Llanto, G.M. (2007), "Overcoming obstacles to agricultural microfinance: looking at broader issues", Asian Journal of Agriculture and Development 4(2):23–39.

Love, I., Peria, M.S.M. (2012) How bank competition affects firms' access to finance. The World Bank, Development Research Group, Policy Research Paper No (6163).

Maurer, K. (2011) Mobilising Capital for the Poor – How Does Structured Finance Fit in Emerging Markets?" In: Köhn, D. (ed.), Mobilising Capital for Emerging Markets. Berlin Heidelberg: Springer, pp. 13–27.

Meyer, R.L. (2002) The demand for flexible microfinance products: Lessons from Bangladesh. Journal of International Development 14(3):351–368.

Pande, R., Cole, S., Sivasankaran, A., Bastian, G.G., Durlacher, K. (2012) Does poor peoples' access to formal banking services raise their incomes? A systematic review. EPPI-Centre, Social Science Research Unit, Institute of Education, University of London, London.

Shankar, S. (2007) Transaction costs in group microcredit in India. Management Decision 45(8):1331–1342.

Taylor, M. (2011) Freedom from poverty is not for free: Rural development and the microfinance crisis in Andhra Pradesh, India. Journal of Agrarian Change. 11(4):484–504.

Vogelgesang, U. (2003) Microfinance in times of crisis: The effects of competition, rising indebtedness, and economic crisis on repayment behavior. World Development 31(12):2085–2114.

Weber, R., Musshoff, O. (2012) Is agricultural microcredit really more risky? Evidence from Tanzania. Agricultural Finance Review 72(3):416–435.

Weber, R., Musshoff, O. (2013) Can flexible microfinance loans improve credit access for farmers? Agricultural Finance Review 73 (in print).

Weber, R., Musshoff, O., Petrick, M. (2013) How flexible repayment schedules affect credit risk in microfinance. Paper presented at the International Agricultural Risk, Finance and Insurance Conference (IARFIC), Vancouver, Canada, June 16–18, 2013.

CHAPTER 8

The Role of DFIs in the Emerging 3.0 Responsible Funding Landscape – Responsible Corporate Governance and Beyond[*]

Klaus Maurer[**]

Abstract

Development Finance Institutions (DFIs) have been a major funder in microfinance since the 1990s when they took over from donors and brought in a more commercial approach, coupled with much needed capacity building at all levels of the financial system. In their role as catalysts, DFIS have been successfully crowding in the private sector which has brought a fundamental change and diversity to the microfinance funding landscape. Most importantly, local deposits have emerged as the main source of funding which is encouraging as financial intermediation to a large extent replaces the channeling of cross-border funds.

In equity finance, private social investors, mostly in the form of Microfinance Investment Vehicles (MIVs), increasingly take the place of DFIs and their standard-setting role in the governance of MFIs. Governance is perceived as a key risk in microfinance, as shown in the Microfinance Banana Skins surveys, with weaknesses prevailing in main governance areas such as clear ownership structure, disclosure and transparency, and the role and responsibilities of the board. Equity investors are not fully capitalizing on the opportunity to strengthen MFI governance. They must more actively engage in and beyond the board room and ensure adequate qualifications, commitment and continuity of their board nominees.

Several trends visible today are likely to gain momentum and shape the microfinance funding landscape of tomorrow: (i) public funding and subsidies for microfinance will decline further, (ii) local funding and especially local deposits will become the dominant funding source, (iii) more investors will shift from debt towards equity finance (iv) the diversity of funders and their comparative advantages provide a fertile ground for complementarity, and finally (v) the DFIs will

---

[*]   The views and opinions expressed in this paper represent the views and opinions of the author. This paper is published by the author in his own personal capacity and does not reflect the opinions or views of Finance in Motion GmbH.

[**]   Chairman of the Supervisory Board, Finance in Motion GmbH.

continue to play a role as catalysts and standard setters, albeit in a more indirect role from the back seat while MIVs and other intermediaries will be more in the driver seat.

1   Introduction

The microfinance industry has experienced a major upsurge in funding over the past couple of years. CGAP estimates that global cross-border funding in 2011 was in the tune of US$ 25 billion. Development finance institutions (DFIs) have been and continue to be the largest group of funders in quantitative terms but perhaps more important has been their impact beyond funding, i.e. their contribution in setting quality standards in many areas including corporate governance and responsible finance. With the rapid institutional change ongoing in the industry but also with the entry of private investors, the funding landscape is undergoing a fundamental change. This development raises a number of questions: With the crowding in of private investors, is the work of DFIs done? And if so, are DFIs ready to exit? Are the private investors able and willing to step into their shoes and can they maintain the impact beyond funding? Or do we rather see a complementarity of different types of investors, including the DFIs, for some time to come? Who will hold corporate governance in microfinance up to standard? These and other questions are being discussed in the following.

The paper is structured in four parts. Section 2 provides an overview and analyses the pattern of the microfinance funding landscape, characterizes the different investors and the complementarity of their funding, and places cross-border funding into perspective with local funding. Section 3 focuses on the specific role of development finance institutions (DFIs), their specific development role, and their important functions as standard-setters and catalysts of crowding in the private sector. Section 4 highlights the importance of good corporate governance, identifies the key dimensions and discusses the current and future role of DFIs and private investors in promoting good governance. Finally, section 5 sketches an outlook to the future microfinance funding landscape, depicting four main trends.

2   The Microfinance Funding Landscape

2.1 Overview of Microfinance Funding

With the growth and evolution of the global microfinance industry, funding of microfinance has increased substantially over the last decade and a highly diversified funding landscape has emerged. Today's microfinance funding landscape can be broadly classified into foreign or cross-border funding on the one hand and local funding on the other hand, with public and private funders present on both sides, as shown in Chart 1 below. With Microfinance Investment Intermediaries (MIIs),

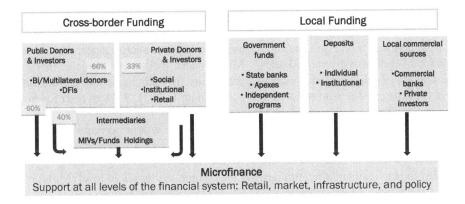

Fig. 1. The Microfinance Funding Landscape
Source: based on CGAP 2010

a new type of player has joined the scene in recent years. These intermediaries comprise Microfinance Investment Vehicles (MIVs) or funds as well as holding companies of MFI or microfinance bank networks.

Obtaining a comprehensive and consistent picture of the funding flows to the microfinance industry remains a major challenge despite a number of laudable initiatives[1] aimed at increasing the transparency of microfinance funding. Partly, this may be due to the fact that a large part of the microfinance industry is still unregulated and hence not reporting to a central supervisor, and partly due to the large number of diverse funders who have entered the scene in recent years. The MFIs reporting to the MIX Market have debt outstanding from close to *one thousand* (!) different lenders (MBB 2012).

2.2 Patterns and Trends of Cross-Border Funding

Total cross-border funding commitments for microfinance has grown considerably to at least US$ 25 billion in 2011 according to CGAP estimates. Ten years ago, cross-border funding was almost exclusively provided by public funders. Even today, public funders still account for the major share of about two thirds. But with microfinance becoming known as an attractive investment opportunity, private investors became a second important source of funding with a current estimated share of one third. Among 59 funders surveyed by CGAP in 2012, DFIs were still the largest group of cross-border funders in microfinance with a share of 55%[2],

---

[1] The major initiatives comprise the annual funder survey by CGAP, the Funding Structure Reports by the MIX Market, MIV surveys by Symbiotics and MicroRate/Luminis.

[2] DFIs committed $9.3 billion out $17.5 billion total cross-border funding of 59 funders participating in the survey.

however, the DFIs' share has been declining from over 60 % in the last three years with private funders increasing their stake.

Funders use *direct* and *indirect* channels to support microfinance. The emergence of specialized intermediaries – Microfinance Investment Vehicles (MIVs) and holdings – has provided a convenient facility for both public and private funders and fostered a trend towards *indirect* funding. In 2011, 37 % of total funding for refinancing was channeled via MIVs and holdings.

Microfinance funding is being allocated to different uses or purposes. Refinancing of MFIs' microcredit portfolios has been – and still is – the major purpose with 77 % of total cross-border funding (CGAP 2012). 15 % of funding is provided for capacity building, primarily at the institutional or micro level (MFIs) but also at the market infrastructure and policy levels (meso and macro).[3]

Debt remains the main financial instrument with 55 % of total commitments in 2011, but its share has been declining. This reduction is compensated by a growing share of equity investments, now reaching 16 %. Among MIVs, this trend towards equity investments in MFIs has been even more pronounced with the share of equity doubling from 12 % in 2008 to 23 % in 2011 (Luminis 2012). Guarantees increased to 9 % while grants account for 15 %. Grants are primarily employed for capacity building while allocating grants to funding of microcredit portfolios has largely been phased out.

The *regional allocation* of cross-border (predominantly public) funding is quite heterogenous while investments by (predominantly private) MIVs are concentrated in Eastern Europe/Central Asia and Latin America (74 % of investments), while Africa, Asia and MENA are highly underserved in view of the potential demand.

Funding in *local currency* presents a major challenge for cross-border funders who are generally not willing or able to absorb currency risk. Only 14 % of the direct debt is provided in local currency. MIVs fare better in making investments in local currency with a share of 28 %, the bulk of which was hedged through various mechanisms. Access to hedging facilities like TCX has enabled MIVs to make significant inroads to local currency investments. However, in the latest survey MIV managers named exchange rate volatility as the top factor hurting MIV performance in 2011 and perceive forex risk and hedging cost as the second main challenge for 2012. Expanding local currency funding will remain a key challenge going forward. In many markets, e.g. in the MENA region, cross-border funding may not be able to compete with local funding.

2.3   Cross-Border Funders Under the Microscope

The global attention and interest in microfinance over the past decade – and further triggered by the 2005 UN Year of Microcredit and the nobel prize to M. Yunus and the Grameen Bank in 2006 – have attracted a variety of funders and

---

[3]   The purpose of the remaining 7 % of funding is unspecified.

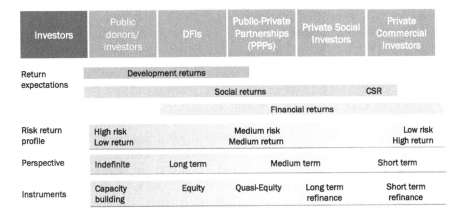

Investors	Public donors/ investors	DFIs	Public-Private Partnerships (PPPs)	Private Social Investors	Private Commercial Investors
Return expectations	Development returns				
	Social returns				CSR
			Financial returns		
Risk return profile	High risk Low return		Medium risk Medium return		Low risk High return
Perspective	Indefinite	Long term		Medium term	Short term
Instruments	Capacity building	Equity	Quasi-Equity	Long term refinance	Short term refinance

Fig. 2. Spectrum of cross-border funders

investors. They differ in objectives and motives, risk and return expectations, time horizon and instruments (see Chart 2) and can be briefly characterized as follows:

- On the left side of the spectrum are purely public funders that are publicly owned and employ public funds. These comprise bi- and multilateral donors such as BMZ, AFD or the IBRD. They combine social and development objectives in their microfinance funding strategy but do not expect any financial return. The definition of "social return" used in this paper refers to outreach and the social impact on the end-clients while "development return" is focused on building institutions and financial systems as a stand-alone objective.

- Development Finance Institutions (DFIs) are publicly owned but employ primarily market funds or a blend of public and market funds, and hence, may be regarded as a hybrid institution. DFIs generally have social, development and financial return expectations ("triple bottom line"). The employment of capital market funds determines the specific risk and (financial) return profile of DFIs and explains why DFIs prefer to invest in safe MFIs.

- On the right side of the spectrum are the private investors which need to be differentiated. Among the private commercial investors there are probably very few who are investing in microfinance for purely financial returns. More prevalent are institutional commercial investors, like insurance companies or pension funds, which take microfinance as an add-on into their portfolios for reasons or corporate social responsibility (CSR).

- The majority of the newly entering private investors are socially responsible investors with a truly double bottom line perspective, i.e. they combine financial returns (with the view of sustainability) and social returns (in terms of outreach and social benefits for the end-clients). Social investors generally do not explicitly pursue the development objective of building institutions and financial systems.

- MIVs and holdings have emerged as new type of players in the microfinance funding landscape and function as intermediaries between asset owners and MFIs. At the end of 2011, there were 115 MIVs with total assets of US$ 7.7 billion (Luminis 2012). Overall, 35 % of MIV funding originated from public and 65 % from private investors. Many MIVs represent a hybrid form where the line between public and private is blurred, e.g. private investor funds with a public guarantee. Some MIVs are set up as public private partnerships, e.g. EFSE or MEF, but there are presumably also many MIVs with private investors only.[4] MIVs are managed by specialized fund managers and investment advisors. Holdings are network structures of either existing or greenfield MFIs or microfinance banks, for example the ProCredit Holding with 21 microfinance banks.[5]

The different types of investors also differ in terms of risk appetite which is highest among donors and lowest among private commercial investors. In terms of investment perspectives, public funders clearly have the longest horizon, private commercial investors the shortest. Each type of investor by nature has its strengths and weaknesses. The long-term horizon of public funders brings stability but public funds are generally scarce while commercial funds from private investors are not limited, at least in principle, but their short-term horizon brings the risk of volatility.

The comparative advantages of different investors can also be read from the type of instruments they provide. While private investors prefer to offer senior (i.e.low-risk) loans with short tenors for refinancing of MFI loan portfolios, donors offer grant funds for long-lasting investments in capacity building and systems development. DFIs, and recently also MIVs, tend to provide subordinate loans, guarantees and equity finance.

Instruments differ greatly in terms of their leverage effect. The leverage tends to be greatest on the left side of the spectrum, e.g. one dollar spent on capacity building might produce a leverage factor 10, and lowest on the very right side, e.g. one dollar expended as one-year loan for refinancing microloans may generate a leverage factor 1 or 2. In between these two poles, a number of high-leverage instruments exist such as equity (with a leverage factor of 8 to 10 depending on the regulatory environment), sub-debt and other hybrid forms.[6] Scarce public funds should therefore maximize their leverage effect.

---

[4]   There were no data available on the number and share of purely private MIVs.

[5]   Other such holdings are Access, Advans, Microcred, and more recently Finca. The greenfield model is discussed in more detail in section 3.

[6]   The various funder surveys by CGAP and others do not reflect this leverage effect. Funding provided through different instruments by different investors is simply added up indiscriminately, thus, clouding the real picture.

Overall, the spectrum is fluid and there are no clear cuts between the different types of investors but rather overlaps. However, the differentiation of investors, their objectives and return expectations, their investment horizon and their specific instruments prepares the ground for an emerging complementarity of public and private funders.

2.4 Local Funding for Microfinance

Although comprehensive and consistent data on local funding sources are still lacking, it is evident from existing data sources that local funding for microfinance has become the primary source of funding, much more important than cross-border funding. This structural change in funding was induced by the changing landscape of microfinance service providers. NGO-MFIs have lost their role as the primary vehicle for microlending, while the relative importance of banks and non-bank financial institutions (NBFIs) has increased. As banks and in some legislations also NBFIs are allowed to take deposits, **local deposits** have advanced to the single most important source of funding in microfinance.

Aggregate MIX Market data provide some order of magnitudes. In 2011, a total of 2,656 MFIs reported total assets of about US$ 115 billion and an aggregate loan portfolio of almost US$ 78 billion. Local deposits mobilized by the same institutions reached US$ 69 billion, or 60% of total assets and over 88% of the loan portfolio. The remaining US$ 46 billion or 40% of assets comprise debt and equity. Earlier analyses found that 60% of debt financing was from local lenders, primarily commercial banks (MBB 2011). Hence, it is safe to conclude that overall some 84% of total funding to MFIs originates from local sources, and the balance 16% or about US$ 18 to 19 billion from cross-border funders which is largely in line with the results from the funder surveys presented in the previous section.[7]

The trend towards local deposit mobilization as the primary source of funding is even more visible in the leading MFIs in the world. The 20 institutions[8] listed in Table 1 below combine a loan portfolio of US$ 25 billion and thus represent one third of the universe, serve 40 million borrowers and 60 million depositors. The results are illustrative when looking at the ratio of deposits to loans (bolded column): In almost half of the cases, local deposits are sufficient to refinance the entire loan portfolios of those institutions. For institutions like Grameen Bank, Acleda Bank or even ProCredit, this picture was unthinkable only ten years ago. The major exception is India at the bottom of the list where credit-only MFIs with funding from local commercial banks have expanded outreach to millions of borrowers but have so far been prevented by a very conservative Reserve Bank of India to accept deposits.

---

[7]   After subtracting the funding provided for capacity building.

[8]   ProCredit is included as the group of 21 banks.

In view of building inclusive financial systems, this development is encouraging in many respects. The shift – in relative terms – from channeling cross-border funds to strengthening local financial intermediation brings stability and reduces the exposure of MFIs and borrowers to currency risk. It clearly confirms that savings are an essential financial service, especially for the poor. In 2011, aggregate MIX Market data recorded 88 million borrowers and an almost identical number of 88 million small savers. For the MFIs, the mobilization of local deposits brings self-sufficiency in funding and imposes greater discipline and prudence in lending operations. In the medium to long term, relatively cheaper local deposits will lower the cost of funds which can be passed on as benefit to the borrowers.

Table 1: The role of local deposits in leading microfinance institutions

		Loan Portfolio US$ bn	Deposits US$ bn	Deposits/ Loans	Borrowers '000	Depositors '000	Ratio Depositors/ Borrowers
Bangladesh	Grameen Bank	1.0	1.6	159%	6,610	8,340	1.3
Indonesia	BRI	3.9	5.9	151%	4,500	19,600	4.4
Colombia	Banca Caja Social	3.0	3.8	127%	625	5,200	8.3
Kenya	Equity bank	1.3	1.5	115%	638	5,700	8.9
Cambodia	Acleda Bank	1.0	1.1	110%	272	822	3.0
Bolivia	Prodem	0.5	0.5	101%	116	688	5.9
SSA, ECA, LAC	ProCredit Group	5.2	4.8	92%	558	3,400	6.1
Bolivia	Bancosol	0.6	0.5	91%	169	485	2.9
Peru	Mibanco	1.6	1.4	88%	435	571	1.3
Bolivia	Banco FIE	0.6	0.5	84%	176	477	2.7
Mongolia	XAC Bank	0.4	0.3	66%	77	382	5.0
Peru	Creditscotia	1.2	0.7	57%	714	529	0.7
Azerbaijan	Access Bank	0.4	0.2	47%	118	110	0.9
Mexico	Compartamos	0.8	0.4	43%	2,300	18	0.0
Bangladesh	BRAC	0.6	0.3	42%	4,960	6,800	1.4
Bangladesh	ASA	0.7	0.2	24%	4,420	6,482	1.5
India	Bandan	0.6	0.0	2%	3,850	0	0.0
India	SKS	0.3	0.0	0%	3,946	0	0.0
India	Spandana	0.6	0.0	0%	3,364	0	0.0
India	Share	0.4	0.0	0%	2,160	0	0.0
TOTAL		24.7	23.5	95%	40,008	59,604	1.5

Source: Own compilation, based on MIX Market data for 2011

Despite the primacy of local funding, cross-border funders will continue to have a role to play. The challenge is rather to seek complementarity of local and cross-border funding along comparative advantages in terms of the different instruments offered to the microfinance sector. It is clear that refinancing of MFI portfolios will be assumed by local sources in local currency, primarily local deposits, or in case of non-deposit-taking MFIs by local financial institutions. For example, India and Morocco are prominent examples where local commercial banks account for the bulk of microfinance funding.[9]

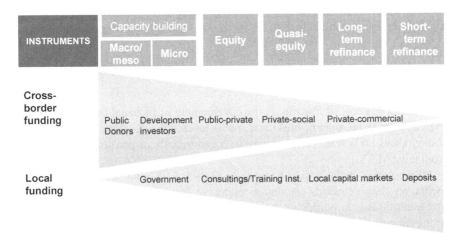

Fig. 3. Complementarity of cross-border and local funders

Cross-border funding is most needed for longer-term refinancing, subordinated and hybrid forms of finance such as mezzanine as well as guarantees, as the local capital markets are still underdeveloped. Equity remains a crucial area where cross-border investors have a role to play in view of the governance that comes with it. Finally, capacity building will be required at all levels of the financial system where cross-border funders have an important role by bringing international good practices and standards.

3   Impact Beyond Funding: Role of DFIs in Promoting an Inclusive Financial System and a Responsible Finance Landscape

DFIs have engaged with microfinance programs and institutions globally, taking the lead in the early 1990s from donor agencies that have been supporting micro-

---

[9]   India due to priority sector lending.

finance initiatives in the early phases. The DFIs assumed the risk of a sector that had an unproven business model, bringing in a more commercial approach, coupled with much needed capacity building and technical know-how.

Beyond this quantitative lead, DFIs have had – and continue to have – an important qualitative role in the funding landscape and have had an impact on the development of microfinance which extends beyond funding. At least three important functions of DFIs should be highlighted: (i) their role as "development investors" focused on building inclusive financial systems at macro, meso and micro levels, (ii) their role as standard setter, e.g. in corporate governance, responsible finance and other fields, and (iii) their role as catalyst and match-maker by crowding in private sector institutions.

3.1 Development Role: Capacity Building for Financial Systems Development

DFIs perform a crucial function in the development of financial systems by building capacity at the macro, meso and micro level. This development role clearly distinguishes DFIs from private investors, even socially responsible investors, and from most MIVs.

DFIs engage at the policy (macro) level and work with lawmakers, governments, regulators towards creating a conducive framework for finance in general and microfinance in particular. At the meso level, DFIs support the development of the financial sector infrastructure. The IFC, for example, has been active in setting up credit bureaus in several countries and has recently supported the establishment of mobile banking platforms. In Bosnia and Herzegovina, KfW and USAID were instrumental in setting up the deposit insurance which has boosted the confidence among small savers to deposit their money in local banks. Another prominent example is the Currency Exchange Fund (TCX), a hedging facility set up in 2007 by a group of leading DFIs which has since played a key role in expanding local currency funding.

At the micro level, DFIs have significantly contributed to institution building of banks and MFIs. To this end, DFIS have pursued a three-pronged strategy of downscaling of commercial banks, transformation of MFIs and setting up of greenfield microfinance banks. Through debt and equity investments coupled with technical assistance many commercial banks were introduced to lending to micro, small and medium enterprises (MSMEs) and after a phase of learning and experimentation have been convinced of the business case of MSME finance. DFIs played a key role in the transformation of former NGO-MFIs into successful microfinance banks which are regarded as the leading players such as Acleda Bank in Cambodia, XAC Bank in Mongolia and Compartamos in Mexico, to name a few.

But the model which DFIs are most prominently associated with, is the establishment of greenfield microfinance banks. The first bank was founded in the mid-1990s and today the model is well-known: Several DFIs join forces and form a club of reputable shareholders, and jointly with a strong technical partner prepare and set up a specialized bank for microfinance. During the start-up phase, the technical partner provides management and technical advisory services. The experience has shown that, within two to three years, a Greenfield bank can reach break even.

ProCredit has been the precursor of this model (Laude 2009) with meanwhile 21 microbanks newly established on three continents over the past fifteen years. In a second stage, the banks were subsumed under a holding company where again DFIs have been key shareholders. In the process, many DFIs swapped their earlier shareholdings in the retail banks with a stake in the holding company. In the meantime, the model has been replicated by other technical operators which have created holding companies with DFI participation: Access, Advans, Microcred, Swiss Microfinance Holding. Together with ProCredit Holding, these five holdings today control 42 microbanks serving 1.2 million borrowers with a combined loan portfolio of US$ 6 billion and 4.3 million savers with a deposit volume of US$ 4.8 billion. This is a remarkable achievement in terms of sustainable massive outreach in a relatively short period of time. The banks are spread across Eastern Europe, Africa and Latin America while the whole of Asia and the MENA region have so far not been a target for the greenfield model. Furthermore, international MFI networks like Opportunity International, Finca and CHF have recently adopted a similar model of transforming retail MFIs into for-profit companies under a holding structure, some with participation of DFIs.

DFIs also provided a major impulse in the field of product development beyond microfinance. They have been pioneering into green finance including energy efficiency, agricultural finance and more recently education finance. In many countries, banks and other financial institutions have integrated these products into their portfolio.

3.2   Setting Standards in Good Governance and Responsible Finance

Impact beyond funding has also been achieved through standard setting in the young industry, and DFIs have played a leading role in many areas. Promoting good corporate governance has been one of the areas where DFIs have set standards across the industry through their engagement as shareholders in the transformation of MFIs and in the greenfield model described above. The promotion of good governance is the special focus of this paper and is discussed in the next section.

Closely linked to good governance is the area of responsible finance where DFIs have been equally instrumental in setting standards and promoting industry norms and codes. Responsible finance is being understood in a wider sense than social performance and client protection.[10] DFIs, and specifically the IFC, were

---

[10]   The term "responsible finance" first appeared in February 2008 as the lead theme of a conference organized by KfW and Frankfurt School of Finance and Management.

the first to set *do no harm* standards and introduce environmental and social exclusion lists. Anti-money laundering requirements and integrity standards are further important elements in a responsible finance framework. These insertions have become important building blocks of the bridge between the microfinance industry and the global ESG (Environment-Social-Governance) standards adopted by the mainstream finance and investment industry.

The holdings, international MFI networks and the MIVs have become a prime platform for DFIs for putting responsible finance on the agenda, thereby reaching out to a large network of retail microfinance institutions. For example, the European Fund for Southeast Europe (EFSE) as one of the largest MIV where all major DFIs are invested conducted a series of high-level responsible finance events jointly with the central banks in several Eastern European countries. EFSE's Development Facility was the first to conduct an in-depth study on over-indebtedness in the microfinance sector in Bosnia and Herzegovina, and further research in other countries has followed since.

3.3 Catalyst and Matchmaker: Crowding in the Private Sector Through Public Private Partnerships

The most important and powerful function of DFIs is their catalyst role of fostering the entry of private sector institutions into areas considered as high risk or unprofitable. This is done through demonstrations ("lighthouse examples"), capacity building and effectively enhancing the institutional governance of their investee companies as shown above, but also through various forms of public private partnerships and arrangements.

The prime comparative advantage of DFIs lies in their enhancement power which derives from the AAA-Rating that most DFIs have. This allows them to provide credit enhancement in financing structures, e.g. subordinate tranches, as well as guarantees which are considered first-class by regulators across the world. In many financing structures which at first sight appear to be private market transactions DFIs have taken catalytic positions by providing enhancement. BOLD (BlueOrchard Loans for Development 2006–1)[11], the first collateralized loan obligation (CLO) in microfinance in 2006 is just one example where a DFI, the Dutch FMO in this case, took a crucial first loss position and made the structure feasible.

As outlined above, over the past ten years DFIs have increasingly taken catalytic positions in holdings and MIVs. In most cases, they take a subordinate stake, typically the mezzanine piece, thus catalyzing private investors who opt for the senior and lower risk tranches. This has been the model for public private fund structures like EFSE, REGMIFA, MEF and others. Interestingly, DFIs act as a catalyst not only for private investors but, in their mezzanine position, also vis-à-

---

[11] BOLD raised a total amount of USD 99.1 million for loans disbursed to 21 MFIs, in 13 different countries, and 5 different currencies.

vis purely public investors and donors who value the leverage power and regard the DFIs as the 'middlemen' to the private sector and the link to the capital markets. When providing valuable first loss funding, some bilateral donors make it a condition that DFIs provide mezzanine investment on top or in parallel.

The participation of DFIs in wholesale structures or retail institutions brings reputation and credibility for the investees and provides a quality seal for other investors and especially for regulators. The fact that a MFI has undergone a thorough due diligence by a DFI is frequently perceived as an entry signal to MIVs and private investors. Most importantly, however, is the DFIs' clout in the negotiations with regulators. The experience with transformation of MFIs and setting up greenfield microbanks has proven that the presence of DFIs as reputable shareholders – direct in the retail institution or indirect via a holding – is crucial for obtaining a license as a deposit-taking institution where shareholders need to be approved by the regulator. While socially responsible investors and MIVs may be well-known in the microfinance community, they are a blank page for most regulators, to say the least. Some regulators are "reluctant" to "suspicious" to approve "investment funds with strange names" as shareholders of banks.[12] On the other hand, as the regulatory environment is not always conducive, the presence of DFIs brings protection for retail MFIs in dealing with the authorities and is very useful in assuring a smooth relationship in volatile political environments.

Crowding in of the private sector is a main pillar in the mandate and raison d'etre of the DFIs. It is intended and encouraged as it demonstrates the sustainability of the business model, and often made a condition for DFI engagement. And the DFIs' role and presence is generally valued by the private investors. Despite good intentions, the relationship between DFIs and private investors is occasionally exposed to some tension. The debate revolves around three contentious issues which are closely interrelated: (i) technical assistance, (ii) the different roles of public and private investors, and (iii) exit.

On (i) technical assistance and capacity building, private investors are somewhat ambiguous. On the one hand, they value the much needed capacity building and technical know-how provided by DFIs in the development stage of MFIs which has brought many institutions to the level of investor-readiness. On the other hand, DFIs are perceived to have a competitive advantage in terms of offering capacity building programs and technical assistant packages as "deal sweeteners" which does not necessarily level the playing field (Sanyoura and Espejo 2011). While the criticism may be valid for single cases, closing down technical assistance by DFIs would be like throwing out the child with the bathwater. More encouraging is the trend among several private investors and MIVs of setting up their own technical assistance facilities for capacity building of their investees. Many investors have realized only during the financial crisis that even well-performing 1st tier and 2nd tier MFIs urgently need institutional strengthening – beyond financial investments alone – in areas such as risk management and internal controls.

---

[12] Personal communication with supervisors from two central banks.

Behind the second issue, concerning the different roles of public and private in-vestors, is the view expressed by some private investors that DFIs have been slow to adapt to the growing appetite of private investors to engage and provide funding for the microfinance sector, not making enough room for the private investors. In the case of senior loans, there seems to be an overlap of DFI funding and private investors in view of the growing yet still limited number of MFIs ready to absorb commercial funding. This could lead to an over-supply of funds to certain market segments, while there is still much unmet demand in others. The critics say that DFIs continue to invest in mature 1st and 2nd tier MFIs while they should make room for the private investors and move "downstream" to small 3rd and 4th tier in-stitutions because DFIs should be assuming the risks that private investors are still not willing or able to assume. The counter-argument is that DFIs, albeit being public-owned institutions, employ capital market funds and hence need to main-tain a certain standard of credit risk rating, thereby inducing the tendency to stay within a relatively conservative circle of mature and well-performing MFIs. This is further reinforced by the DFIs' limitations – given their operating cost structures – of making small ticket investments as needed by early stage MFIs. These risk and cost considerations prevent DFIs from expand the frontier beyond a certain limit. Going forward, it will be important to ensure that there is no overlap but complementarity.

This discussion leads to the third issue, exit by DFIs. Long-term commitment in a certain geographic region or a certain sector is crucial to any DFI's development mission. Especially during the financial crisis of 2008 when private investors sig-nificantly reduced their commitments, the DFIs' motto "we are here to stay" was welcome and appropriate. The DFIs' ability to act as lenders of last resort und thus help stabilize unsettled funding markets is recognized also by private investors who generally have a much shorter investment horizon than DFIs. The theory is straight-forward: *When a MFI has the capacity to mobilize resources from finan-cial markets by the quality of its financial statements, the aim of the DFI may be considered as having been reached. It is then time for the DFI to withdraw. It is then desirable for it to recycle its equity investment and allow its client to bring in carefully selected private institutional investors. This will undoubtedly make the mission more sustainable.* (Laude 2009) However, in practice it is not always ob-vious – particularly when it comes to equity positions. The case for debt, espe-cially short-term senior debt to refinance microcredit portfolios, is clear: in many cases the time is right to now leave the field to the private sector and especially to local fund providers including depositors.

The situation is more complex with equity investments. While DFIs may have an initial investment horizon of say eight years, there seem to be little or no spe-cific internal guidelines in terms of the stage of the investment at which a DFI should exit. As a consequence, DFIs tend to stay longer than anticipated (Sany-oura and Espejo 2011).[13] The governance role associated with an equity invest-

---

[13]   More research would be required to firmly substantiate this statement.

ment adds a further dimension and raises the question of *responsible* exit strategies to be discussed below.

The ongoing trend in the greenfield model of DFIs consolidating their individual equity stakes in retail microbanks into one larger stake at the holding level can be seen as a first stage of exit. In addition, this "upstream" consolidation brings cost savings through economies of scale. Occasionally, however, a DFI is already invested at the holding level and yet takes another major stake in a retail greenfield bank newly to be established under the same holding. This is useful in order to create value at holding level; however it is critical for DFIs to consider when to exit the affiliate, once it has matured and reached full sustainability.

3.4 Future Role of DFIs

Financial systems in most countries are far from being inclusive. The work is not done and, going forward, DFIs will have a role to play. DFIs need to sharpen their instruments and interventions, strictly adhering to their comparative advantages and additionality: remain a development investor, standard-setter and catalyst. This is when DFIs achieve the greatest impact beyond funding.

DFIs can provide additionality in funding by developing and providing a variety of financing instruments so far not offered by private investors, for example subordinate and mezzanine finance, guarantees and other enhancement products. There is a role for building local capital and bond markets to allow such products to be offered locally in the medium and long term.

DFIs continue to have a role as equity investors, at least in the back seat of MIVs and holdings. Especially in deposit-taking institutions where regulators look for reputable shareholders before granting a license DFIs can offer additionality in credibility and standing. MIVs, particularly closed-ended equity funds are often not the preferred candidates as shareholders in banks as they are less able to respond to a capital call in an emergency. When MIVs have the backing of DFIs, the notion of patient capital and deep pockets are convincing factors.

Should DFIs move "downstream" to smaller 3rd and 4th tier MFIs? The answer would be: generally no, for three reasons. Firstly, it is not their comparative advantage to work directly with very small and high-risk MFIs for reasons mentioned earlier. DFIs have started to delegate this work to privately managed MIVs and holdings in which they invest, and these are more agile and flexible in dealing with smaller institutions. Secondly, the business case has been made that microfinance is a sustainable and profitable venture in the pioneering work by the DFIs since the 1990s. Especially the greenfield model has shown that microfinance banks set up as a franchise can reach profitability within 2 to 3 years. Also, DFIs have demonstrated how to develop and transform small MFIs into successful profitable operations. In this respect, the demonstration work of DFIs is done, and the time is right for the private sector to replicate the approach. Thirdly, there is a general trend among DFIs to move "upstream" and focus resources and effort on the specialized intermediaries, i.e. MIVs and holdings. This trend is also visible in the DFI funding flows: the share of indirect funding through MIVs and holdings increased from 38% (2007) to 48% (2011). It is clear that DFIs are increasingly taking the backseat and invite MIVs, holdings and their managers to take the driver seats.

Could or should these private sector vehicles not take over the breeding of small existing or new MFIs? In fact, early initiatives in this regard are emerging. Several MIVs formed a working group in 2011 to explore ways and means to support smaller MFIs. The group plans to build a directory of 2nd and 3rd tier MFIs, to reflect on foreign exchange hedging and small transactions sizes, and to coordinate much-needed technical assistance (e-MFP 2011). With the development blue print on the table, the demonstration of the business case done, the know how and tools available, the case and the vision for private venture capital to take over may be ripe: *It is time for the sector to come to terms with the reality that more venture capital type investors are needed to ramp up the business model in order for it to become truly mainstream.* (Sanyoura and Espejo 2011)

4   Special Focus: Promoting Good Corporate Governance

4.1   Why Is Corporate Governance so Important in Microfinance?

The quality of corporate governance is a key factor – and also a key risk – for the performance of MFIs. Some piece of evidence to support this is annual Microfinance Banana Skins' survey conducted among several hundred microfinance practitioners, analysts and regulators. Since the first survey in 2008, corporate governance has consistently ranked high on the scale of perceived risks. In the latest survey in 2012, it ranked second overall (see Chart 4) while some key stakeholders – regulators and investors – even named corporate governance as the number one risk in MFIs.

2008	2009	2011	2012
1. Management quality	1. Credit risk	1. Credit risk	1. Overindebtedness
2. Corporate governance	2. Liquidity	2. Reputation	**2. Corporate governance**
3. Inappropriate regulation	3. Macroeconomic trends	3. Competition	3. Management quality
4. Cost control	4. Management quality	**4. Corporate governance**	4. Credit risk
5. Staffing	5. Refinancing	5. Political interference	5. Political interference
6. Interest rates	6. Too little funding	6. Inappropriate regulation	6. Risk management
7. Competition	**7. Corporate governance**	7. Management quality	7. Client management
8. Managing technology	8. Foreign currency	8. Staffing	8. Competition
9. Political interference	9. Competition	9. Mission drift	9. Regulation
10. Credit risk	10. Political interference	10. Unrealisable expectations	10. Liquidity

Fig. 4. Corporate Governance in Microfinance Banana Skins Surveys

The growing importance of corporate governance is also induced by the ongoing transformation of the microfinance sector and the resulting institutional change. Many MFIs are in transition to larger and more professional institutions with a more differentiated organizational structure, delegation of authority and wider array of checks and balances. As the institutions mature, they gradually formalize functions previously executed informally, in their boards, their management and among their staff.

In particular, the transformation of MFIs into deposit-taking institutions demands greater responsibility and prudence where strong shareholders, a solid capital basis and good governance are key factors, on the one hand. On the other hand, by being able to offer a wider range of services, especially savings, MFIs expand their client outreach to poorer segments who do not have the capacity for microcredit. In this respect, good governance is directly linked to client outreach and social performance.

Finally, good governance is central to the overall performance of an MFI. In a recent pilot project, the MIX tested a new set of governance indicators among a sample of 162 MFIs across 57 countries. Reporting on these indicators showed a positive correlation among factors such as the presence of risk management functions, internal auditing, and Board committees, suggesting that good MFI governance procedures do not exist in isolation from each other (Pistelli et al. 2012).

BANEX in Nicaragua is an example where more effective governance could have mitigated the impact or even averted failure (McKee 2012). Other examples show that crises and financial distress can create huge additional strains on governance.

4.2 Principles, Dimensions and Areas of Good Corporate Governance

Broadly defined by the OECD, corporate governance involves a set of relationships between a company's management, its board, its shareholders and other stakeholders. Corporate governance also provides the structure through which the objectives of the company are set, and the means of attaining those objectives and monitoring performance. The OECD Principles of Corporate Governance issued in 1999 have become an international benchmark for policy makers, investors, corporations and other stakeholders worldwide. They focus on the following key dimensions: (i) ensuring the basis for an effective corporate governance framework including legal and regulatory requirements, (ii) key ownership functions and the rights of shareholders and their equitable treatment, (iii) disclosure and transparency, and (iv) responsibilities of the board. The Financial Stability Forum has designated the OECD Principles as one of the twelve key standards for sound financial systems.

An effective corporate governance framework should promote transparency and efficiency, be consistent with the rule of law and clearly articulate the division of responsibilities among different supervisory, regulatory and enforcement authorities (OECD 2004). The internal governance framework comprises – in addition to the board as the key element – different organs and actors, including specific board committees, executive management, risk management separated from operations and an independent internal audit. In addition to the key governance dimensions listed above, corporate governance covers a wide range of areas such as internal and external reporting (linked to the dimension of disclosure and transparency), non-financial and financial incentive structures including compensation schemes, addressing conflicts of interest, internal systems of accountability, code of conduct among staff and several more. From the range of areas it becomes clear that the topic of governance is multi-facetted and, while there are generally accepted principles, the governance structure in an organization also has to fit to the business culture of that organization.

Governance in microfinance is inherently more complex than in other sectors due to the industry's implicit double bottom line. In recent years, governance has become a prime topic for research and discussion and a growing consensus on principles of good corporate governance has emerged in the industry, both on the importance of good governance – as reflected in the results of the Microfinance Banana Skins Surveys – as well as on their implementation – as reflected in several implementation guidelines and tools published recently.[14] However, recent research has revealed a considerable gap between the ideal of effective MFI governance and the reality on the ground (CGAP 2012). Some of these shortcomings relate to the key dimensions of governance selected for further discussion: ownership and shareholder structure, the role of the board and shareholder exit.

4.3   Clear Ownership Structure and Shareholder Rights

Good corporate governance starts with clear ownership. This provides the essential basis for accountability and responsibility in an organization. The absence of clear ownership and an often diffuse stakeholder structure have been inherent weaknesses of NGO-MFIs, and with it, the greatest vulnerability of a large part of the microfinance industry. In the past, most MFIs have been incorporated as foundations, trust funds or associations, i.e. all of them legal forms with no real owners. Over the years, these institutions have accumulated donor grants which were further grown by retained earnings into a sizable capital base which one might want to call "donorship". The transformation of "donorship" into real ownership remains a key challenge for NGO-MFIs. In most cases, it involves a complex, painful and lengthy process. Several examples of a successful transformation exist, e.g. Bancosol in Bolivia, Acleda in Cambodia or Compartamos in Mexico, but in many environments NGO-MFIs are struggling with legal and/or political obstacles. In countries like Bosnia and Herzegovina, Kosovo, Egypt and lately Iraq the transformation process has been stalled for years.

---

[14]   These include Rock et al 1998, CMEF 2012, Fundación Mikrofinanzas BBVA 2011, IFC 2010, Vita and Gonzalez 2011.

The greenfield approach pursued by DFIs in cooperation with strong technical partners over the past decade has been straightforward in terms of ownership. The key element and a major success factor of this approach has been the gathering of strategic and like-minded shareholders with common objectives, primarily DFIs[15] and lately also private socially responsible investors. This club of DFI shareholders has enacted a highly effective governance structure, initially through direct shareholding and board membership in the early greenfield operations and today largely in an indirect manner via the respective holding company.

The DFIs have been the pioneers in microfinance equity investments, and through this ownership participation have had a key role in promoting good corporate governance through active engagement. Even today, DFIs are still the largest equity investors with US$2.3 billion in microfinance equity in 2011 (CGAP 2012). However, in the rapidly changing funding landscape MIVs have grown to become the second most important source of equity capital with almost US$ one billion in 2011 (Symbiotics 2012).

4.4   Role and Responsibilities of the Board

A key element of good governance is the functional separation of board and management. The guiding concept is a two-tier system of accountability where a supervisory body holds an executive body accountable for performance. The challenges are (i) to structure an effective board in terms of size, composition, qualification, responsibilities, compensation, adoption of a conflict of interest policy, and with the right balance of governance and management, and (ii) to structure effective board processes including the preparation and conduct of meetings, decision-making etc.

The reality on the ground is still far from this ideal and many MFIs have a long way to go in order to achieve those standards. Governance by the board is particularly weak in NGO-MFIs in several respects. Firstly, accountability of board members is structurally weak due to the absence of clear ownership. Secondly, board members are often volunteers with social background and little know how in finance. Thirdly, management capture is the greatest vulnerability in MFIs with weak board governance. It happens often that a charismatic CEO or general manager dominates the board, thus weakening the board's oversight of the MFI and the board merely serving as a rubber stamp for the management.

The opposite may also be the case where the board dominates governance, especially where charismatic founders are in the chair position. Such board may try to manage and not govern. Especially, when the management is perceived as weak the board may engage in operational issues – become a *hands-on* board as the other extreme to the *rubber-stamp* board (Rock 1998) – and hence depart from its govern-

---

15   Many of the greenfield banks had the same or a similar composition of DFI shareholders dubbed as "the usual suspects" which comprised KfW, IFC, EBRD, FMO and EIB.

ance function of setting the policy and strategic framework. One of the most important and delicate tasks in creating good governance is to achieve a proper balance of functions between the board and management, avoiding either board or management capture (CMEF 2012).

Again, equity investors have an important role in strengthening governance through active engagement on the board. A key function of the board is the definition and subsequent implementation of the organization's mission. DFIs have had a pioneering role by appointing representatives to the boards of MFIs whose primary concern has been to keep the organization oriented towards the double bottom line of social and financial returns. Their role within these boards is almost like that of an "activist" constantly working for a dual social and financial objective (Laude 2009).

Setting the responsible finance agenda has become another important topic for the board room. In the wake of some recent excesses and local crises, MFI boards need to provide policy guidance to management on thorny issues such as responsible portfolio growth, transparent pricing and balanced returns. This includes also a debate about overheated markets or market segments in an increasingly competitive environment and the formulation of an appropriate response strategy. In a recent research (MCKee 2012), CGAP found the hot button strategic decisions in the boardroom of MFIs surprisingly consistent among a diverse pool of interviewees (see Box below).

Which Decisions Are Reported to Generate the Most Controversy in the Board Room?

- How fast to grow and where

- Which new products to offer and which client segments to prioritize

- How to price products and ensure long-term client protection

- What profit targets are appropriate and how should profits be allocated

- What level of executive remuneration is appropriate

- How to handle capital increases, entry of new owners, and responsible exit

- How to handle crisis

Source: McKee 2012

With the growing diversification of the funding landscape, the investors' role and influence in the governance of microfinance is shifting from DFIs to intermediaries like MIVs and holdings. Recent research by CGAP (McKee 2012) found that MIVs and holdings today assume 208 (64 %) out of 325 board seats, with DFIs taking 29 % or 93 board seats. The research concludes that equity in-

vestors are not fully capitalizing on the opportunity to strengthen MFI governance. It concluded that investors should (i) more actively engage in and beyond
the board room, (ii) ensure adequate qualifications, time commitment and continuity of their board nominees, and (iii) increase efforts towards aligning shareholder interests. It seems that the new investors have some way to go to step into
the DFIs' shoes, to fully assume responsibilities as actively engaged board
members and to live up to the expectations associated with their role as active
promoters of good corporate governance.

This then raises the question of corporate governance at the next higher level,
i.e. the MIVs and their private fund managers, where essentially the same principles and crucial governance issues apply. Apart from anecdotal evidence, little insight is available on the governance in over 115 MIVs. The EFSE, for example,
has developed and adopted comprehensive guidelines on good corporate governance. The MIV surveys make an attempt to capture ESG aspects but only two indicators focus on governance, transparency and anti-corruption policy. Accordingly, 86 % of MIVs report on ESG aspects to their investors and 84 % of MIVs
apply anti-☐corruption and/or internal whistleblowing policies to their investments (Symbiotics 2012).

4.5 Responsible Exit Strategies

The double bottom line in microfinance introduces the dimension of equity investors' responsibility with regard to exit strategies. Two aspects are particularly relevant in this regard: the timing of the exit and how to preserve the mission after exit.

When is the right time for an exit from a MFI? There is no universal answer to
this question as it differs for different investors. Intuitively, it should neither be too
early nor too late. The risk of a too early exit is associated primarily with private
commercial investors who tend to have a short-term investment horizon. To mitigate
this risk, some shareholder agreements will include a "lock up clause" that prevents
shareholders from exiting within a pre-determined period, eg. five years. This en-
sures that shareholders in ad advance agree to remain vested in the mission of the
MFI for a longer time horizon (CMEF 2012). Exit provisions also help to protect
minority shareholders and to maintain a continuity of like-minded ownership. Key
exit issues should be anticipated and negotiated early in the shareholders' agreement. With DFI shareholders rather the opposite is the case: as patient investors they
tend to exit later than initially anticipated. While this may not pose a risk to the respective investee but it prevents precious DFI equity capital being recycled to other
MFIs. In this regard, the gradual exit of DFIs in the greenfield model from retail
MFIs and the consolidation at the holding level is a first important step.

The other challenge of microfinance exits is the need to preserve the social mission. DFIs are particularly concerned, given the amount and effort invested in the
institution, to sell their stake to carefully selected investors. Some socially responsible investors may prefer to exit by selling their shares to other socially responsible investors, even at lower return (CMEF 2012). Therefore, investor screening

and selection constitutes a key element of responsible exit strategies. Selection criteria would include their objectives and mission, risk and return expectations, investment horizon, ownership structure, integrity and reputation, and their track record in microfinance.

4.6 Promoting Good Corporate Governance: Whose Role in the Future?

The changing landscape of microfinance funding is naturally bringing a change in roles of different funders. MIVs and their private managers as well as the holding companies are increasingly taking the driver seats in the governance of MFIs. DFIs are taking the back seats and continue to exert influence more indirectly through their stakes and board seats in the holdings and the MIVs. DFIs must make sure that MIVs and their representatives on the boards of MFIs are professionally and actively engaged. CGAP's recent finding that most microfinance investors are not taking an active enough role should be taken as an early warning.

The other element for promoting good governance in the future is strengthening the "sector governance" through investor coordination (e-MFP 2011). Lenders groups and other peer groups may play a more active role in setting standards and defining codes for the industry. It is encouraging that most of the principles and guidelines on corporate governance, previously the domain of DFIs, come from such peer groups and industry associations.

Most crucial for future governance, however, is the growing importance of a completely stakeholder group, the local savers and depositors who already are or will be the main funders of microfinance in the future. They are represented by the prudential regulators and supervisors in the respective countries. While regulators are generally aligned on principles and practices of corporate governance as they relate to the financial, fiduciary and prudential side, many of them are on a steep learning curve when it comes to social side and how to balance both sides under the microfinance industry's double bottom line. This opens a new dimension for promoting good corporate governance in the future.

5   Outlook: The Microfinance Funding Landscape of Tomorrow

The paper has illustrated the microfinance landscape today and its evolution in the past years. It has identified some main trends and some of these will gain momentum in the future.

5.1 Further Decreasing Public Funds and Subsidies for Microfinance

The role of public funders in microfinance will further decrease, particularly in the field of debt financing and with it the amount of truly public funds and subsidies while private investors, mostly socially responsible investors, are likely to further increase their presence and commitment to the sector.

This trend implies that the scarce public resources should be employed in a highly effective manner. This implies two things: (i) to maximize the leverage of public funds and (ii) to use subsidies in a highly targeted and "smart" way. For example, employing scarce public funds as *first loss* tranches in structured funds or similar public-private-partnership arrangements can create a significant leverage. When such structure is further enhanced through mezzanine finance from DFIs the risk threshold is lowered to a level that is attractive for private investors, or that is even acceptable to more commercial institutional investors, thus pushing the frontier even further.

Creating conducive frameworks through capacity building at sector and macro levels have probably the highest leverage as will enable the private sector to flourish. A lot of work is to be done in many countries to make regulations conducive to microfinance, to introduce secured transactions frameworks including collateral registries, to establish or open up credit bureaus for micro borrowers, to name a few activities where public subsidies should be targeted in a smart and effective way.

Going forward, therefore the allocation of public funds for microfinance should be critically scrutinized in terms of their leverage and additionality effects.

5.2 Ongoing Trend Towards Increased Local Funding: Local Deposits and Capital Markets

The issue of financial inclusion has been put on the agenda of high-level fora such as the G20 and of many national governments. More and more countries are expected to enact conducive laws and regulations to allow for deposit-taking MFIs. This will enable many more MFIs to offer a whole range of services to clients beyond microcredit, especially savings. There are many more potential savers than potential borrowers among the 2.7 billion poor of this world. Recent research on the state of the microfinance industry concludes that the latent demand for microcredit seems to be limited and the actual gap in serving the poor is much smaller than the estimates frequently put forward (Lützenkirchen and Weistoffer 2012).

What is the ideal share of local versus cross-border funding over time? The experience of the most successful microfinance institutions clearly shows that loan portfolios – which are mostly short-term – can over time be entirely funded by local deposits. Building inclusive and sustainable financial systems is about fostering financial intermediation rather than channeling of cross-border funds. Therefore, the role of cross-border funders *for the refinancing of microcredit portfolios* will clearly diminish. Their market niche will shrink to those countries where MFIs are not permitted to accept local deposits. And even there, as the cases of India or Morocco demonstrate, the local financial institutions with their comparative advantage of local currency financing will likely pick up a larger share in the future.

What role then for the private social investors that have entered the microfinance field with so much enthusiasm and appetite? They will need to seek additionality by offering different instruments such as equity, subordinated debt and other hybrid forms of risk capital (see below). If their mandate allows, they should also look into longer-term loans to refinance e.g. investment loans to very small and small enterprises, so far the domain of DFIs. Many of these enterprises have graduated from the microenterprise segment and require loan amounts above the microfinance threshold and longer tenors. Most of the greenfield banks are already serving these clients and many existing MFIs look into upscaling into the small enterprise market.

In most countries, local capital markets are highly underdeveloped and in a nascent state. This holds true for both bond and equity markets. Cross-border funders have an important role in filling the gap but also in catalyzing local capital market transactions and building local bond and equity markets.

5.3   Increasing Trend Towards Equity and Other Forms of Risk Capital

The current trend towards equity and other forms of risk capital will further increase. From 2008 to 2011, MIVs have doubled the share of equity financing in their overall funding from 12 % to 23 % while the share of debt declined to 76 % (Luminis 2012). The rising demand for equity is a reflection of the ongoing transformation of NGO-MFIs into for-profit companies and microfinance banks. Banks and other deposit-taking institutions per se have higher minimum capital and capital adequacy requirements. Moreover, the recently established microfinance holdings plan to establish at least two additional greenfield banks per year which will create a surge in capital. But also other forms of risk capital will be required such as mezzanine finance or subordinated loans, e.g. in regulatory regimes that acknowledge sub-debt as tier-2 capital, and other hybrid instruments.

5.4   Working Towards Complementarity Between Public and Private Funders

As the market for cross-border funders will narrow down, particularly in the field of debt finance, and become more focused, the likelihood of overlaps of different types of investors will also increase. Yet it is important to acknowledge the different roles played by the purely public funders, the DFIs, the MIVs and the private social investors, with a view to foster more differentiation and complementarity. What comparative advantages do different funders bring to the table? What do private investors expect from public funders and DFIs, and vice versa, what do MFIs and public funders expect from private investors? A constructive debate among the different funders on these issues would help pave the way to greater complementarity in a market which – in any case – will be increasingly covered by local funders and local deposits and where cross-border funders will have to sharpen the additionality of their respective offers.

5.5   What Future Role for DFIs?

As outlined earlier, DFIs will continue to have a role to play in the future as cata-lysts and match-makers but also in capacity building, especially at the macro and sector levels, and in promoting high standards in areas like corporate governance or responsible finance. What will change is the level of engagement. The current trend of DFIs working increasingly through intermediaries such as MIVs and holdings will likely gain further momentum and the tendency of working directly with retail MFIs will likely diminish. DFIs will operate more indirectly – from the back seat – while MIVs and private investors will be more in the driving seat.

DFIs will maintain additionality in funding by providing financing instruments, for example subordinate and mezzanine finance, guarantees and other enhance-ment products, as long as these products are not offered by private investors. Fi-nally, there is a key role of DFIs in building local capital and bond markets to al-low such products to be offered locally in the medium and long term. While some of these products may seem overly sophisticated for microfinance today they are an important building block of an inclusive financial system in the future.

References

CGAP (2011) Cross-Border Funding of Microfinance. Global Trends 2007–2010. December 2011.

Council of Microfinance Equity Funds (CMEF) (2012) The practice of corporate governance in microfinance institutions.

European Microfinance Platform (e-MFP) (2011) Sharing innovative practices for responsible microfinance investment. Brief No.2: Strengthening governance for responsible finance: Examples from European investment funds. October 2011.

Fundación Microfinanzas BBVA (2011) Guide for the Adoption of Good Govern-ance Principles in Microfinance Institutions. March 2011 1st edition. Madrid.

International Finance Corporation (IFC) (2010) Corporate Governance.

Lapenu, C., Pierret, D. (2006) Handbook for the analysis of the governance of ofi-nance institutions. IFAD, GTZ, BMZ, CERISE, IRAM.

Lascelles, D. (2012) Microfinance – A Risky Business. A Time for Strong Lead-ership. Center for Financial Inclusion. May 2012.

Laude, A. (2009) The role of development finance institutions in good governance for microfinance. In: Private Sector & Development. Issue 3, September 2009. Proparco.

Luminis (2012) Microfinance Trends and Innovations. MicroRate.

Lützenkirchen, C., Weistoffer, C. (2012) Microfinance in evolution: An industry between crisis and advancement. Deutsche Bank Research.

McKee, K. (2012) Voting the Double Bottom Line: Active Governance by Microfinance Equity Investors. CGAP Focus Note No.79. May 2012.

Microbanking Bulletin (MBB) (2012) Funding Microfinance – a Focus on Debt Financing.

OECD (2004) OECD Principles of Corporate Governance.

Pistelli, M., Geake, S., Gonzalez, A. (2012) Assuring Governance in Microfinance: Initial Findings from a Pilot Project. MIX Market. April 2012.

Rock, R., Otero, M., S. Saltzmann (1998) Principles and Practices of Microfinance Governance. ACCION International.

Sanyoura, Z., Espejo, E. (2011) The Role and Impact of Private Sector Capital in the Global Microfinance Sector. Commissioned Workshop Paper presented at the Global Microcredit Summit November 14–17, 2011, Valladolid, Spain.

Symbiotics (2012) 2012 Symbiotics MIV Survey. Maket Data & Peer Group Analysis. July 2012.

Vita, M., Gonzales, J.V. (2011) Methodological Guide: Evaluation and Development of Good Governance in Microfinance Institutions. Managua, Nicaragua: Promifin.

Von Stauffenberg, D., Rozas, D. (2011) Role Reversal Revisited. Are Public Development Finance Institutions Still Crowding Out Private Investments in Microfinance? Microrate.

World Microfinance Forum Geneva (2010) The Future Risks and Opportunities in Investible Microfinance. Debate on Corporate Governance in Microfinance. 14 October 2011, Geneva.

CHAPTER 9

The Microfinance Approach: Does It Deliver on Its Promise?

Eva Terberger[*]

Abstract

Microfinance, formerly celebrated as a most successful development tool, has been confronted with harsh criticism in recent years. It is claimed to have contributed to clients' over-indebtedness while having failed to deliver on its promise of reducing poverty. By reviewing recent evidence, this paper aims for a more realistic assessment of the microfinance approach. It is argued that borrowing always goes along with risk. Accordingly, the danger of over-indebtedness can be ameliorated by responsible finance practices, but never eliminated. Nevertheless, microfinance deserves its place as a development tool. Even if positive impacts are much smaller than claimed in the past, the impact stream is able to flow for as long as the microfinance supplier survives. As there is proof that temporary support can build sustainable institutions, the cost-benefit ratio still seems to speak in favour of the microfinance approach.

1 Motivation: Impact Crisis in Microfinance

"The Promise of Microfinance" was the title of *Jonathan Morduch's* seminal paper in the Journal of Economic Literature in 1999, for the first time introducing microfinance to a broader academic public. At the time, the title reflected rather accurately the spirit of all those politicians, donors or practitioners supporting the microfinance approach as a means to fight poverty in developing countries. A little more than a decade later, public opinion on microfinance has dramatically changed. Microfinance is accused of absorbing billions of donor funds while showing little or no effect on improving the livelihoods of the poor (*Drake* 2009; *Harford* 2009). Even more alarming, reports on microfinance clients in India appeared in the media who, in desperate situations of over-indebtedness, took to suicide as the apparent last resort (*Biswas* 2010). The question is posed in public 358 Die Unternehmung,

---

[*] Professor, University of Mannheim.

66. Jg., 4/2012 whether for the poor microfinance has turned "from a blessing to a curse" (*Wade 2010)*. In a nutshell, the utmost praise of microfinance in 2006, when *Muhammad Yunus* and the Grameen Bank were awarded the Nobel Peace Prize, became scepticism and even outright criticism merely a few years later.

The trigger, which caused this back swing in microfinance's media coverage, was twofold. On the one hand, the first few academic studies were published that attempted to rigorously measure the impact of microfinance by comparing the livelihoods of microfinance clients to a control group, which is similar to the client group in every respect except for a lack of financial access. The reported results fell short of what some promoters of microfinance had claimed, and made the hope of microfinance lifting millions out of poverty look like a mere illusion. On the other hand, the financial crisis in 2008/2009 revealed to everybody that microcredit is not without risk for its clients. In some overheated microfinance markets, which had shown annual growth rates in the double digits previous to the crisis, repayment rates dropped drastically and left an unknown number of clients in the state of over-indebtedness. Those who gave early warnings about the dangers of commercialisation in microfinance felt substantiated in their reasoning.

It is far from obvious, however, that the new evidence brought forward by rigorous impact studies and the aftermath of the financial crisis gives sufficient cause to overthrow everything supposedly known about microfinance, and to abandon all hopes of microfinance as an effective tool to improve the lives of low-income people in the developing world. After all, the financial crisis was a singular shock, and the evidence from over-indebted clients is primarily based on anecdotal evidence. Likewise, the evidence produced by rigorous impact studies is still scarce, and these studies are rather limited in what they can measure. Therefore, rather than premature rejection, recent evidence calls for a reassessment of the microfinance approach, of its potential achievements and its risks.

Contributing to such a reassessment is the motivation for this paper. A recapitulation of how the microfinance approach originated and what spurred the hopes going along with it will be combined with a review of what we know about microfinance's impact and what we don't. This shall form the basis of a realistic judgement on what can be expected when opening access to finance for those, who formerly had been excluded from formal financial services.

The rest of the paper is organised as follows. Section 2 briefly revisits the emergence of the microfinance approach in the 1990s; section 3 summarises the current knowledge on the risk of over-indebtedness which goes along with microcredit; section 4 puts the new evidence produced by rigorous impact analyses into perspective; section 5 concludes with some remarks on the virtues, the vices, and new challenges of the microfinance approach.

2   The Microfinance Revolution – Revisited

What was the "promise of microfinance" all about, raising the hopes of access to finance as a way out of poverty? Following a period of disappointing results in all attempts to foster micro and small enterprise via directed lending in the 1970s and 1980s, a paradigm shift in the development approach brought about a change for the better. The provision of concessional credit lines reserved for those who were thought to be too poor to be bankable was replaced by the approach of building financial institutions (*Krahnen/Schmidt* 1994) specialised on serving the target groups formerly excluded from access to the formal financial system. The results of this paradigm shift, which took place in the early 1990s, were actually promising.

Donor funds, provided by means of directed lending, often went along with dismal repayment performance and frequently never even reached the target group due to adverse incentives produced by low interest rates. In sharp contrast, microfinance institutions (MFIs) supported by donor money for institution building managed to recapture the loans disbursed to micro entrepreneurs. Thanks to a credit-technology based on cash-flow assessment and graduation, rates of arrears stayed even below those of established banks in the same region. By the end of the 1990s, the 'microfinance revolution' – as it was frequently called – held the promise of offering a 'win-win' solution of suppliers and customers likewise profiting: After an initial phase of support for institution building, MFIs seemed to be able to offer financial services to the formerly underserved while covering costs or even producing moderate profits; and microfinance clients were receiving a sustainable access to formal financial services going along with new opportunities to smooth income and enlarge their businesses, thereby improving the livelihoods of their families or even transcending poverty. As such, microfinance appeared to be an extremely cost-effective approach to fight poverty: Once an MFI was built up and working, it was able to survive in the financial market on its own account. There was no need for further subsidies to keep open the window of opportunity which access to finance was offering to the poor.

The success story of microfinance spreading around the developing world seemed to confirm this way of thinking. Flagship MFIs were transforming into licensed banks without abandoning their target group of micro entrepreneurs and low-income households. At least in urban areas, these clients were getting access not only to microcredit, but also to other financial services like savings accounts and transfers of payments. Time intensive transformation of non-governmental organisations into professional banks was more and more often replaced by a 'greenfielding' approach, i.e. the foundation of fully-fledged microfinance banks right from the start. MFIs were getting less and less dependent on refinancing lines by donors, development banks or ethical investors. Instead, they were collecting local deposits or even tapping the capital market by issuing bonds. Singular micro banks in different countries were united in networks or under a holding to form micro banking groups, adding to knowledge sharing as well as improved liquidity and risk management. Since the turn of the millennium, specialised microfinance investment vehicles, refinanced by development finance institutions and ethical investors, have offered debt and equity finance to advanced MFIs; and on 20th April 2007, another milestone in the development of the microfinance sector was marked by the Initial Public Offering of the Mexican Banco Compartamos, an MFI founded in 1990 with grants from several donor sources (*Rosenberg* 2007). Microfinance was certainly on the way to becoming an integral part of the financial market.

By the end of 2008, shortly before the effects of the financial crisis had reached microfinance, the Microfinance Information eXchange, the most comprehensive database on microfinance, reported, based on the data of almost 1400 MFIs, that these institutions were reaching out to over 86m borrowers and almost 96m voluntary savers worldwide (*Gonzalez* 2009). The average loan balance per customer, a common proxy or target group orientation, was below USD 1,600. Furthermore, on average institutions were earning profits (return on equity 1.4 % on average, median 8.9 %). There were regional differences as microfinance in Africa was clearly lagging behind. Furthermore, data on the Microfinance Information eXchange are positively biased as more successful MFIs are more likely to report. Nevertheless, hundreds of MFIs around the world were giving proof of what had seemed impossible before the microfinance revolution: The target group of micro entrepreneurs and low-income households can be financially served without continually loosing money.

However, progress in financial performance of MFIs was not equally welcomed as a success by all protagonists of the microfinance idea. With the IPO of Banco Compartamos in 2007, which attracted commercial investors not least because of the bank's high return on equity, warnings were getting louder that microfinance is loosing out on its original mission of helping the poor. Being hit by the financial crisis in 2009 put a definite halt to microfinance's boom. Reports on clients' over-indebtedness in the aftermath of the crisis as well as rigorous impact studies failing to prove noticeable poverty reduction effects of microfinance added to the doubts about financial success of MFIs automatically going hand in hand with benefits for the poor.

3   Over-Indebtedness – A Widespread Phenomenon in Microfinance?

3.1 The Downside Risk in Microcredit

While microfinance now covers a wide range of financial services for low-income households, initially the microfinance movement was mainly associated with access to credit for micro entrepreneurs. Notwithstanding all the potential positive impacts of access to loans, borrowing money is never without risk.

On the creditor's side, risk is pretty well documented by rates of arrears and loan writeoffs. On the borrower's side, however, risk going along with borrowing is much more difficult to capture; its documentation is correspondingly weak. Often, information from the MFIs about repayment rates was and still is taken as a proxy for the degree to which borrowers have debt problems. The excellent repayment performance, which contributed to the high expectations put into the microfinance approach, was taken as a reliable signal for risks being rather low on the borrowers' side. However, there always were occasional warnings that taking arrears as a proxy might be missing out on something.

Back in 1996, *Hulme and Mosley* in their well-known book "Finance against Poverty" had already pointed out that borrowers might be worse off than before if they fail to repay, and they called for more intensified research on the livelihood of borrowers who drop out of a credit scheme (*Hulme/Mosley* 1996, 119–121). The authors were asking MFI staff for their estimations on the percentage of borrowers who have trouble meeting their loan obligations and who are likely to go bankrupt. Additionally, *Hulme and Mosley* collected anecdotal evidence on delinquent borrowers' suffering, e.g. when collateral was seized.

Actually, this is the borrower's downside risk of a credit contract. In contrast to equity finance, which shares the business risk between entrepreneur and equity provider more or less symmetrically, a credit contract does not spell out an equal participation in entrepreneurial risk. If the business goes well, the earnings exceeding the loan obligations will belong to the entrepreneur. If the business fails, however, it will always be the borrower who takes the first loss while the creditor only looses out once the borrower's repayment capacity is exhausted. Supporters of microfinance were well aware of this risk, commonly called financial leverage risk, when in the beginning of the 1990s the institution building approach was developed. There were even some pilots and studies on micro equity finance in the form of venture capital. It just turned out to be too expensive, however, to provide small financial volumes as equity participation.[1] There would not have been a realistic chance to turn micro venture capital into a cost-covering endeavour. Therefore, microcredit seemed to be the only option to create access to finance for the target group without the need for continual subsidies. Excellent repayment rates of microcredit as well as huge demand for this service laid remaining concerns to rest.

This changed, however, with microfinance turning into a business, particularly as suppliers entered the market that, under the flag of microfinance, started to roll out small consumer loans on a big scale. Already before the outbreak of the financial crisis, when microcredit was growing in double-digit annual rates, warnings

---

[1]   Pretes (2002) promotes micro equity to avoid financial leverage risk. However, he underlines that micro equity in his definition is provided as a grant, and not as cost covering venture capital.

on the danger of households' over-indebtedness were surfacing.[2] Promoters of the microfinance approach as a development tool reacted with campaigns and principles for responsible finance (www.smartcampaign.org), to which institutions with a double mission, i.e. financial and social, readily committed themselves. This might not have been sufficient to protect microfinance clients, however, as the aftermath of the financial crisis made apparent.

3.2   Household Over-Indebtedness – A Phenomenon Difficult to Capture

Whether the spreading of microcredit actually led to an increase in human tragedies most likely will never be clarified with certainty. However, knowing about the downside risk of borrowing provides sufficient cause to try to find effective ways for client protection. This is all the more important as the microfinance movement is spreading in low income countries, where the legal framework aiming at client protection is not yet very sophisticated. Even if laws, often initiated through the microfinance donors, to promote transparency of interest rates are more frequently put in place, and even if microcredit institutions are obliged to explain risks, e.g. going along with foreign currency loans, clients often have difficulties in understanding their contract terms nevertheless, due to a lack in financial literacy. The most important corner stones of client protection, which would have the power to effectively protect borrowers if they fail, are still missing in almost all microcredit markets in the developing world: A consumer insolvency law with debt relief combined with a formal social safety net. With these in place, an income on the subsistence level and the opportunity for a fresh start would be guaranteed also to those borrowers who get caught in a debt trap.

It is difficult to define at which point debt service becomes unbearable and the fine line is crossed between indebtedness and over-indebtedness (*Hottenrott* 2002, *Alam* 2012). Even functioning insolvency laws in developed countries face this challenge. Over-indebtedness as a legal term is usually reserved for companies with limited liabilities, describing a state in which liabilities exceed assets, and accordingly the company's equity is negative. When translating this definition into the context of an individual borrower, two difficulties arise. The inventory of an individual borrower's liabilities not only has to cover all personal debt, but also has to pin down a financial figure to represent future expenses to guarantee a living at least on the subsistence level. Likewise, on the asset side, beside all tangible and financial assets to the borrower's name, the inventory will have to include an item for the human capital, representing the capacity to earn future income. Naturally, estimations of future income, most likely forming the most important asset of borrowers without material wealth, as well as an estimation of future living ex-

---

[2]   Potential problems coming along with growth rates of that magnitude can be manifold. A very important one in microfinance was a shortage in qualified staff. Recruiting and training could not keep up with the same pace as the portfolios were growing without loosing out on quality.

penses is afflicted with a relatively high degree of uncertainty. That is why even in developed countries individual borrower's over-indebtedness is not a juridical term. Instead, not meeting debt obligations is taken as the trigger for individual insolvency procedures, which takes us back to where we started, that is arrears as a proxy for over-indebtedness.

Some countries, however, allow individuals to file for insolvency if they can prove it to be unlikely that they will be able to meet debt obligations in the future. This seems to be more adequate to protect clients from downside credit risk. Debt entanglement is likely to start much earlier than at the point in time when it becomes impossible to serve debt obligations. Not being able to turn anywhere for legal help when debt burdens are starting to become unbearable is particularly devastating for low-income borrowers in developing countries. As there is no formal social safety net, unlucky borrowers whose businesses fail might even continue the debt service although they urgently would need the little money they have for basic living expenses like food, school fees or medical expenses. Hardly anything systematic is known about the extent of struggling before borrowers actually fail on their debt obligations. A recent contribution to closing this knowledge gap, which *Hulme and Mosley* had pointed out more than 15 years ago, is an empirical research by *Jessica Schicks* (2010).

3.3   The Extent of Over-Indebtedness

The extent of over-indebtedness, which is found in microfinance markets, clearly depends on the definition employed as well as on the research design. *Schicks'* research (*Schicks* 2010, 2012) aims at grasping over-indebtedness from a clients' perspective, and thereby laying the foundations for a pragmatic definition of over-indebtedness, which does not draw on the insufficient proxies of delinquency or failure to meet payment obligations. The research relies on 2010 data gained from structured interviews of more than 500 urban micro borrowers in Ghana. The interviewees were randomly sampled from the customer base of five well-known Ghanaian MFIs. Clients who were in arrears were slightly over-sampled to have a sufficient representation. The over-sampling was corrected for in the subsequent analysis by assigning weights to the different sample groups. During the interview, clients were confronted with a given list of potential "sacrifices", e.g. working more, eating less, taking children out of school, and they were asked to pick out those sacrifices, which they experienced in the context of recent loan repayments. In a second step, they were asked to rank on a scale of one to five whether they considered their individual sacrifices as acceptable (1) or totally unacceptable (5). In the case that a client frequently (3 times or more) suffered sacrifices rated as unacceptable, he or she was counted as overindebted. About 30 percent of the sample fell under this pragmatic and client-focussed definition of over-indebtedness. Interestingly enough, the urban Ghanaian microfinance market does not count as particularly riddled by problems of over-indebtedness, and according to the information systems of MFIs, rates of arrears were on a much lower and from their creditor's point of view a rather acceptable level.

Obviously, this research is but a first step, and it is certainly no proof that borrower struggling is caused by micro loans. Being able to draw conclusions in that direction requires comparing interview results to those of a control group who is similar to the client group, except for not having to serve a loan. Actually, more rigorous research relying on a control-group approach could even reveal that households without any micro debt suffer even more because they are lacking the opportunity to smooth their consumption stream via borrowing. Almost all of the clients who took part in the interviews in Ghana and were classified as over-indebted firmly stated that they want to borrow again, some of them even higher amounts if possible. This is quite a firm indication that even those clients who suffer in serving their debt put a high value on financial access. Nevertheless, *Schicks'* results substantiate the suspicion that something important is left out when figures about portfolio risk and failure rates are the only inputs relied upon when estimating the extent of over-indebtedness.

More research, and specifically more research of a rigorous kind is needed to say more; and unfortunately the few results we do have (see *Alam* 2012, *Schicks/ Rosenberg* 2011 for an overview) give few new ideas on what more could be done against the problem of overindebtedness. Closing the credit window is obviously not a viable option, as it would cut clients off from the upside potential of loans at the same time. Commitment to principles of responsible finance still seem to be the best preventive measure from the MFIs' side, including a careful assessment of clients' repayment capacity, an abdication of unethical methods of loan collection, an adaption of payment schemes to borrowers income streams, and an assessment of options for rescheduling in case of problems.

However, there is no way that responsible finance can compensate for a lack of official help for debt-trapped households, i.e. via an insolvency law providing a fresh start, or via formal social safety nets. As the downside risk of credit cannot be ruled out ex ante, it seems all the more important that for the vast majority of clients the potential positive impact of microfinance more than compensates for its risk. In this light, the existing evidence on microfinance's impact on the livelihood of the poor deserves the utmost attention.

4   Impact Measurement in Microfinance – Results and Limitations

4.1   Control Group Designs to Capture Impact on Microfinance Beneficiaries

The success story of microfinance as a tool to fight poverty was based predominantly on two pillars: Firstly, the achievements in building financially viable MFIs serving millions of customers formerly excluded from the formal financial system, and secondly an unaccounted number of anecdotes about how microfinance changed the lives of beneficiaries. The latter, however, are far from providing rigorous evidence that access to finance brought about the change for the better. Firstly, a before-after comparison, which is typical for anecdotes, fails to single out the influence of microfinance. It might have been simply an extraordinary entrepreneurial spirit of the owner (or something else), and not a microloan, which was pivotal in turning a tiny market stall into a thriving business. Secondly, the occasional story about a successful client might be cherry-picked from a pool of clients who on average were by far less fortunate.

Impact studies of an experimental or quasi-experimental design (*Duflo et al.* 2007) are promising to provide a more reliable foundation for microfinance's claim of benefitting the poor. Inspired by the methodology of pharmaceutical studies, these impact studies statistically mimic a comparison between the situation with and without access to finance. With anecdotal evidence, a 'with versus without' comparison is impossible; it is contrafactual because a single person either can, or cannot, have access to finance. However, experimental impact studies circumvent this problem by comparing the target group of an intervention, in our case the customers of a microfinance institution, with a suitable control group. Ideally, the control group is as good as identical to the target group, except for the latter having access to finance, while the former is lacking it. The most reliable method to gain a target and a control group, which at least from a statistical point of view are identical, is to randomly divide a large group of individuals into those who receive the 'treatment' and those who do not. This random selection is reflected in the name of that experimental method, which is classified as most reliable, the so-called Randomised Controlled Trials (RCT). As can easily be imagined, it is as good as impossible to apply this method when aiming to measure the impact of microfinance. A random selection of individuals into target and control group might be possible if two financial products are tested against each other, but it hardly seems realistic to use a random selection if it is a question of access versus non-access. However, the strict methodology of RCT can be relaxed by applying a quasi-experimental design. There is a wide range of methods to define a control group in a quasi-experiment. The pipeline approach makes use of similar groups receiving the 'treatment' at different points in time. Accordingly, the group treated later in time can serve as the control group for those who are treated first. Propensity score matching is a method to artificially create a control group by finding an 'untreated' statistical twin for each target group member. In impact studies of microfinance, researchers usually try to identify a control town quarter or village, which is inhabited by community members very similar to those in the target area where a new branch of an MFI is going to open.

In the course of the (quasi-)experiment, data is collected from both groups, ideally before the intervention as well as afterwards. The 'double' difference in the average livelihoods of the two groups – given that both are large enough to statistically eliminate any random influence through the law of large numbers – allows for the isolation of microfinance's impact: The first difference of potential impact variables, e.g. business activities, income, education or health, is taken before the new financial window opens, and this difference will be close to zero if the two groups are selected well and accordingly are (almost) identical in a statistical sense. The second difference is taken after the target group receives access to finance. The improvement or deterioration in livelihoods in comparison to the control group, measured at the same point in time, gives the impact of microfinance (after correction for any difference between target and control group which was detected by the comparison before the intervention).

Experimental as well as quasi-experimental designs result in much more reliable impact measurements than any before versus after comparison can offer. However, the measurement is valid exclusively for the single intervention, which was the object of the study (internal validity). A larger number of impact studies of a similar kind are necessary to gain insights on whether results are of a more general nature and whether similar effects can be expected when the intervention in question is replicated in other settings (external validity). Systematic reviews offer a framework to analyse the question of external validity, given that a sufficient number of impact studies on a certain intervention type is entering into the review. According to the methodology of systematic reviews, only impact studies meeting the experimental or quasi-experimental standard are to form the base of analyses. The quality standard applied as well as the search process and range must be documented exante. Depending on the number and quality of studies, which enter a systematic review, it will deliver conclusions on whether impacts of the intervention in question show a low or a high variability subject to the regional, cultural or socio-economic setting.

4.2   Rigorous Impact Studies on Microfinance – Results

What is the rigorous evidence then, on which the microfinance approach can rely when trying to prove its benefit? While a few years back there was not even a handful of microfinance studies applying a control-group-approach, the body of evidence has become much larger in the last two years. Three systematic reviews have been published at this point. The first one, published in 2010, focussed on Sub-Saharan Africa (*van Roojen et al.* 2012); it is based on 15 impact studies in 10 countries. The second review by *Duvendack et al.* (2011) relies on evidence worldwide provided by 58 studies in 19 countries. The third review (*Pande et al.* 2012) includes 12 studies in 10 countries worldwide. At least one more systematic review focussing on evidence from the Asian region is in the process of being conducted (*Stewart et al.* 2011). Only a small minority of the individual studies actually follows the gold standard of RCT design. Most studies aim at measuring the impact of microcredit; in single cases the question of impact is addressed for agricultural credit, micro savings, micro insurance, micro leasing or new banking technologies.

All in all, the impact of microfinance, which was observed, was rather moderate, and certainly fell short of the "Microfinance Promise" of lifting millions of people out of poverty. There is quite reliable evidence from several studies that access to microcredit actually had positive effects on entrepreneurial activities, e.g. the foundation of new businesses or the enlargement of existing ones. Likewise, positive effects on acquiring durable goods were found. There is little evidence, however, that microfinance led to a general improvement of livelihoods. Several studies find no effect on income or general well being; single studies, particularly in Sub-Saharan Africa, conclude positive effects on income, health or the quality of housing and food. However, there is occasional evidence as well that access to microloans, particularly if the money was not invested, but used for consumption purposes, increased vulnerability or had negative effects on the schooling of children. Parallels to the results of *Schicks'* study on over-indebtedness are evident.

Quite frankly, this is no overwhelming proof of microfinance's power to fundamentally change the lives of the poor. It can be concluded that microfinance certainly is no magic bullet to fight poverty, and there is no rigorous evidence that microfinance turns subsistence-level enterprises into flourishing small firms on a large scale. However, microcredit can support entrepreneurial activity on a moderate level, and it can help to accumulate durable assets, perhaps even help to moderately improve income and living conditions in general. These potential benefits come for the price of additional risk, particularly if the loan is used for consumption.

Certainly, the evidence provided by rigorous impact studies is still preliminary, but it seems sufficient to put "The Promise of Microfinance" into a more realistic perspective. Advocates of the microfinance approach need to be much more moderate about what can be achieved by providing access to financial services.

However, existing evidence neither seems to justify extremely negative media coverage, nor gives it any reason to abandon the microfinance approach as a development tool altogether. Even the pioneers of RCT who, besides other interventions, have conducted the probably most well-known impact studies on microfinance, come to conclude:

"As economists, we were quite pleased with these results: The main objective of microfinance seemed to have been achieved. It was not miraculous, but it was working. In our minds, microcredit has earned its rightful place as one of the key instruments in the fight against poverty." (Banerjee/Duflo 2011, chap. 7)

4.3 Limits of Rigorous Impact Studies in Microfinance

A pessimistic outlook on the future of microfinance based on existing rigorous evidence seems unjustified, especially as the systematic reviews clearly point out that there are a very limited number of studies yet which meet the required quality standard. This is not really astonishing, as building microfinance institutions is a type of intervention, which is not ideally suited to apply experimental or quasi-experimental designs. In contrast to clearly targeted 'treatments', microfinance interventions serve the target group in a more indirect way. MFIs open a window to access financial services; the clients decide by themselves whether they want to use that opportunity. This causes a problem of selection bias, which is difficult to eliminate in impact studies.

There are other shortcomings of existing impact studies that are unlikely to be overcome by future research. Most importantly, almost all of them were conducted during the last few years. However, the Microfinance Revolution started more than two decades ago. By now, MFIs have long spread out all over the developing world, most likely placing branches in the most promising locations for their mission. Accordingly, it will hardly be possible anymore to find a target group and a control group untouched by microfinance exactly in those locations, which had the highest impact potential in the past. Methods of rigorous impact analyses were simply applied too late; most probably, more impact would have been found if measurement had taken place when microfinance was still in its infant shoes. Indirectly, this hypothesis is gaining some support by the latest systematic review (*Pande* 2012). It reports particularly high impacts found in studies on financial services which were introduced as an innovation in the respective development context, i.e. agricultural loans or mobile banking. Beside the shortcoming of measuring the impact, particularly of microcredit interventions in urban areas, too late, it seems of minor importance that the vast majority of existing studies cover timeframes of no more than 18 month, which is too short to discover potential long-term impact.

What rigorous impact studies fail to capture as well, are all potential impacts of microfinance interventions on the financial system as a whole. Besides its direct benefit for microfinance clients, financial system development is usually an additional goal associated with microfinance interventions. Undoubtedly, the microfinance approach has served this purpose in several respects. Beside micro clients, MFIs offer their service to small and even medium enterprise, which were not adequately served by the banking system before. These clients, not having been the subject of rigorous impact analyses yet, might have a much higher potential in job creation than micro clients. Additionally, tens of thousands of MFI staff members were trained, often with donor support. This most likely contributed to the professional standard in the financial sector, all the more as trained staff often moved on to other banks. Furthermore, in many developing and transition countries MFIs served as role models for good governance: they were actively pushing for client protection, and they were pioneers in their commitment to principles of responsible finance.

5   Conclusions

Without doubt, the reputation of microfinance suffered during its crisis. However, microfinance survived the crisis, and, in my view, it came out of it healthier than before. Support for microfinance or any other development tool that is based on naïve perceptions, unrealistic expectations, or a lack of knowledge of the public can hardly be a solid foundation for development success in the long run. Before the crisis, there was a certain degree of over-promising concerning microfinance's impact on the livelihoods of the poor, at least by some advocates of the microfinance approach; and the remarkable growth rates of microcredit portfolios gave further nourishment to over-optimistic expectations. The microfinance crisis with its financial and its impact dimension has put this back into perspective. Microfinance certainly is no magic bullet against poverty, and its positive potentials for improving the livelihoods of low-income people do not come without risk.

The downside risk of credit on the borrower's side, namely the risk of having to struggle to repay or even being caught in a debt-trap, can be mitigated by means of thorough credit analysis, transparency, and customers' education in financial matters. However, the risk hardly ever can be eliminated because it cannot be ruled out that the client suffers a severe shock and repayment capacity falls well below former expectations. Actually, the spreading of microfinance and MFIs diminished the scope of individual MFIs for controlling credit risk of single customers as competition in the microfinance market usually comes along with a rising number of clients borrowing from multiple sources. This is all the more worrying as the success of the microfinance approach has attracted other players who just try to make a business, not least with consumer loans, without safeguarding against the dangers of over-indebtedness which are borne by the low-income customer. Credit bureaus are important agents that can help MFIs keeping track of clients' overall credit history; that is why the establishment of such bureaus has been promoted by the same donors for quite some time that are supporting microfinance. Despite of these improvements, it will still take a lot more in developing countries to round off the institutional set-up of client protection, namely by the establishment of insolvency laws for private individuals allowing relief from unsustainable debt, and of social security systems which can guarantee an income on the subsistence level. Therefore, it will remain of utmost importance that MFIs with a financial and a social mission use all their options to secure positive impacts for their clients as best as they can, first and foremost by providing financial services in a responsible way.

Microfinance's potential for positive impacts on clients' livelihoods has been demonstrated, even if measured impacts, particularly of microcredit, stayed well behind of what was hoped for. Impacts of microfinance on financial sector development, i.e. via training of staff, the promotion of transparency, good governance, or principles for responsible finance, have never been measured; nevertheless, they are existent. Last but not least, when assessing the achievements and the future potential of microfinance, it is not to be forgotten how it all began. Without doubt, there is a striking success that the microfinance approach can righteously claim as its own: The creation of viable target-group-oriented financial institutions, which after an initial phase of institution building can survive without continually being fuelled with additional subsidies. As long as access to finance goes along with predominantly positive impacts for its clients, these impacts will flow for as long as the MFI survives. Accordingly, the microfinance approach seems to offer a very favourable cost-benefit relation, even if impact on individual clients in a single time period is small. The example of the German savings banks,3 founded in the beginning of the 19th century with a mission very similar to that of the MFIs of today, give vivid evidence of sustainable institutions serving the target group of micro and small enterprises as well as low- and medium-income households, by now for as long as about two centuries.

References

Alam, S.M. (2012) Does Microfinance create over-indebtedness? Working Paper, under http://ssrn. com/abstract=2070616.

Banerjee, A.V., Duflo, E. (2011) Poor Economics: A Radical Rethinking of the Way to Fight Global Poverty. New York.

Biswas, S. (2010) India's micro-finance suicide epidemic, under www.bbc.co.uk/news/world-southasia-11997571 (12.8.2012).

Drake, B. (2009) Small Change. In: The Boston Globe 20.9.2009, under http://www.boston.com/bostonglobe/ideas/articles/2009/09/20/small_change_d oes_microlending_actually_fight_poverty/(12.8.2012).

Duflo, E., Glennerster, R., Kremer, M. (2007) Using Randomization in Development Economics Research: A Tool-Kit. In: Gonzalez, A., Handbook of Development Economics, vol. 4, pp. 3895–3962. (2009) Microfinance at a glance – 2008. Microfinance Information eXchange, Washington D.C.

Duvendack, M., et al. (2011) What is the evidence of the impact of microfinance on the well-being of poor people? Research Report, EPPI-Centre, Social Science Research Unit, Institute of Education, University of London.

Guinnane, T.W. (2011) The Early German Credit Cooperatives and Microfinance Institutions Today: Similarities and Differences. In: Armendáriz, B., Lapie, M. (eds) Handbook of Microfinance, London-Singapore, pp. 77–100.

Harford, T. (2009) Perhaps microfinance isn't such a big deal after all. In: Financial Times 5.12.2009, under http://www.ft.com/cms/s/0/ae4211e8-dee7-11de-adff-00144feab49a.html (12.8.2012).

Hottenrott, V. (2002) Die Überschuldung privater Haushalte in Deutschland vor dem Hintergrund der neuen Insolvenzordnung. Diss., University of Heidelberg.

Hulme, D., Mosley, P. (1996) Finance against poverty, Vol. 1, London.

Krahnen, J.P., Schmidt, R.H. (1994) Development Finance as Institution Building. Boulder, Col.

Morduch, J. (1999) The Promise of Microfinance. Journal of Economic Literature 37:1569–1614.

Pande R., et al. (2012) Does Poor People's Access to Formal Banking Services Raise their Incomes? EPPI-Centre, Social Science Research Unit, Institute of Education, University of London.

Pretes, M. (2002) Microequity and Microfinance. World Development 30(8):341–1352.

Rosenberg, R. (2007) CGAP reflections on the Compartamos Initial Public Offering: A case study on microfinance interest rates and profits, CGAP Focus Note No. 42, Washington D.C.

Schicks, J. (2010) Microfinance Over-Indebtedness: Understanding its drivers and challenging the common myths. Centre Emile Bernheim (CEB) Working Paper No. 10/048.

Schicks, J. (2012) Over-indebtedness in Microfinance – an empirical analysis of related factors on the borrower level. Centre Emile Bernheim (CEB), Working Paper No. 12/017.

Schicks, J., Rosenberg, R. (2011) Too much Microcredit? A Survey of the Evidence on Over-Indebtedness. CGAP Occasional Paper No. 19.

Stewart, R., van Roojen, C., de Wet, T. (2011) Do micro-credit, micro-savings and micro-leasing serve as effective financial inclusion interventions enabling poor people, and especially women, to engage in meaningful economic opportunities in LMICs? EPPI-Centre, Social Science Research Unit, Institute of Education, University of London.

Van Roojen, C., Stewart R., de Wet, T. (2012) The Impact of Microfinance in Sub-Saharan Africa: A Systematic Review of the Evidence. In: World Development, forthcoming.

Wade, M. (2010) From a Blessing to a Curse, underhttp://www.theage.com.au/national/from-a-blessing-to-a-curse-20101213-18vjo.html (12.8.2010).

Index

Keywords

Access to finance 58, 59, 125, 135, 182, 183, 189
Andhra Pradesh 3, 7–9, 14, 16, 18, 23–25, 31, 35, 39, 55, 61, 71, 82, 93, 95, 99, 125, 153
Branchless banking 106, 116
Business models 47, 62, 105, 109, 120, 125, 137, 164, 167, 170
Clients
  Client needs 108, 129
  Client protection 11, 165, 174, 186, 192, 193
Commercial investors 159, 160, 175, 184
Commercial microfinance 47, 136, 141, 144
Competition 25, 31, 76, 85, 93, 123, 125, 135, 153, 193
Control systems 123, 128
Corporate governance 128, 136, 137, 155, 156, 170–172, 176, 179
Credit bureau 10, 13, 15, 31, 34, 36, 37, 110, 132, 164, 177, 193
Cross-border funding 14, 133, 156–158, 161, 163
Debt crisis management 132
Development finance 39, 50, 57–59, 61, 64, 66, 110, 119, 124, 133, 141, 152, 155, 156, 159, 179, 180, 184, 194
Downscaling 135, 164
Equity 6, 18–21, 35, 36, 47, 60–63, 65, 71, 80, 93–96, 99, 101, 102, 107, 117, 119, 123, 128, 133–135, 155, 158, 160–164, 168, 173–175, 177, 178–180, 184, 185, 186
Fair treatment 126
Financial ecosystem 127
Financial frontier 136
Financial inclusion 35, 39, 107, 109, 110, 113, 116, 117, 119–121, 136, 140, 146, 149, 177, 179, 195

Financial literacy 131, 186
Financial services 12–14, 22, 27, 29–31, 36, 37, 48, 49, 60, 64, 69, 97, 105, 106, 108–111, 113, 115, 117, 119, 121–127, 129, 130, 131, 133, 134, 136, 137, 140, 162, 182–184, 191, 192, 193
Funder 133, 155, 157, 160, 161
Funding 5, 10, 12, 29, 36, 45, 47, 49, 80–82, 130, 132–134, 136, 155–158, 161, 162–164, 167, 168, 174, 176, 179
Funds 4, 6, 11, 12, 36, 37, 43, 45, 46, 51, 54, 57, 60, 62, 63, 71, 74, 80, 81, 94, 95, 98, 102, 107, 108, 112–115, 118, 119, 123, 129, 130, 133–135, 144, 155, 157, 159, 160, 162, 164, 166–169, 172, 175–177, 179, 181, 183
Grants 62, 133, 134, 158, 160, 172
Green finance 165
Guarantee 119, 151, 160, 186, 193
Impact 8, 13, 14, 22, 23, 27–30, 38, 39, 50, 52, 53, 56, 58, 60, 73, 85, 86, 92, 93, 113, 115, 118, 123–126, 135, 136, 152, 156, 159, 164, 165, 169, 180–182, 184, 188–194
Industry building 28, 35, 58, 123, 136
Institution building 37, 39, 49, 50, 52, 58, 133–135, 152, 164, 183, 185, 193, 194
Institutional investors 14, 47, 61, 62, 130, 168, 177
Insurance
  Microinsurance 133
Interest rates
  Flat interest rates 131
  Interest rate caps 11, 80, 132, 151
Loans
  Agricultural loans 146, 192
  Consumer loans 185, 193
  Education loans 129, 130, 134
  Energy efficiency loans 129

Market environment 133, 135
Mezzanine finance 169, 177–179
Microcredit 5, 6, 13–16, 20, 22–30, 34,
    37–39, 66, 69, 70, 72, 74–76, 79, 82,
    85, 90, 92, 99–101, 107, 108, 112, 115,
    120, 123, 126, 127, 129, 130, 137, 139,
    152, 153, 158, 168, 171, 177, 180,
    182–186, 190, 191–193, 195
Micro-enterprises 57
Microfinance investment vehicle (MIV)
    6, 20, 22, 34, 40, 120, 123, 134, 155,
    157, 158, 160, 166, 175, 180, 184
Minimum capital requirements 132
Mobile banking 164, 192
Networks 1, 2, 10, 62, 64, 106, 108, 110,
    115–118, 120, 123, 134, 135, 144, 157,
    160, 165, 166, 183
Outreach 5, 6, 49, 50, 60, 64, 99, 103,
    105, 117, 119, 123–128, 130, 133, 137,
    141–143, 152, 159, 161, 165, 171
Overheating 36, 123, 132, 133
Over-indebtedness 7, 9, 12, 55, 126, 131,
    132, 135, 140, 166, 181, 182, 184,
    186–188, 191, 193–195
Payment services 130, 133
Portfolio at risk 18
Portfolio quality 18, 36, 37, 125
Poverty reduction 58, 126, 184
Private sector 5, 6, 54, 56, 125, 126,
    133, 135, 155, 156, 164, 166–170,
    177, 179, 180
Profits 6, 12–15, 18, 20, 22–24, 26, 35, 40,
    44, 47, 54–56, 59, 61–63, 65, 70–72,
    74, 77, 78, 80, 84, 91–96, 98, 99, 103,
    107, 114, 116, 117, 122, 125, 126, 150,
    165, 174, 178, 183, 184
Rating(s) 36, 166, 168
Regulation
    Responsible regulation 132

Responsibility
    Responsible exit 133, 169, 174–176
    Responsible finance 10, 131, 136,
        164–166, 181, 188, 193
    Responsible practices 128, 131
Return(s) 3, 6, 12, 18, 19, 46, 51, 55, 63,
    64, 69, 71, 89, 92–96, 99, 101, 102,
    122, 125, 128, 133, 140, 142, 143, 145,
    148–150, 159, 161, 174–176, 184
Risk
    Risk management 106, 128, 172, 184
Rural finance 41, 134
Savings 3, 11, 14, 16, 21, 22, 24, 27, 28,
    36–38, 58, 66, 69, 70, 72, 73, 80, 82,
    90–92, 101, 103, 107, 108, 112–114,
    117, 121, 126, 130–134, 136, 162, 169,
    171, 177, 183, 190, 195
Small business 48, 50, 59, 63, 64, 73, 78,
    103, 110, 111, 126, 129, 134
Social investors 13, 15, 30–32, 35, 36,
    61, 155, 159, 177, 178
Staff training 64, 127
Sustainability 1, 2, 5, 45, 49, 60, 100,
    101, 103, 105, 115, 124, 127, 128, 132,
    137, 146, 151, 159, 167, 169
Technology 131, 134, 183
Transaction costs 5, 51, 82, 106, 117–121,
    125, 127, 129–131, 153
Transformation 12, 35, 43, 115, 164, 165,
    167, 178, 183
Transparency 11, 30, 34, 59, 60, 73, 74,
    124, 155, 157, 171, 172, 175, 186, 193
Transparent treatment 131
Upgrading 46, 135
Values 16, 24, 31, 34, 37, 41–49, 52, 53,
    54, 58–60, 63, 64, 65, 82, 106, 108,
    112, 114, 115, 119, 125, 136, 137, 144,
    150, 167, 169, 188

Countries

Azerbaijan 162
Bangladesh 5–7, 21, 22, 28, 29, 39, 55,
    75, 142, 143, 152, 153, 162
Bolivia 22, 29, 34, 76, 162, 172
Bosnia and Herzegovina 23, 25, 29, 38,
    76, 99, 110, 164, 166, 172

Brazil 106, 116, 118
Cambodia 21, 76, 162, 164, 172
China 6, 14, 16, 27, 29, 72, 101, 152
Colombia 14, 16, 21, 162
Ecuador 29
El Salvador 114

Ethiopia 21, 118
Ghana 110, 187, 188
India 1–6, 8, 9–11, 14, 18, 22–25, 27,
    29, 35, 39, 47, 59, 64, 65, 82, 83, 95,
    98, 135, 143, 152, 153, 161–163, 177,
    181, 194
Indonesia 3, 21, 29, 49, 72, 76, 100, 110,
    162
Jordan 115
Kenya 14, 16, 21, 22, 29, 38, 117, 118,
    162
Laos 135
Madagascar 139, 144, 145, 147, 150,
    151

Malawi 27, 38, 114, 115
Mexico 21, 24, 59, 76, 82, 114, 162,
    164, 172
Mongolia 21, 23, 38, 162, 164
Morocco 25, 26, 29, 35, 38, 110, 163,
    177
Nicaragua 22, 25, 29, 35, 76, 171, 180
Pakistan 14, 16, 25, 29
Peru 21, 29, 135
Philippines 87, 88
Tanzania 118, 139, 141, 144–146, 149,
    153
Turkey 135
Vietnam 14, 16, 72, 101

Regions

Asia 16, 21, 24, 75, 77, 103, 108, 110,
    129, 153, 158, 165
Europe 5, 12, 16, 24, 29, 52, 75, 103,
    129, 135, 152, 158, 165, 166, 179
Latin America 20, 75, 77, 78, 103, 110,
    114, 123, 158, 165

MENA Region 70, 75, 103, 158, 165
Sub-Saharan Africa 22, 103, 110, 123,
    190, 191, 195

CPSIA information can be obtained at www.ICGtesting.com
Printed in the USA
LVOW01*0308171214

419196LV00009B/82/P

DATE DUE	RETURNED